"Sister Aquinata Böckmann is herself a treasure in our worldwide Benedictine Order. Once again in her newest book, *A Listening Community*, she continues to share that treasure by unpacking the heights and depths of the heart and mind of St. Benedict, explaining clearly the origins and meaning of the Prologue and first three chapters of the Rule of St. Benedict. As we plunge into her book, new meanings emerge to challenge all of us who wish to live in the daily our Benedictine spirituality to a new level of communal sensitivities. Thank you, Sr. Aquinata, for all the wisdom you have shared with so many of us around the globe!"

—Karen Joseph, OSB
Assistant Director of Spirituality Ministry
Sisters of Saint Benedict
Ferdinand, Indiana

"*A Listening Community* is Sister Aquinata Böckmann's best so far. Her research is German—thorough as usual. Her editors and translators have exceeded my expectations by bringing forward an English text that feels native. Most of us will not have the opportunity to live forty years in Rome and do the in-depth research that Sister Aquinata has done, but we can read this book. I thought I knew the Rule of Benedict since I've lived as a nun for more than fifty years. Ever new, this classic text is brought forward by an expert wordsmith. Sister Aquinata is our contemporary Hildegard of Bingen."

—Mary Margaret Funk, OSB
Our Lady of Grace Monastery
Beech Grove, Indiana

"This book is a must read for Benedictines old and new and for all who cherish the way of life taught in the Rule of Benedict. Once again, Aquinata Böckmann confirms her reputation as a top scholar of the Rule and one whose work is readable and accessible. She does not impose her ideas but lets the text speak for itself, giving close scrutiny to each word and phrase and then backing away to view their role in the overall structure and context of the Rule and the monastic tradition."

—Jerome Kodell, OSB
Abbot
Subiaco Abbey

"In an earlier book, *Perspectives on the Rule of Saint Benedict*, Sister Aquinata analyzes verses 1-4 and 45-50 of the Prologue with attention to the humanizing impulse of Benedict of Nursia, as distinct from the Rule of the Master's more ascetical tone. In this volume the reader is gifted with an extensive commentary on the entire Prologue plus chapters 1–3. The author contends that the Prologue and chapters 1–3, viewed as a unit, form Benedict's unique apologetic for cenobitic life—for the formation of 'a listening community' under a rule and a superior. Characteristically, Sister Aquinata is meticulous in her scholarship as she follows the principles of biblical exegesis applied to the Rule and consistently allows the text to speak for itself. She never loses sight, however, of the need for contemporary applications—in comments like 'today this line of thought would have to be further expanded,' or 'how might we aptly translate this [understanding] for our time.' Readers of *A Listening Community* will rejoice with gratitude for the Christ-centered relationality that is the soul of St. Benedict's call to live in community."

—S. Ephrem Hollermann, OSB
Saint Benedict's Monastery
Saint Joseph, Minnesota

Aquinata Böckmann, OSB

A Listening Community

A Commentary on the Prologue and Chapters 1–3 of Benedict's Rule

Translated by

Matilda Handl, OSB, and Marianne Burkhard, OSB
Edited by Marianne Burkhard, OSB

LITURGICAL PRESS
Collegeville, Minnesota

www.litpress.org

This work was previously published in German as *Christus hören: Prolog bis Kapitel 7* (Editions Sankt Ottilien, 2011).

Cover design by Ann Blattner. Cover photo by Judith Sutera, OSB. "Last Meeting of Sts. Benedict and Scholastica," Choir chapel window at Mount St. Scholastica, Atchison, Kansas. Used with permission.

1   2   3   4   5   6   7   8   9

Library of Congress Cataloging-in-Publication Data

Böckmann, Aquinata.
　　[Christus hören. English]
　　A listening community : a commentary on the prologue and chapters 1–3 of Benedict's Rule / Aquinata Böckmann, OSB ; translated by Matilda Handl, OSB and Marianne Burkhard, OSB ; edited by Marianne Burkhard, OSB.
　　　　pages   cm.
　　Includes bibliographical references.
　　ISBN 978-0-8146-4922-0 (pbk.) — ISBN 978-0-8146-4947-3 (ebook)
　　1. Benedict, Saint, Abbot of Monte Cassino. Regula. Prologus.   2. Benedict, Saint, Abbot of Monte Cassino. Regula. Caput 1–3.   3. Benedictines—Spiritual life.   4. Benedictines—Rules.   5. Listening—Religious aspects—Christianity.   I. Burkhard, Marianne.   II. Title.

BX3004.Z5B625   2015
255'.106—dc23   2014024561

Contents

Preface

This book contains a commentary to the entire Prologue and the first three chapters of the Rule of Benedict. The Prologue is important because it contains, as it were, the overall content of the Rule in the form of an oral homily pointing out the basic attitudes of a person who wants to live as a monk according to this Rule. But it is interesting that just after having finished the Prologue, Benedict feels the need to propose the main organization of this monastic community: It is for cenobites, living under the Rule and an abbot (RB 1); then he describes the abbot, his task and pastoral care, and his important role in guaranteeing the unity of the community (RB 2). Up to this point Benedict more or less follows the Rule of the Master. But RB 3 is a clear departure, presenting an entire chapter on the counsel the brothers give to the abbot. In describing this Benedict emphasizes community life in a new way.

We can presume that in a prologue the author presents us with important values so that it becomes like the key to a musical piece. From this first text we might learn already how to interpret the following chapters. And these first three chapters present us with the most important organizational elements of this community. They form a certain unity since each of them is written as a circular composition around an essential core or nucleus. The core of RB 1 contains the importance of the Rule (v. 8); the core of RB 2 shows that this very heterogeneous community, which is entrusted to the abbot, finds unity only in Christ (v. 20); and the core of RB 3 talks about the fact that both the abbot and the brothers are to follow the same law of the Rule (v. 7). We become aware that Rule, abbot, and community are closely related and form the three pillars of RB.

The Rule of the Master forms an underlying basis for these three chapters. This Rule was written around 530 which can be deduced from the fact that the Master did not seem to know certain documents known to Benedict. It also has indications that it comes from southern Italy, e.g., by its use of local saints. Especially for the first chapters of RB it is very important (most important?) to read both Rules line by line and side by side, comparing them with each other.[1] Perhaps the change concerns only some words—yet it can indicate a whole mentality if in the spirit of this change, additions, omissions or rewordings are repeated. In this way a close reading shows us the person of St. Benedict in a deeper way.

I know that it is not easy for us today to follow an old text step by step. With regard to this difficulty, I want to quote a passage from Michael Casey's book *Strangers to the City*:

> A line-by-line, word-by-word analysis must be undertaken. . . . The hardest thing of all is the simplest to formulate: every word must be understood. It is hard because the eye tends to skip over just those things which are the most shocking or most call into question our way of looking at things. . . . One passes over such things unless one takes pencil and paper, outlines, counts, stops at everything and tries to wonder.[2]

I want to let the text speak. This happens, among others things, in observing the structure of the text. Through the style the personality of the author is expressed, and in the structures of texts the author shows what is important to him. Not that each word has the same weight, but we can recognize the differences between the two Rules only if, again and again, we closely look at the text.

I follow the principles of biblical exegesis. First I look at the text and analyze it (synchronic reading). Then I look at its sources (diachronic reading). After having done this I can raise the question of what the text says to us, to people of today. Two images helped me in working with texts in this manner. The first image comes from my friend Jacques Dupont, a biblical exegete, who said that reading a text is like blowing softly again and again into ashes until the flame emerges. In a second image I compare this way of reading with rubbing matches, or rubbing two uneven stones—the text and our feeling—until the flame appears.

Most of the commentaries on RB we use were written by abbots or monks. Up to now we have only a few written by Benedictine women living in their community. The common life does not leave much time for writing, but it has the advantage that the commentary remains near the "earth" and its

---

1. The English translation of RM is taken from Luke Eberle, *The Rule of the Master* (Kalamazoo, MI: Cistercian, 1977); a concordance in Latin is from Benedict Guevin, *Synopsis Fontesque: RM – RB* (St. Ottilien: Eos Verlag, 1999).

2. Allan Bloom, "The Study of Texts," in *Giants and Dwarfs: Essays 1960–1990* (New York: Simon and Schuster, 1990), 306–7, as quoted in Michael Casey, *Strangers to the City: Reflections on the Beliefs and Values of the Rule of Saint Benedict* (Brewster, MA: Paraclete, 2005), 46.

reality. Since 1973 I have been living in Rome and have for nearly forty years given lectures on the Rule of Benedict at the University of San Anselmo; yet I have also presented innumerable seminars and retreats on topics from RB in various parts of the world and on all the continents. I am very grateful to all the students and participants in such seminars. I was constantly challenged to delve even more deeply into the texts and into our Benedictine life. I am also grateful that living in Rome I was able to profit from its international libraries.

My thanks go to all and especially to my international community in Rome and to my superiors who supported my work on the Rule. Thanks also to Sr. Matilda Handl from my community in Rome who translated a part of this book. Profound gratitude goes to Sr. Marianne Burkhard from St. Mary Monastery, Rock Island, Illinois, who translated the other part and edited the entire book with much skill and conscientiousness.

To find a title for this book on the first part of the Rule was not easy. The title contains two significant words: "listening," which summarizes the Prologue but also the attitude of the abbot, and "community." Listening builds community, and in the first three chapters of his Rule, Benedict strongly recommends living in community.

Rome, February 10, Feast of St. Scholastica
Sr. Aquinata Böckmann

The Prologue to the Rule of Benedict

THE PROLOGUE IN THE RULE OF BENEDICT
AND IN HIS MAIN SOURCE

Following his main source, the *Regula Magistri* (RM), Benedict prefaces his Rule with a prologue, a spoken word (this is the literal meaning of Latin *prologus*). We do not know what occasioned it, nor to whom it was originally addressed. Perhaps it was connected to baptism. The focus is on a beginner and a new beginning; thus, in both RB and RM it could be an exhortation for a person who is entering the community or for a candidate preparing for monastic profession. We can assume that this allocution addresses some of the important concerns regarding the monastic life as Benedict is teaching it.

The Rule of the Master also has a prologue that is followed by several introductory passages. Its origin is probably a baptismal catechesis[1] in which the person to be baptized was given the Our Father and some psalms, e.g., Psalms 14/15 and 33/34, which was apparently a custom in Southern Italy. The Prologue in RM exhorts to listen and to act accordingly and closes by presenting the Rule. The Master's "theme" follows in three parts (Th, Thp, Ths). The theme of the source (in Th) is shaped by baptism. The Lord invites us all: "Come to me," and we throw off the burden of sins and come to the source. After having been refreshed in the joy of resurrection, we hear the second call: "Learn from me," or, in other words: "enter my school and follow me." Thus we no longer look for a father in the flesh but instead pray

---

1. See A. Böckmann, *Perspectives*, 13. In footnotes, author and the first significant word of the title refer to the corresponding entry in Bibliography III: Secondary Sources and Studies; author followed by page number refers to commentaries of the Rule.

in a new way the Our Father which is explained in the second part (Thp = theme *pater*).

The Our Father is addressed to Christ who in baptism has begotten us as his children. In practice this means that by doing God's will we begin to resemble him. In its substance this explanation is close to Cyprian's *De Dominica Oratione*, which also accords the largest space to the plea of doing God's will.[2] This is particularly important when introducing someone to monastic life, and later the Master can resume this thread in the chapters on obedience. One's own will (*voluntas propria*) must be uprooted and be replaced by the will of God; in this way monks will slowly grow to be more spiritual by shedding all that belongs to the flesh. The model of obedience is Christ. In all these explanations the thought of judgment is strong. In accordance with the explanation of baptism the Our Father is now interpreted in terms of the Christian-monastic life.

"Listen"—this was applied to the call to come to the source (Matt 11:28 in Th), then it is applied to the Our Father (Thp) and also to the psalms, especially Psalms 33/34 and 14/15 which are explained in the third part of the explanation (Ths = theme sequence). While the Prologue of RM concludes by mentioning the Rule, the thematic explanation concludes by mentioning the school of the Lord's service (Ths 46-47). The Master greatly values smooth transitions from one part to the next. Benedict does away with these literary constructions.

THE STRUCTURE OF THE PROLOGUE IN RB

Benedict's Prologue is constructed around a center in a chiastic manner which is not as clear in RM, even though Benedict basically follows the third part (Ths) of RM.

A: **1-7 Listening (heart) and practicing**; obedience to the precepts

Service, fight—return, resp. follow

Christ, the true king—eternal punishment or glory

Prayer that HE will grant completion

  B: **8-13 Introduction to the explanation of the psalms**: invitation to
    listen (heart)

  and to come/run with a first quote of Psalm 33/34 (v. 12)

---

2. *De Dominica Oratione* (*De dom. or*). For a list of abbreviations of patristic texts, refer to Bibliography II: Patristic and Monastic Texts; abbreviations are listed alphabetically under author or source.

C: **14-20 The way to life (3x) (explanation of Ps 33/34)**

a (14) the Lord is seeking . . . calling

b (15-18) the tongue is not to speak lies,

　　turn from evil—do good

　　the eyes of the Lord are upon us (*ecce adsum,* here I am)

c (19-20) Brothers . . . the Lord shows us the way to life

　D: **21-22 Thus, gird your loins with faith**

　and the practice of good works

　　E: **let us go forward on his ways under the guidance of the Gospel**

　D': so that we may be worthy to see

　the one who has called us into his kingdom.

　If we desire—then . . .

C': **23-35 The way to dwelling in the tent (3x) (explanation of Ps 14/15)**

c' (23-24) Brothers . . . the Lord shows us the way to the tent

b' (24-34) to walk without blame—be just—speak no lies

　　the Lord himself works in us—through grace I am what I am

a' (35) the Lord, concluding (completing) . . . waits

B' **36-39 Conclusion of the psalm explanation**: invitation to practice

what was heard—conversion

allusion to the preceding psalm

A': **40-50 Listening (heart) and practicing**—obedience to the precepts

Fight (*militia, servitium*)—to walk, resp. to run, the way

Escaping hell, doing what will profit us in eternity; Christ's kingdom and eternity

Prayer for the help of grace

Beginning and end (A, A': 1-7, 40-50) repeat the same topics: there are two ways leading either to glory or to hell. We are to listen, to obey, to walk on the right way. Obedience can also be described as fighting/struggling, or serving. Christ stands before us in a commanding position as king in his kingdom. We can only respond by grace, and thus we address him with our earnest prayer.

Two parts follow leading toward the center; they can be described as an introduction to the first psalm explanation (B: 8-13) and as the end of the second psalm explanation (B': 36-39). In the introduction the invitation to listen is dominant; at the end it is the invitation to practice what was heard. Both parts take up a thought of the respective psalm.

Closer to the center we have C (14-20) and C' (23-35), two passages about the way to life and the way to the Lord's tent. They explain Psalm 33/34 (C) and Psalm 14/15 (C'). Formally they begin and end in similar ways: a (14): "The Lord seeing . . . calls" and a' (35): "The Lord, concluding (completing) . . . waits." Toward their center both parts contain an invitation to avoid evil, to do good (b), and also to give glory to God (b').

In the center of the entire Prologue we find verses 21-22. They are skillfully framed by two verses with similar expressions: c (18-19): "Brothers . . . the Lord shows us the way to life" and c' (24, cf. 23): "Brothers . . . the Lord shows us the way to the tent." The center states what is at stake, namely, "to walk our ways under the guidance of the Gospel." It is in this sense that we have to read the psalm explanations and the entire Prologue (see the detailed explanations of its individual parts).

PROLOGUE 1-7

Let us now look more closely at the beginning of the Prologue, first in RM, then in RB. "Having then completed the Lord's Prayer, brothers, let us now, as the Lord commands, treat also the performance of our service [*servitii opera*] so that he who has deigned to include us among his sons may never be distressed by our evil deeds" (RM, Ths 1-2). The Master is very logical as he transitions from the Our Father to the concrete service to God who has adopted us. In his Prologue, Benedict prefaces the text from RM with four verses that conclude with the words: "that [*ut*] it [the good work] be completed by HIM" (4b), and then adds verse 5 rather awkwardly: "that [*ut*] he, who counts us among his sons, need not be angry." It would be easier to read this text without this "that" (*ut*); moreover, there is a change from the second person singular ("you" in 1-4a) to the third person (he) and from the singular "you" (1-4) to the plural "us" (5). In RB we can clearly sense a break between verse 4 and 5.

These initial four verses are very carefully crafted; they summarize the long introductory parts of the Master and are also inspired by PsBasil and Wisdom literature.[3] They emphasize the following: *Listening* (with three expressions)—*obeying* as listening and doing, as returning, and finally as fighting—*praying*. In reference to the Latin words, one could speak of three initial O's: *obsculta, oboedientia,* and *oratio.* In all this, Christ's commanding figure is placed in the foreground because it is under his guidance that we take up our weapons by renouncing our self-will. The last verse (4) stresses the

---

3. For an extensive discussion of these four verses see Böckmann, *Perspectives*, 12–32. The interpretation of the various parts of the Prologue were first published in *EA* and subsequently reworked (cf. Bibliography III).

importance of a "most earnest prayer" (*oratio instantissima*) even before any action is undertaken and also shows that grace is indispensable by indicating that HE (Christ?) is to complete the work.

Benedict then abruptly begins to follow the text of RM. Verses 5-7 form a unit: they begin with our being adopted and a possibly positive response to this adoption until they eventually intensify to a negative expression "hand us over to punishment" (*ad poenam*). Yet the last word of verse 7 "to glory" (*ad gloriam*) shows the final goal of Christian and monastic life. Except for small changes (see below for the detailed interpretation) Benedict closely follows RM.

Prologue 5-7 does show continuity with Prologue 1-4:

(a) Both parts deal with the relationship between father and son in which Christ is the father (in my view this is already true in v. 1).

(b) The negative pole is explicitly named, first as the laziness of disobedience (Prol 2), then as instances of self will (Prol 3), or as misdeeds (Prol 7).

(c) As a positive attitude, obedience is mentioned as a practice in various shades: labor of obedience (*labor obedientiae*), weapons of obedience (*arma obedientiae*), and in addition, already in verse 1 in the binary expression "listen—put into practice (*obsculta—comple*) and in verse 6, again obedience (here expressed by another Latin verb, *parere*).

(d) What is at stake is Christ, first the service for Christ (*Christo militare*), then the following of Christ into glory (*sequi eum*). The human persons doing this are called "servants" (*servi*).

Thus we can understand why some editions of RB print verses 1-7 as one paragraph.

The Structure of Prologue 1-7 can be presented in the following manner:

a Listen—obey—father
  b serve (*militare*)—Lord
    c pray (v. 4)
a' obey—father
  b' follow him to glory—Lord

Presenting the text in this manner shows more clearly that verse 4 (c) is the center while the other elements are repeated. Verses 1-4 appear to criticize, or to establish a balance to the following verses. Prologue 5-7 describes a gradual development from being a son to being a servant and finally to eternal punishment. In this regard, Prologue 2 in particular seems to correct a one-sided understanding, since there disobedience is already behind us and it is assumed that we desire to return through obedience. The two ways—leading to damnation or to glory—are presented differently. Earlier we were on the way, descending toward the negative, but through the Lord's call the return to the positive is presented to us. As a whole, verses 1-4 present basically the positive side: obey, serve Christ, yet in all this you must pray that he may bring it to completion. What verse 7 expresses negatively—those who do not want to follow him to glory—could be seen as a parallel to verse 4: He accomplishes it, that is, we will follow him to glory.

PROLOGUE 1-4[4]

V. 1: Listen, my son, to the precepts of the master and incline the ear of your heart; willingly receive the admonition of the loving father and put it into practice. (*Obsculta, o fili, praecepta magistri, et inclina aurem cordis tui, et admonitionem pii patris libenter excipe et efficaciter conple.*)

It is characteristic for Benedictine spirituality that receptivity is emphasized before even mentioning activity. Here in particular, the emphasis is on listening with its consequences, and this listening is then further deepened in two synonymous expressions. For Benedict the human being is essentially a "hearer of the word." In his anthropological treatise (RM 8) the Master speaks about the soul which has its roots in the heart and is activated through the seeing of the eyes, the speaking of the mouth, and the hearing of the ears (RM 8.17). The principal reason for keeping silence lies in the fact that it enables the disciple to listen (RM 8.37; RB 6.6).

For Benedict, listening is the fundamental attitude from which all other attitudes flow. Listening leads to obedience; silence, listening is humility; yet listening is—as Benedict adds in the penultimate chapter—equally indispensable for the communal life. Without listening we cannot anticipate one another with respect, nor obey one another; we cannot do what is useful for the other nor show each other pure fraternal love (RB 72.3-8). In the council meeting it is important to listen to the abbot, the community, and the least of the members (RB 3); yet we also listen to someone who comes from outside (RB 61.4), and the porter, as the symbolic representative of the entire community, shows that he listens to the "call of the visitors and the poor" (RB 66.3). Today this line of thought would have to be further expanded: to have the ear of our heart on the pulse of the world, incline it toward the human beings in the entire world as a complement to our listening to the Lord!

---

4. This will be only a summary explanation since my earlier book *Perspectives* contains a detailed exegesis of Prol 1-4 (Böckmann, 12–32).

The particular ways of living out monastic life are shaped by listening: *lectio divina* means primarily listening—we have our ear *in* Sacred Scripture—and liturgy consists to a great extent of listening to the Word of God; even communal singing is essentially a listening to each other. In this way *lectio* and liturgy are practices that lead us ever deeper into this fundamental attitude (cf. 19.1f.: God is always present, especially now in the Liturgy of the Hours).

Listening as a fundamental attitude presupposes faith that God is not mute but rather promises to give us his life-giving word; this is a sign of his love. An appropriate response is a person's listening in undivided attention, a listening heart (Prol 1). Listening is more than just hearing. We are able to hear externally and at the same time do something else, as is already customary in our present-day culture. Yet listening goes deeper and is more demanding. It presupposes that I am not filled to the brim with my own needs, desires, and activities but rather have some empty space in me allowing myself to be surprised and startled (cf. Prol 9 "with thunder-struck ears"). Listening can easily be blocked. The Word of God again and again calls me out of my certainty, doesn't leave me alone. Our listening is also a concrete form of our love for God as it shows that we trust him and entrust ourselves to him. All this, however, is not only the result of our efforts but also a gift of God with which he wants to gift us every day, "today." Consequently the Word of God can also transform us. The ear of the heart then is entirely turned toward God and to all human beings.[5] Presence of God (cf. Prol 18; RB 19.1) and full presence of the human being!

This first verse of the Prologue asks us to listen to the precepts of the master and the admonitions of a loving father. These are words which provide our life with guidance that derives from experience. Thus, the last expression here is also logical: put them into practice.

V. 2: so that by the labor of obedience you may return to him from whom you had wandered by the laziness of disobedience. (*ut ad eum per oboedientiae laborem redeas, a quo per inoboedientiae desidiam recesseras.*)

While verse 1 describes obedience as listening and putting into practice what was heard, obedience in verse 2 is described as the way to the Lord, alluding to the great plan of salvation. Obedience is considered as the primary means which leads to this return home. The expression "laziness of disobedience"

---

5. For listening cf., e.g., Choi, "Listening"; Schwager, "Hörer"; Malone, "Listening." In cases where the author does not refer to specific pages *within* an article, only the author and the title of the article are given in the footnote; for full reference cf. Bibliography III.

(*desidia*) could be alarming: a lethargic laissez-faire attitude leads to sliding off and missing our return to the Lord.

V. 3: To you, therefore, my word is now directed, whoever you are, renouncing self-will, who in order to serve the Lord Christ, the true King, are taking up the very strong and splendid weapons of obedience. (*Ad te ergo nunc mihi sermo dirigitur, quisquis abrenuntians propriis voluntatibus, Domino Christo vero regi militaturus, oboedientiae fortissimo atque praeclara arma sumis.*)

As in PsBasil, the focus here is on the service (*militia*) for the king. Yet Benedict is more precise and first speaks about the negative sounding condition for such service, i.e., renouncing all acts of self-will, which means to be free for practicing the obedience that is rendered to Christ, the true King. Amid the various kings of the times, the true and only king, Christ, appears in radiance. Here Christ is placed in a dominant position at the beginning of the Prologue, just as he appears also at its end (Prol 50) and at the end of the Rule (73.8). Thus after listening a second central point of RB emerges, that is, its Christocentric orientation.

Although *militare* can be translated as "to serve," a militant element is also present. Obedience has very strong and splendid weapons; they are not only very strong in their effect but also splendid! With this Benedict presumably appeals to young people's capacity for enthusiasm. We may ask how we might aptly translate this for our time and how we might show in a persuasive and motivating way why it is still worth it to take up monastic life. After these first two central points a third one appears: prayer.

V. 4: First of all, whenever you begin a good work, you are to pray most earnestly that he will complete it. (*In primis, ut quidquid agendum inchoas bonum, ab eo perfici instantissima oratione deposcas.*)

The adverbial expression "first of all" points to the primacy of prayer that precedes our actions, accompanies and completes them. This is the third central point that Benedict introduces at the very beginning of his text to his hearers: the primacy of prayer that is the expression of his faith in the Lord who is always efficaciously present, to whom we are turned and without whom "we can do nothing" (cf. John 15:5). The most earnest prayer could be, for instance, a kind of ejaculatory prayer such as "O God, come to my assistance, O Lord, make haste to help me" (cf. 18.1; 35.17). It is first prayed with our lips and then descends ever deeper, even to the bottom of our heart and so becomes a lived attitude. These four verses that Benedict himself placed at the very beginning of the Prologue present his main concerns and already point to the end of the Prologue (40-50) as well as of the Rule (RB 72–73).

PROLOGUE 5-7

We can also write Prologue 5-7 as a circular composition. Parts A and A' form the greatest contrasts while B and B' emphasize the same or a similar content. In Latin both B and B' contain the word *aliquando*.

A 5 so that he, who already now graciously counts us among his sons,

   B must not at some time be saddened over our evil actions.

      C 6 Therefore we are to obey him at all times with his good gifts he implanted in us

   B' so that he as an angry father may not at some time disinherit his sons

   7 nor as a Lord who is to be feared may be enraged over our evil actions and

A' hand us over to eternal punishment as worthless servants who refused to follow him to glory.

This entire passage consists of two sentences, though the first one, as seen above, is only a "hanging" second part of verse 4 (in comparison with its source in RM). The main clause (v. 6) summarizes the fundamental attitude of obedience that is presented as the best means to avoid being disinherited and, worse yet, being eternally punished.

God-Christ is first indirectly called "father" since he has accepted us as his children, yet he can also be an angry father or even a Lord who is to be feared and who becomes angry. His actions are first positive: he deigns to count us among his sons; but after he is distressed by evil deeds, he may also disinherit his sons, or even deliver them to eternal punishment.

Human beings are first sons whom the father has endowed with good things, and as sons they can and should obey him. Yet when they produce evil deeds (mentioned twice), they will be disinherited as sons or even cast away as useless, truly evil servants or slaves who refuse to follow him. A monk is not only a son but also a servant/slave of Christ. According to Roman concepts, a son does not need to work (*operari*), yet is to show his father love and obedience and must not distress him through evil actions (*malis actibus*). As servant/slave, he first has to obey and then also to produce profits with the goods of his master (as does the servant with the talents). Moreover, he has to accompany his master wherever he goes.

The word "now" (*iam*) in verse 5 has a counterpart in the expression "at all times" in verse 6 (*omni tempore*) and in the warning that it should not happen that at some time (*aliquando* used with two examples) God needs to have recourse to the worst punishment. This is strong language that also contains a strong appeal to listen and obey. All this is expressed in contrasts:

- Sons—truly evil servants (*filii—nequissimi servi*);
- his good gifts in us—with evil actions, our evil (*de bonis suis in nobis—de malis actibus, a malis nostris)*;
- he graciously counts us among his sons—an angry father, a lord to be feared (*iratus pater, metuendus dominus*);
- to glory—to punishment (*ad gloriam—ad poenam*).

The two negative consequences are expressed in parallels and their similarity seems to accentuate the intensification:

The father	saddened over the evil actions	disinherits his sons
The Lord who is to be feared	angry because of our evil actions	hands over his servants to punishment.

Shown as a sequence of actions this would take the following form:

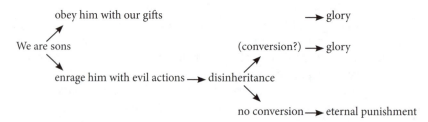

This sequence of actions reveals God's ways of acting which always anticipates us and our free will that may choose a good or a bad response to God's gifts and his adopting us as his children. Only one answer is appropriate to being a son: obeying with his good gifts that he has implanted in us. If we do not do this, and on the contrary, do evil things, disinheritance will follow. This passage might awaken in us the forces that bring us to conversion. We are still servants who, at least, are able to serve him well. We may think of the prodigal son who, in Luke 15:19, begs: "Treat me as you would treat one of your hired workers." But if the servant is truly evil and refuses to follow, even though the goal is very attractive, then punishment will eventually follow.

V. 5: so that he, who already now graciously counts us among his sons, must not at some time be saddened over our evil actions. *(ut qui nos iam filiorum dignatus est numero conputare, non debet aliquando de malis actibus nostris contristari.)*

He graciously counts us among his sons.[6] Here the emphasis is first on God's grace, on what he has already done for us. He has "deigned" *(dignatus)* to adopt us. This is his freedom and gracious love. Again, as in verses 1-4 Christ here appears as father who begets new children in baptism. The church was born from his side, thus the newly baptized can legitimately call him father (cf. comments on RB 2.3). A Scripture passage such as Wisdom 5:5 may have influenced this verse even in the choice of words. This is more readily evident in Latin: *Ecce quomodo conputati sunt inter filios Dei et inter sanctos sors illorum est.* "See how he is accounted among the sons of God; how his lot is with the saints!"[7]

It is certain that RM and RB allude to baptism in which we were accepted as children. In the explanation of the Our Father RM says "the Lord destroyed the sting of death . . . after restoring us to the grace of adoption by him, he has not ceased to invite us to the kingdom of heaven. Hence the voice of the Lord says: 'If you keep my commandments, I will be your father and you shall be my sons.' So it is that we, though unworthy but aware of our baptism, dare in his prayer to call him father (Thp 7-10; it is remarkable how everything is centered on Christ!). To be sons also means that our will conforms to his, in everything we are to resemble the father (Thp 13-14). We also can compare this with Scripture: the great opportunity to be God's children appears in 1 John 3:1: "See what love the Father has bestowed on us in that we may be called children of God! Yet so we are" (cf. John 1:12). In Romans 8:15 Paul says that "you received a spirit of adoption through which we cry 'Abba, Father.'" This also offers the wonderful promise: "if [we are] children, then heirs as well, heirs of God" (Rom 8:17)—a text to which Benedict returns at the end of the Prologue (50) as well as RB 2.3.

Not at some time saddening [God] by our evil actions. Being a child of God corresponds to good actions as the following verse explicitly states. When such actions are mainly described as obedience, we may see evil actions as

---

6. In the detailed explanations the author focuses on specific ideas *(in italics)*, therefore their formulation does not always correspond to the translation of the verse at the beginning of the section.

7. The second epistle of Clement to the Corinthians says the following with reference to Christ: "As father he called us his children, and when we were in danger to perish, he saved us" (1.1.4). The Latin translation reads: *tamquam pater filios nos appellavit, pereuntes nos servavit.* Funk, 1, 147.

disobedience, or as in Prologue 2, the "laziness of disobedience." This may be laziness or even resistance or rebellion. To sadden, enrage: this is an anthropomorphic way of speaking about God. Scripture says that God is delighted with us, saddened, gets angry. If he truly is a father, then he is involved, his "guts" tremble with us (cf. Hos 11:8). When explaining this verse Smaragdus (67) refers to Proverbs 10:1: "The wise son gives joy to his father, but the foolish son is the grief of his mother." And Ephesians 4:30 states: "Do nothing to sadden the Holy Spirit of God with which you were sealed."

At some time (aliquando). Expressions of time are significant in this paragraph: "now—at some time—at all times—at some time." The time of now is emphatically contrasted with eternal punishment or glory. This is a prophetic admonition to get serious!

V. 6a: Therefore we are to obey him at all times with his good gifts he implanted in us. (*Ita enim ei omni tempore de bonis suis in nobis parendum est.*)

To obey him at all times: Obedience is directed to Christ, the father who, as RB 2 demonstrates, has a privileged mediator in the abbot (he, too, is called "father" and "Lord"). This also corresponds to Prologue 3 where the newcomer is challenged to take up the battle of obedience for Christ, the true king.

With his good gifts he implanted in us (de bonis suis in nobis).[8] The Lord implanted good things in us, they belong completely to him. Now we are called to let them flourish, develop them, work with them, yet it is still his work. Thus all boasting is excluded (cf. Prol 29-32; 4.42). We may think of our abilities, our strengths, and the graces which are all God's gifts to us. God asks us for nothing except for what he has already given us. In other words: before making a demand of us, he has already given us the strength and grace to fulfill it. This obedience is the main command addressed to the newcomer and to all monastics. It corresponds to the first verses of the Prologue: listen, obey, labor of obedience, weapons of obedience. It is interesting to compare different translations: the one published by the Conference of Abbots of Salzburg deviates most from the Latin: "Because he is effecting good things in us, we must obey him always." In this translation the connection between the good things and obedience is no longer very clear.[9] What is expressed

---

8. According to Quartiroli, 7, the Latin preposition *de* in *de bonis suis* has an instrumental meaning.

9. Steidle (1975) translated: "we are to obey him with the gifts that he has given us." The American translation of RB 1980 emphasizes the goodness of the gifts: "with his good gifts which are in us, we must obey." Quartiroli: "using the good gifts which he himself has given us." Kardong: "By means of the good things he has given us, we should

in this concise Latin text and ought to be expressed in the translations is the following:

1. The gifts are good (*de bonis*).
2. They come from him, belong to him, are implanted in us or given as gifts to us, us by him (*de bonis suis*).
3. By means of these gifts we obey. These gifts give us the possibility of obeying.

V. 6b: So that he as an angry father may not at some time disinherit his sons. (*Ut non solum iratus pater suos non aliquando filios exheredet.*)[10]

The Hebrew Scriptures often speak of the wrath of God, and the Christian Scriptures also mention the possibility of being disinherited. 1 Corinthians 6:9: "Do you not know that the unjust will not inherit the kingdom of God?" Galatians 5:21: "those who do such things [idolatry, dissensions, envy] will not inherit the kingdom of God." Smaragdus points out (70) that our inheritance is actually Christ. The imperishable inheritance is preserved for us in heaven (1 Pet 1:4), yet we may lose it.

V. 7a: nor as a Lord who is to be feared may be enraged at our evil actions and hand us over to eternal punishment as worthless servants. (*sed nec ut metuendus dominus inritatus a malis nostris, ut nequissimos servos perpetuam tradat ad poenam.*)

Now it is not only the angry, enraged father but also the Lord who is to be feared who is truly indignant at our evil actions. The Lord "who is to be feared" occurs in this form only once in the Latin Vulgate, namely, in Eccl 1:8 *Unus est metuendus Dominus*, literally translated: One is the Lord who is to be feared. The expression "evil servants" reminds us of parables such as Matthew 18:32 where the king says: "You wicked servant! I forgave you your entire debt," or the parable of the gold coins which one servant hid because

---

obey." Vogüé emphasizes the instrumentality: "to obey him with the means of the good things that he put in us." The edition of RB in *français fondamental [basic French]* is clearest: "The gifts which he has implanted in us, we must always use in order to obey him." We can also compare this with Augustine *In Ps.* 25.2.12: "*in quibus ergo sic habitat dominus ut et de bonis suis ipse glorificetur, ut non sibi velint tribuere, et quasi proprium vindicare quod ab illo acceperunt*" (in whom therefore the Lord resides in such a way that he himself is glorified by his good gifts so that they may not attribute them to themselves and, as it were, claim as their own what they had received from him).

10. RM has *nos . . . filios*, that is, "disinherit us, his sons" (Ths 3). The textual transmission is uncertain, cf. Hanslik, 2.

he feared his master. The Latin text of Luke 19:22, *serve nequam*, is in RB intensified to a superlative *nequissimi servi.*[11]

To hand over to eternal punishment or, as RM says, to hand over to punishment for all eternity! This, too, is found as an admonition in the gospels. "Eternal punishment" sounds very menacing. RB mentions it several times, and the Master threatens it quite often. But Benedict also uses this as motivation in order to encourage monks to practice doing what is good (cf. RB 7.11).

V. 7b: who refused to follow him into glory. (*eum sequi noluerint ad gloriam.*)

The pronoun "him" clearly designates Christ even though he already was visible behind the father and the Lord (also in Prol 1-4). To follow him into glory—this would describe the essence of our Christian and monastic life. This sentence recalls 1 Peter 5:10: "The God of all grace who called you to his eternal glory."

This passage contrasts "father—son" and "Lord—servant" with their respective semantic fields of adoption, to obey, inheritance, on the one hand and, on the other, to be feared, enraged, worthless servants. In the context of the two Rules the contrast between son and servant is less clearly delineated as, for example, in Galatians 4–5, but the semantic fields still bear their specific marks. According to the explanation of the Our Father in RM, it is the mark of the son that he observes the father's commandments (Thp 9). "For he who resembles his father not only in appearance but also in conduct is his son" (Thp 14). In practice, it is essential to do the will of the father. The monk is called simultaneously "son" and "servant/slave" (*servus*) though the servant may also be attentive (*diligens*, Prol 14 in RM). For the authors of both Rules another biblical passage certainly also plays a part here, namely, Romans 8:15 which is then quoted in RB 2.3: "you received a spirit of adoption through which we cry, *Abba*, Father!" As Romans 8:15-17 states more fully: "For you did not receive a spirit of slavery to fall back into fear" and "if [we are] children, then [we are also] heirs."

After doing some checks in the works of Cyprian, Ambrose, and Augustine,[12] we can add some clarifications with regard to this text: We are children of God through grace, servants through creation. A son remains in the house, a servant does not always remain there; the son is also heir, but the servant is not. If the son already obeys, the servant obeys even more so. The son's obedience seems to be of a special kind, it is a loving obedience without fear. It would be good if the servant could also serve his lord in love, but it is sufficient if he obeys out of fear. A bad servant does not do the

11. Only in these two places is *nequam* = worthless, bad used as an adjective to *servus*.
12. Cf. Cetedoc 1.

lord's will. To be the Lord's servants is not negative in itself. The pathway of conversion leads a bad servant to become a good one until God again revives a parent-child relationship. Here we can also recall that the Lord humbled himself to being a servant in order to accept us into the relationship between his son and the Father.[13]

Yet it would be artificial to put a clear demarcation line between these two semantic fields. Each one reflects one aspect of the relationship Christ—human person/monk—but does not exhaust it. Our two Rules may also allude to the double fear which characterizes RB 7[14] (and even more so RM 10). The fear of the servant (*timor servilis*) leads to the fear of love (*timor amoris*).[15] This finds its culmination in RB 72.9 when Benedict says that monks are to fear God in love (*amore Deum timeant*).

The two ways are set out clearly for the baptized when they begin (or renew) monastic life: eternal torment or glory. The way to the latter is clear: obedience, imitation of Christ, prayer. The other way offers: doing evil, letting everything go (laziness, *desidia*), not listening. In accordance with the two ways we can construct a semiotic chart for Prologue 5-7:

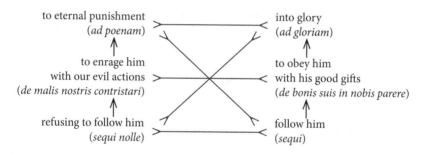

Even with the threats that sound negative, Benedict wants to achieve only this: to draw our attention to the one thing necessary: to Christ, the Lord, to listening to him, obeying and following him as it befits a Christian and monastic life. With the expression "to follow him into glory," Benedict presumably alludes to the service for Christ the true King (Prol 3) whom one follows over the heights and through the depths, or to the one who completes

---

13. Some characteristic passages are Ambrose, *In Ps* 118.9.2; Cyprian, *De dom. or* 14; Augustine, *In Ps* 122.5; 32.2.1.

14. The first step of humility emphasizes the "fear of God" (*timor Dei*), but in the third step, which deals with obedience, Benedict already interrupts the schema of RM by inserting the expression "for the love of God" (*pro Dei amore*); he seems to find it difficult to conceive of an obedience that is located only in fear.

15. Cf. the classical passage in the *Conferences* of Cassian (*Conf.* 11.11-13).

everything. Furthermore, he clarified the connection to the center of the Prologue: "to walk in his ways" (Prol 21). The following passages demonstrate that the Gospel leads us and the psalms guide us.

PROLOGUE 8-13

After the introductory part of the Prologue (Prol 1-4, 5-7), which focuses on the decision to serve Christ in obedience, the Prologue now leads into explanations of psalms. Verses 8-13 are an introduction to the first psalm explanation. The text wants to invite the addressee first of all to listen but also to see and to run. There is a dialogue between the addressee and Sacred Scripture. After having listened to the father/master in Prologue 1 and having put into practice what was heard; after having set out clearly the possibility of being a child of God and the final goal, yet also the potential failure, Scripture is now explicitly placed into the foreground as a force that acts. In contrast to RM, Benedict's text begins with a clearly accented "then" (*ergo*) which presumably indicates that if we are and want to be what the text said, then it is extremely important to expose ourselves to Sacred Scripture.

In comparing this with RM, it is immediately evident that Benedict places a quote from Psalm 95 in the center of this part. This means that God's voice daily calls out, "Today, when you hear his voice" (a word from a psalm) and not "Whoever has ears" (Matt, Rev, Prol 11). Thus the verse from the psalm is also characterized as divinizing light.

We can also write these verses as a chiasm:

A 8-9a Therefore let us at last get up; Scripture arouses us saying: "The hour is already here to rise up from sleep;"

And, with eyes opened to the divinizing light,

B 9b we hear with thunder-struck ears God's loud voice admonishing us daily by saying:

C 10 "Today, when you hear his voice, do not harden your hearts!"

B' 11 And again: "Whoever has ears to hear, is to listen to what the Spirit tells the churches."

A' 12 And what does the spirit say? "Come, sons, listen to me. I will teach you the fear of the Lord."

13 Run while you have the light of life so that the darkness of death may not seize you.

A and A' mention a negative reality (sleep, darkness of death) and its opposite, the divinizing light and the light of life. Getting up in A is intensified in A' to running. Common to B and B' are the ears and listening to Scripture.

In the center (C) we find precisely what Benedict adds. Verse 10 mirrors the thought of the entire passage: the word "today" (*hodie*) sums up the urgency which was already present in verse 8 in "therefore at last—the hour is here" (*ergo tandem . . . hora est iam*); this is taken up again in verse 13 in the imperative "run while" (*currite dum*). The "voice" summarizes both the words and the warning of the entire passage (see also "voice" in v. 9b). The theme of listening is present throughout the entire passage, but its opposite is also emphasized in the "hardening of the heart," and in A and A': sleep, darkness of death. As in A and A', both negative and positive realities are mentioned, and it is characteristic that the heart again appears in the center!

Benedict's insertion (v. 10) states more clearly that the divine voice daily calls out to us in a word from a psalm (invitatory, Vigils), and that in the psalm Christ speaks as God (divine voice). Nowack is of the opinion that this is also indicated in the orientation to the east in the invitatory, and thus he sees in this psalm a celebration of an encounter with Christ.[16] In this context we can also think of the corresponding antiphons to this invitatory psalm in the Liturgy of the Hours. They indicate that at least in a later period (perhaps resuming an older tradition?) this invitatory was addressed to Christ and that it is Christ who is speaking in it.

Verses 8-13 can also be read as a section in itself which begins with sleeping (and getting up) and ends with a call to run and an eschatological look at the "darkness of death." The paragraph contains all the elements that are typical for the Prologue:

- The anticipating action of God (Scripture arouses, addresses and illuminates us)
- listening as our answer and
- seen negatively: stop sleeping and not to harden our heart
- furthermore the coming and running
- and the final remark that the light of life is a gift and that running prevents us from being seized by the darkness of death

In the scriptural quotes the Hebrew and Christian Scriptures alternate without distinguishing who is speaking through these words: it is God, the Holy Spirit, or Christ. The view of Scripture as a unity clearly prevails.[17]

---

16. Nowack, "Quid," 462f.

17. M. Marrion, "Perichoresis," 28, thinks this lack of distinction indicates that the Father gives the Son the teaching, which the Son articulates and the Father repeats, and the Holy Spirit also repeats the words of the Father. In my opinion this seems a rather exaggerated view.

It is instructive to pay attention to the semantic fields and to gather their respective expressions. First we are struck by the fact that this text speaks primarily about listening and the ears: "let us hear with thunder-struck (*at-tonitis*) ears, hear his voice, ears to hear, hear; come and hear." On the other hand we have voice (twice), saying (four times), calling, admonish, teaching.[18] The Latin word *audire* = to hear/listen occurs five times in this short paragraph alone! And only verse 13 is devoid of an expression of hearing. In addition, there is the field of seeing: verse 9 mentions the eyes and the "divinizing light" (*deificum lumen*) and the last verse speaks of "the light of life and the darkness of death" (*lumen vitae—tenebrae mortis*). A third semantic field is that of moving: rise up (two times), come, run (*exsurgere—surgere*; *venite—currite*) and its opposite: sleep, harden (*somnum, obdurare*). Indications of time are also important: at last, hour, daily, today, while (*tandem aliquando, hora, iam, cotidie, hodie, dum . . . ne*). This creates the urgency in this paragraph! Ears and eyes of the human person are mentioned, both are connected with the heart (cf. RM 8, and biblical anthropology).[19]

V. 8: Therefore let us at long last get up; Scripture arouses us saying: "The hour is already here to rise up from sleep." (*Exsurgamus ergo tandem aliquando excitante nos scriptura ac dicente: hora est iam nos de somno surgere.*)

The text continues in the first person plural. The first verb in Latin *exsurgere* = to get up is stronger than the following *surgere*; it denotes an urgent admonition to get up at last, to "rise up." RM says here that we are "sluggish, slothful,"[20] yet Benedict omits this word just as he omits almost all the contemptuous words RM uses for the monks. Scripture arouses us to get up (*excitare—exsurgere*). In the Latin Bible the word *exsurgere* occurs often in reference to God but also in reference to human beings. The psalmist (Christ) slept and arose (Ps 3:6);[21] Joseph rose from sleep and took Mary into his home (Matt 1:24); Mary set out to visit Elizabeth (Luke 1:39); Jesus awoke from sleep and rebuked the storm (Mark 4:39). Each time this is a decisive new

18. *Dicente . . . attonitis auribus audiamus . . . divina . . . clamans . . . admonet vox dicens . . . vocem eius audieritis . . . aures audiendi audiat . . . dicat . . . dicit . . . audite . . . docebo.*

19. E.g., Isa 32:3-4: "The *eyes* of those who see will not be closed; the *ears* of those who hear will be attentive. The *heart* of the flighty will become wise and capable, and the stutterers will speak fluently and clearly" (emphasis added).

20. RM Ths 5: *Exsurgamus tandem aliquando ut pigri.* Benedict omits the last two words but adds *ergo* = therefore.

21. In Latin the verb is *exsurrexi*; presumably it was this word that prompted Benedict to use this psalm as the first psalm for Vigils.

beginning. Ephesians 5:14 certainly is an important background element for this passage: "Awake, O sleeper, and arise from the dead, and Christ will give you light."[22] One can sense a strong faith that Scripture may, as it were, raise us from the dead and bring us to new life. In his commentary on this verse, Smaragdus (72f.) points out that the *tandem aliquando* also indicates how much time has already passed. Everything here alludes to baptism.[23] Ephesians 5:14 is an old baptismal hymn. The newcomer in monastic life is challenged to intensify the reality of baptism. Augustine says in his commentary on the Gospel of John (34.9): "The way itself has come to you and has aroused you from sleep."[24]

Perhaps we would never say on our own that Scripture arouses us from sleep. For us Scripture is a book, yet this was not true for the old church. The Bible is truly a living person who, so to speak, walks up to the bed of a sleeping person arousing, even shaking him up. The Latin word *excitare* is a frequentative form of the verb *exciere* = to drive out of a quiet situation, and not just once; rather, it is a call for every day. In the Latin Scripture, *excitare* can be found side by side with *exsurgere*.[25] Sacred Scripture shakes us up, addresses us, thunders and admonishes.

"The hour is already here to rise up from sleep."[26] Here the decisive, awakening word from Scripture is Romans 13:11: "the hour is here" (*hora est*). Similar expressions often occur in RB. We have to be watchful at every moment (4.48), guard ourselves against sins at every hour since God also looks down on us every hour and the angels report everything to God at every hour (7.12-13). Among these instances of "at every hour," there are some particularly decisive hours or even moments (*kairoi*). Some manuscripts say that from "the hour" of profession the monk entirely belongs to the community.[27] Augustine experienced his decisive "hour" of conversion with the text of Romans 13:11-14 which allowed him to be "raised from death": "It is the hour now for you to awake from sleep. For our salvation is nearer now than when we first believed; the night is advanced, the day is at hand. Let us then throw off the works of darkness [and] put on the armor of light; let us conduct ourselves properly as in the day." "The hour is here"—this reminds

22. In Latin: *Surge, qui dormis, et exsurge a mortuis, et inluminabit tibi Christus.*

23. Cf. M. Puzicha, "Leitworte," 22.

24. *In Joh.* 34.9: *Surge! Via ipsa ad te venit, et te de somno dormientem excitavit.*

25. Mark 4:38-39; both verbs have the same prefix and occur only once in RB (*hapax legomena*).

26. Benedict quotes the Vulgate verbatim while the Master inserted the word *enim.* Since Benedict had already added *ergo* = therefore, he can leave the quote in its original form.

27. RB 58.23; Hanslik, 150.

us of the "hour" in the Gospel of John. Yet the hour in which we hear the call of Scripture is also the hour of deciding between death and life. Indirectly, the light already appears in this scriptural text. Baptism is called enlightenment (*photismos*), and it is in reality a resurrection from death and a being enlightened by the light which is Christ. In a derivative sense this is also true for the newcomer to monastic life, and true for us anew every day.

From sleep. What might this mean? It might be doing evil things (see Hildemar, 26), but also doing nothing, neglecting to do good, a certain laziness similar to the "sluggishness" (*desidia*) in Prologue 2. In this sense RM had added the expression "you sluggish ones." We may also recall 1 Thessalonians 5:4-6: "You . . . are not in darkness for that day to overtake you like a thief. For all of you are children of the light and children of the day. Therefore, let us not sleep as the rest, but let us stay alert and sober." Smaragdus says the following: "To love sleep is to embrace torpor of mind through sloth, and to give no thought to the future" (74). When life here on earth is compared with night, as is often the case in biblical and monastic literature, we can certainly say that whoever thinks only of this life is asleep. Scripture and the Rule open a deeper and wider perspective for us. Baptism and entering monastic life intend to direct us toward this eschatological reality and to convey within it new way of seeing the present.

V. 9: And, with eyes opened to the divinizing light, we hear with thunderstruck ears God's loud voice admonishing us daily by saying . . . (*et apertis oculis nostris ad deificum lumen adtonitis auribus audiamus divina cotidie clamans quid nos admonet vox dicens . . .*)

Clearly the sleeper has to open his eyes to see the light. We can think of Ephesians 1:18: "may the eyes of your hearts be enlightened that you may know what is the hope that belongs to his call, what are the riches of glory in his inheritance among the holy ones."

To the divinizing light (*ad deificum lumen*). The translations of this expression vary. Some say "the light from God" (Vogüé; RB 1980), others "divine light" (Salzburg, Steidle, Holzherr), and yet others translate its original sense: "the light that makes divine, divinizing" (Herwegen, Colombás, Penco). Vogüé refers to the *Life of Saint Anthony* where the word occurs several times and to Cyprian who is closer to Benedict than PsDionysius (as Miquel emphasized).[28] In general, scholars point to the connection with Eastern theology.[29] Perhaps this is already a first precursor of Psalm 34 which in Latin says in 33:6: *accedite*

28. Vogüé, "Trois expressions," 207–12 (with bibliographical references).
29. E.g., Holzherr, 2007, 52–53; M. Puzicha, 52; P. Miquel, "Lumière."

ad eum et inluminamini et vultus vestri non erubescent. Literally translated this means: "Come near to him and you will be illuminated, and your faces will not blush." In the Prologue enlightenment is seen together with Scripture which sometimes is given the adjective *deificus* = divinizing, e.g., "divinizing words [*verba deifica*], divinizing books [*libri deifici*], divinizing instruments [*deifica instrumenta*]" and "divinizing writings [*scripturae deificae*]."[30]

We can also think of the "light for the revelation to the Gentiles" (Luke 2:32) or of Psalm 119:105: "Your word is a lamp for my feet, a light for my path." Holzherr quotes Origen who refers to God as the teacher of wisdom: "Yet it is God who teaches by sending light into the soul of the one learning from him and enlightening the learner's spirit with his own words. . . . Insight itself and the opening of our heart for accepting divine teaching occur through divine grace."[31] In his Rule Basil describes the love between God and human beings as an inner light. "I am experiencing the love of God in an entirely inexpressible way. It can be experienced rather than expressed. This love is an indescribable light. If my words should use a comparison with lightning or thunder, my ears would not be able to tolerate or receive it. . . . With our bodily eyes we do not see this brightness, but soul and spirit see it. When this brightness permeates the soul and spirit of saints, it deeply infuses them with the burning desire to love him."[32] Describing Sacred Scripture as a "divinizing light" means that the more we expose ourselves to this light and allow ourselves to be permeated by it, the more we will resemble the Lord our God and thus may be able to radiate some of his light.

We hear with thunder-struck ears God's loud voice admonishing us daily by saying: In addition to the light there is now the divine voice, the voice of God, of Christ. Behind this voice a person emerges who calls, admonishes, and speaks. This voice speaks to us every day, we hear it in *lectio divina*, in the liturgy, in words of commands or instruction from superiors and fellow community members, in table readings. Later Benedict quotes Psalm 95:8, which the monks sing every day at the beginning of Vigils. We are to hear with "thunder-struck ears."[33] Peter Chrysologus says that the sheep hear the voice of their good shepherd with "thunder-struck ears" and that they always follow him and do his will.[34]

---

30. Cf. Blaise, *Dictionnaire*, 250.

31. Holzherr, 2007, 52, quotes Origen, *Job Fragm.* 22.2. The Latin quote in PG 17 says: *Docet vere deus affulgens animae discentis ab ipso, et mentem illuminans lumine, veraci nempe verbo suo.*

32. Basil, *Regula* 2.18-21: This translation follows the one by Holzherr, 2007, 34.

33. Lentini comments this expression as follows: "*attonitus* is used for a person who is stunned by a thunderbolt and the roar of its sound . . . the adjective is very common" (13).

34. *s.* 173.1.

In RB acoustical elements prevail. There are far more allusions to listening than to seeing, and this corresponds to a biblical mentality. In the Greek world, however, the eye was more highly valued than the ear, which was connected more with the feminine in its form as well as its ability. The ear always receives one thing after another while the eye masters everything in one instant, one "look of the eye."[35] It is important to note here that both, eye and ear, are in action. This reminds us of the divine revelations on Sinai and the mountain of Tabor. Thus we could see this passage of the Prologue as an epiphany of the Word of God. On Sinai, thunder and lightning are revelations of God; in the transfiguration, Christ stands in the center between the law and the prophets. The eyes perceive the luminous cloud and his brilliant clothes, the ears hear the voice from heaven. Both point to the divine nature of Christ. The divinizing light and the divine voice act together on Sinai and Tabor.

Returning to the Prologue, we may think of an inner enlightenment that occurs primarily in contact with Sacred Scripture.[36] According to commentaries of the church fathers about the transfiguration, we could say even more precisely: epiphany occurs when we hear the law and the prophets with their center, Christ, for without Christ they do not have luminous clothes. Thus Sacred Scripture can make us "divine" and is at every hour our divine partner in conversation who enlightens and motivates us to pass on the word and the light. We might also connect verses 8 and 9 with the conversion of Saul: first, hardening and darkness, then the clear divine light which blinded him, together with the voice of the Lord who awakened him, raised him from the dead, and gave him new life (Acts 9:3-8; 22:8-11; 26:13-18).

Again—as in the entire Prologue—we are reminded of baptism. The newly baptized are given a burning candle and a white garment. Their ears are opened. In the same way the twofold theme of light and word appears also at a new beginning in monastic life. Figuratively, our eyes will droop again and again and we will close our ears again and again. Therefore we need God who will always open our eyes and ears anew (cf. Isa 50:4). Yet voice and light do not coerce human beings. And what the Gospel of John describes may hap-

---

35. Philo of Alexandria says that "the ears are slower than the eyes which are the first to turn courageously towards the visible objects" (*De migr Abr,* 150, quoted from the French in Philon d'Alexandrie, *Oeuvres* [Paris: Cerf, 1966], 95). P. Miquel "L'oeil" concludes: "an image fascinates before it is controlled; the ear is the organ of silence and of night, the eye needs the light" (16). He connects the ears more with the occident and the synoptics while the emphasis on the eyes belongs more to the orient and the Johannine works.

36. Cf. homilies of the Church Fathers about the transfiguration, e.g., Jerome, *In Eph* 2.4.21; *In Mc* 9.1-7; Ambrose, *In Luc* 7.10-13; Augustine, *s.* 125.9. For seeing this passage as an epiphany, cf. Holzherr, 2007, 34; Michels, "Attonitis"; cf. also Kardong, 11; M. Bozzi, 1:202f.

pen: "In him was life, and this life was the light of the human race; the light shines in the darkness, and the darkness has not overcome it" (John 1:4-5).

In the Prologue of RM (Ths 7) the loudly thundering voice says: "if anyone has ears to hear, let him listen to what the spirit says to the churches" (Rev 2:7; Matt 11:15); in RB it is the word of a psalm that is apparently very dear to Benedict.

V. 10: "Today, when you hear his voice, do not harden your hearts!" (*Hodie si vocem audieritis, nolite obdurare corda vestra* [Ps 95:8]!)[37]

Benedict seems to have placed this verse very deliberately in the center of this passage: it is the verse that is sung every morning in the invitatory. The psalm for the invitatory was presumably chosen for this very verse, at least in RB.[38] Every morning this verse rings out like a fanfare calling for a full awakening. Today! The Letter to the Hebrews says that thanks to God's grace, there is still a today (Heb 3:7–4:11) that is renewed every morning. Therefore we are to seize this opportunity, to live in the today[39] rather than to delay things until tomorrow. We hear the divine voice, the voice of Christ in this psalm as well as in the other texts of the liturgy.

Do not harden your hearts! Being hard of heart can be connected with sleeping, laziness, and insensitivity (*pigritia, desidia*), yet the heart can also be hardened in refusal and pride. We may deliberately plug up our ears and let everything slide off us. Perhaps we fear the consequences of what we hear. Here, however, it is not the voice of a tyrant but that of the loving and inviting Lord (Prol 19), though we may harden our heart precisely against love and choose to remain frozen and be left alone.

Positively stated, this verse admonishes us to be sensitive to the Word of God, to let our heart be softened, pierced, and wounded, and to open it to the voice of Sacred Scripture, the liturgy, and in all of this to the voice of the Lord himself. Alone we cannot protect our heart against hardening. Often we are a stony soil on which the seed of the divine word dries up (cf. Mark 4:13-20). Yet the Bible consoles us, as for instance in the promise of Ezekiel: "I will give you a new heart . . . taking from your bodies your stony hearts and giving you natural hearts" (Ezek 36:26). With regard to this verse Smaragdus (75) says that an actual hardening of heart occurs when we do not

37. For the content of this verse see the dissertation of Hannah Quakebeke, "Du coeur endurci au coeur dilaté," Rome 2008 (written under the direction of Aquinata Böckmann).

38. In this context RM emphasizes verse 1 of Ps 94/95: through a responsory the abbot is to invite the monks to praise the Lord saying: "Come, let us rejoice in the Lord: let us joyfully sing to God our Savior" (RM 32.14-15).

39. Cf. A. Schmidt, "Jetzt" [Now].

want to do what the divine voice points out, e.g., as Prologue 17 says, "turn away from evil and do good." Hardened hearts are found in those who refuse to put on the new person in their actions.[40]

It is again characteristic for Benedict that listening goes hand in hand with the heart: we are not dealing with an external hearing but rather with an opening of our internal being. In a similar manner this is also true of the following verse. Lettmann quotes the following: "When I hear God's word with the ear of my heart, God's own heart can be opened to me."[41]

V. 11: And again: "Whoever has ears to hear, is to listen to what the Spirit tells the churches." (*Et iterum: qui habet aures audiendi audiat, quid spiritus dicat ecclesiis* [Acts 2:7; Matt 11:15].)

Only now, after the exhortation to open our heart, this verse follows. It is fused together from Matthew 11:15 ("Whoever has ears ought to hear") and Revelation 2:7 ("Whoever has ears ought to hear what the spirit says to the churches"). It was apparently not a significant problem for Benedict and his source that in the first quote, it is first God or the Lord who is speaking, in the second, the Holy Spirit through Sacred Scripture. The emphasis is on the unity of Sacred Scripture.

Churches: The Latin word *ecclesiae*—derived from the root verb "to call out"—may remind us that in baptism we are called out of our old life and that God's call leads us into a new community, first the church, then the monastic community. In his explanation of Psalm 33/34 Augustine says: "We are not to open our ears of flesh and close the ears of our heart; rather, as the Lord himself says in the Gospel: 'Whoever has ears to hear . . .' Who will not want to hear Christ as he is teaching through the prophet?"[42]

After the word "listen" has been sounded for the third and fourth time, we may consider once more how important this fundamental attitude is for Benedictine spirituality. From its first word almost to its end, the Prologue is permeated by listening: to the word, to the presence of God, obedience to him, doing the good that grows out of obeying/listening, fighting against what is negative, and finally running on the way while listening to the Gospel. Again it is evident that this open listening with the heart is a gift of God and of baptism.[43]

---

40. Cf. Art. "Endurcissement," in *DS*.
41. R. Lettmann. *Frau im Mantel von Licht* [Kevelaer 2004, 24].
42. *In Ps.* 33.2.16-18.
43. See the comments on Prol 1 in Böckmann, *Perspectives*, 15–18.

V. 12: And what does the spirit say? "Come, sons, listen to me. I will teach you the fear of the Lord. (*Et quid dicit? Venite, filii, audite me; timorem Domini docebo vos* [Ps 33/34:12].)

Here we have the first quote from Psalm 34.[44] All the preceding verses have been leading to this quote. The name "son, sons" is picked up again (cf. Prol 5). "Listen to me"—the word "listen" appears for a fifth time in this short paragraph. Our Rules see the psalmist as the Wisdom teacher Christ who is wisdom personified. "Hear the parable, hear and understand" (Matt 13:18, 21:33; 15:10) "Listen to me"—this recalls the first verse of the Prologue and of Proverbs: "Come, listen" (e.g., Prov 9:5; Wis 2:6). The word "come" reminds us of how the disciples were called (e.g., Mark 1:17; John 1:39), but above all of Matthew 11:28 on which the theme of the source in RM is based: "Come to me all of you." In commenting on this verse Hildemar (32) points out that the sequence "come, listen" is deliberate. Come believing, come in faith! Smaragdus (75 on Prol 9) calls our attention to the sermon of the good shepherd: "My sheep hear my voice; I know them, and they follow me. I give them eternal life" (John 10:27). Here coming precedes listening; yet listening to the voice will also bring someone ever closer to the Master. Perhaps this psalm verse also indicates that the voice is not intrusive; this time it is not a thundering voice but rather a small one so that we first have to come closer. This is not a contradiction. Sometimes the voice of Sacred Scripture thunders at us, but at other times it is like "a tiny whispering sound" (1 Kgs 19:12) so that we have to turn fully toward it. Come—this is addressed to all those to be baptized;[45] come, listen and be converted—this is true for every Christian and every monastic.

I will teach you the fear of the Lord. The central concept of the fear of the Lord appears here for the first time in RB. Its meaning will become clear in the following passage which explains Psalm 33/34. Already here, however, we may assume that this is not a servile fear but a filial fear.[46] This fear implies

44. This may be the reason that the edition of Salzburg Abbots' Conference (SÄK) begins a new paragraph here. Yet, as we have seen, vv. 12-13 do belong to the unit which begins with v. 8, and the new paragraph begins with v. 14 (cf. the diagram, pp. 2–3).

45. Cassiodor, *In Ps.* 3:12: "he comes to the third part where he addresses those who have accepted the first rudiments of the faith."

46. Smaragdus commenting on this verse says: "For this is a fear that causes love, not dread. Human fear is marked by bitterness, this fear by sweetness; the former compels us to slavery, the latter draws us to freedom. . . . For it is written: 'Those who fear the Lord, have put their hope in the Lord; he is their helper and protector' [Ps 115:11] and 'The fullness of wisdom is to fear God' [Sir 1:20]" (77, 78). Cf. RB 7, first step. Smaragdus also connects this fear with the light: "O monk, you must fear the name of the Lord, so that Christ the Sun of Justice may rise for you to drive out the darkness of your mind . . . and pour in the light of understanding" (78). For the content cf. also Cassian *Inst.*

that we recognize God's will and carry it out. According to this text the fear of the Lord can be acquired and learned by listening to the Word of God. Concretely we are listening to a psalm (cf. Prol 14-18), but within it we are listening to a wisdom teacher, Christ, who is speaking in all of Sacred Scripture but especially in the psalms.

I will teach you. With regard to teaching, we can think of the "twofold teaching" the abbot is to use. Scripture also has a twofold teaching: teaching by words but even more so by examples. Christ himself is a wisdom teacher in this sense. He is himself filled with the fear of the Lord (Isa 11:1-5) which Cassian also points out.[47] As the one crucified and risen, he became the personified wisdom of God (1 Cor 1:30). Here the vocabulary of "school" appears for the first time. In the school of the Lord's service, we enjoy the privilege of being taught by Christ and we will remain in it until death (Prol 50).

V. 13: "Run while you have the light of life so that the darkness of death may not seize you." (*currite dum lumen vitae habetis, ne tenebrae mortis vos conprehendant* [cf. John 12:35].)

Already RM changed the scriptural quote.[48] John 12:35 says: "The light will be among you only a little while. Walk while you have the light, so that darkness may not overcome you." John points to Christ as the light. In our Rules this is interpreted as the light of life although in the background Christ too appears as the light of life. Smaragdus comments on this verse in a similar manner: "For that person has in himself the light of life . . . who has him who said *I am the light of the world*" (79).[49] We are not just to walk—*ambulare* in John's text—but to run toward our goal (Latin *currere*). Time presses us to hurry. Benedict wants to motivate us to take some real action now. Now as there is still time, make good use of it (cf. Prol 42-44)—this is a characteristic trait of the entire Prologue.

The darkness is now called darkness of death (*tenebrae mortis*). Thus the light of life is opposed to the darkness of death (both are genitives of identity). In this passage both RM and RB have a negative eschatological outlook:

4.39.1: "The beginning of our salvation and the preservation of it is the fear of the Lord. For by this the rudiments of conversion, the purgation of vice and the preservation of virtue are acquired by those who are being schooled for the way of perfection."

47. *Conf.* 11.13.6f.

48. Cf. also Caesarius, *s.* 130.2: *Et quia nullis praecedentibus bonis meritis de tenebris producti sumus ad lucem, de mortem ad vitam revocati . . . curramus dum lucem habemus, ne praetereuntia salutis tempora neglegamus . . .*; also *s.* 197.4 and 209.1.

49. Cf. John 8:12. Vogüé *IV,* 53, thinks that the two quotes in Prol 11 and 13—divinizing light, light of life—are not well matched, yet it seems to me that the "light of life" means more than physical life.

things may turn out badly. Therefore we are now to do our best in listening and obeying, in running while doing good works! According to John 1:5, darkness has not overcome the word. Thus, if darkness is identical with evil, or even eternal evil, then running is, at the same time, an escaping from evil toward the good and thus toward the eternal light.

A semiotic carré can serve as a summary of this entire passage:

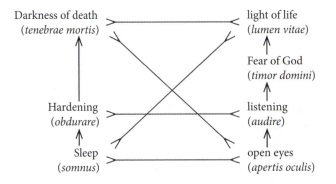

The starkest contrast is between the darkness of death and the light of life. The way to the realm of death is sleeping, letting everything slide and, more aggressively, hardening ourselves. Benedict, however, urgently wants to show us the way of life as long as we have the light of life as a gift. We need to open the eyes and ears of our heart so as to come, and even to run, to Christ. The fear of God is not yet given a specific content. In everything we see that these verses are of a preparatory nature and point toward the following psalm explanations and to the center of the Prologue: to walk our ways with the guidance of the Gospel (v. 21). There is barely another paragraph that stresses the function of Scripture as strongly as this one. According to the Prologue in John's Gospel, word, light, and life are descriptions of Christ (John 1:1-12), and in him and in listening to Sacred Scripture everything is decided: "Today, this is the time!" (*Hodie, hora est!*)

PROLOGUE 14-20

After Prologue 8-13 reminded us to listen to the wisdom teacher Christ, to whom we are invited to come, the explanation of Psalm 33/34 could immediately begin. Yet the authors of both Rules first present the psalm's dialogue between the Lord and the human person in the image of the owner of a vineyard who seeks workers. By doing so, the words of the psalm are again put in Christ's mouth and, in regard to the human person, are interpreted as a new beginning either in baptism or in monastic life. It is Christ himself who seeks his disciples, not the other way around.

On the whole, Benedict follows RM except for some additions, changes, and omissions. Especially at the beginning, the Master shows more clearly how these verses are connected to the preceding ones, for the Lord seeks the listener (*auditorem*) and he calls again (*iterum reclamat dicens*), thus emphasizing that this is the second call. This first psalm explanation is very similar to the second one in Prologue 23-36 (cf. the presentation of the Prologue's chiastic structure 2–3). We can write the text in the following way:

A 14 And the Lord, seeking his worker in the crowds, calls out to them, saying again:

15 "Who is the human being who desires life and longs for good days?"

  B 16 If you [sing.] hear this and answer: "I do," then God says to you:

  17 If you desire true and eternal life,

    C restrain your tongue from evil

    And your lips may not speak deceit,

      D turn away from evil and do good,

    C' seek peace and pursue it."

  B' 18 And when you [plural] do this, my eyes are upon you

  And my ears [turned] to your prayers,

  And before you invoke me, I will say to you: "Here I am."

A' 19 What could be sweeter, dearest brothers,

Than this voice of the Lord inviting us?

20 See, in his kindness the Lord shows us the way of life.

The paragraph begins with the Lord's seeking and returns again to the same subject, i.e., the Lord (A: 14-15; A': 19-20). He shows us the way to life as an answer to the initial question of who would want life. At the beginning and the end the emphasis is on the Lord's kindness and on what he does. The Lord's voice is mentioned, which invites (directly in A' and indirectly in A). The worker (A) has an equivalent in "dearest brothers" (A', v. 19). B (16-17a) and B' (18) contain a change in grammatical subject: "you [sg.], you [pl.], God, I." This is a very personal dialogue in words or actions: "If you [sg.] hearing this, answer 'I,' then God says to you [sg.]" (B); then in B' "when you [pl.] do this, my eyes are upon you . . . before you invoke me, I will say to you 'Here I am.'" The true and real life (B) could be described by verse 18: his eyes are upon us and his ears are open to us; he is present for us.

Thus in the center of the paragraph there would be a moral catalogue (end of v. 17: C, D, and C'). Beginning and end mention contrasts: deceitful speech/peace, and the short sentence (D) forms the center. This sentence is easy to remember: "Turn away from evil and do good." At first we may be disappointed about this core sentence, yet it shows how our authors read the psalms with an eye to practical actions. This sentence describes the two phases of the "practical" life (*praktiké*): negatively by turning away from evil, and positively, by doing good. We can call this a tropological or monastic interpretation. The psalms teach us everything, including that which matters in everyday life, and in this we would also have a plain description of the fear of the Lord (Prol 12). In addition, this center is to be seen together with the center of the entire Prologue (Prol 21): Walking in the way of Christ with the guidance of the Gospel is here first described in a strong manner as avoiding evil and doing good. What is at stake here is an enthusiastic consent to Christ which, however, must also become rooted in sober, everyday actions.

It is worthwhile to consider the entire Psalm 33/34 as a backdrop for this passage in the Prologue. Although only verses 12-15 and 16 are explicitly quoted or described, other verses have also left an echo. The words "come to him and you will be enlightened"—a literal translation of the Latin version of Psalm 33:6—*accedite ad eum et inluminamini*—are mirrored in the "divinizing light" of Prologue 9. And when Benedict speaks of the sweet voice of the Lord inviting us (Prol 19f.), we think of Psalm 33/34:9: "learn to savor how sweet/good the Lord is" (*gustate et videte quoniam suavis est Dominus*).

In the old Latin translation of the First Letter to the Corinthians, Clement of Rome quotes Psalm 33:12-18 as words of Christ and then adds (in n. 22f): "To those who fear him the merciful and forgiving father shows compassion and will give his grace with peace and gentleness to those who approach him with a simple and sincere will."

A narrative sequence might look like this: a new line begins wherever a decision is made.

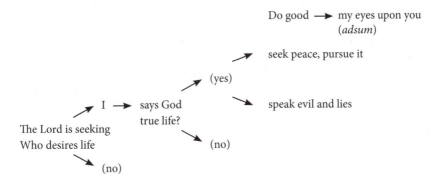

As this narrative sequence shows, some decisions are to be made by us, either for good or for evil. We may leave the call unanswered or answer in the negative. Yet if we accept it and let our longing for true life deepen, then our decision focuses on how to draw its consequences now in our actions; and after having chosen the good and peace, we will experience the Lord's loving presence.

V. 14: And the Lord, seeking his worker in the crowds, calls out to them, saying again. (*et quarens Dominus in multitudine populi, cui haec clamat, operarium suum iterum dicit.*)

This passage begins with the Lord's initiative, similarly to verse 8 where Sacred Scripture initiated the new beginning. Now it is the Lord himself who is seeking his worker in the crowds. Matthew 20:1-6 forms the background where the owner of the vineyard goes out seeking workers for his vineyard. If the crowds stand for all human beings, then this verse articulates the universal call to become a Christian of which religious life is but a more intense form. In RB (together with RM) the crowds presumably denote the Christians, thus we would have here a second call to a closer following of Christ.[50] Again we can recall Matthew 11:28-30 and the two calls the Master had developed on the basis of this text in his parable of the source: "Come to me all you . . . (1, Th 10) . . . shoulder my yoke and learn from me (2, Th 14). Yet what follows is not specifically monastic but simply Christian. This is another reminder of the baptismal catechesis that also used Psalm 33/34.[51] This is a second call to a closer following; its content, however, is an intensive Christian life that is entirely focused on Christ.

Here the Lord (Christ) is presented as the one who is seeking us. And we realize that our seeking him (RB 58.6 "to seek God [*quarere Deum*]") is but a response to his seeking which precedes our own (cf. RB 27.8-9 where the good shepherd searches the one who is lost). The Lord seeks his worker: the monastery is a workshop (4.78), where the main concern is the spiritual craft that is practiced with the tools of good works. Such work means cooperating with God as we are to develop the good gifts God gave us (Prol 6) in obedience and service. This is not a question about particular functions in the kingdom of God. Logically the Lord should ask: "who wants to work in my vineyard?" Or "Who is a good worker?" or "Who has the skills for this or that task?" Yet the question here takes another direction.

---

50. This seems to be the case in RM which explicitly states that this is the second call "And the Lord, seeking from among the many people a workman to hear him, again calls out saying . . ." (Ths 10).

51. Cf. Vogüé, *IV,* 42f.; also Peter Chrysologus, *s.* 62; Cassiodor, *In Ps.* 33.12; Augustine, *In Ps.* 33.2.17-20; PsJerome, *In Ps.* 33.

V. 15: "Who is the human being who desires life and longs for good days?" (*Quis est homo, qui vult vitam et cupit videre dies bonos?* [Ps 33/34:13])

The focus is on the human person him/herself who is then led from one step to the next. The human person has a strong will and is eager in his/her desires. According to Psalm 33/34:13, the goal is described as "life" and "good days." It is characteristic that God does not begin with high ideals but rather with very real needs: life and good days. While this at first may not sound very supernatural, it does show God's human side.

Vv. 16-17a: If you [sg.] hear this and answer: "I do," then God says to you: "If you desire true and eternal life . . ." (*Quod si tu audiens respondeas: "Ego," dicit tibi Deus: "Si vis habere veram et perpetuam vitam . . ."*)

Here we have reached the dialogue in which RB and RM introduce into the psalm quotes as was customary among the patristic authors whose aim it was to make the biblical texts come alive. RM challenged the one listening: "You who are listening, reply: 'I do'" (Ths 12). Benedict, however, says: "*If you . . .* answer, 'I do,' then . . ." and thus puts greater emphasis on the personal decision; he does not want to coerce us. "If you desire true and eternal life": God takes our vital needs seriously, yet deepens them by asking further whether we may not want more and more profound things. He wants to give to us in abundance.

This verse does not come from the psalm, rather the authors of our two Rules added it. Perhaps they felt that the first question was too ambivalent, or that wanting "only" life and good days was not sufficiently spiritual. With this added verse, the following imperatives show not simply a way that leads to a happy life on earth but rather a way that leads to the eschatological goal. It may also be, as Smaragdus (82) indicates, that life and "true life" actually mean Christ: "I am the way, the truth, and the life" (John 14:6). This corresponds to patristic commentaries on the psalm that see in "life" more than just a full life on earth.[52]

The human person now responds with a very personal "I do." She or he is called by name, is addressed very personally. Responding in this manner, the person exposes him/herself to the divine enticement and becomes available in obedience.

Then God says to you: The Master said "And the Lord will say to you" (Ths 12). Speaking in the present tense, Benedict actualizes God's address which thus breaks into the here and now. Why is "Lord" (*Dominus*) changed into "God" (*Deus*)? On the one hand, we could explain this as Benedict's attempt

---

52. Cf. Cassiodorus, *In Ps.* 33.13; PsJerome, *In Ps.* 33; Augustine, *In Ps.* 33.2.17.

to emphasize Christ's divinity. On the other hand, we could say that he wants to refrain from making the psalms overly christological.[53] If we see here a deliberate change, the first possibility seems more plausible to me since the same voice is called in Prologue 19 the "voice of the Lord" (*vox Domini*), the Lord (Christ) will show us the way of life. Thus it is Christ who says "Here I am" and Christ is the speaker in the psalm. Yet it might also be that Benedict changes *Dominus* into *Deus* for reasons of rhythm; in literature *dicit tibi Deus* occurs much more frequently than *dicit tibi Dominus*.[54]

V. 17b: If you desire true and eternal life, restrain your tongue from evil and your lips from speaking deceit. (*Si vis habere veram et perpetuam vitam, prohibe linguam tuam a malo et labia tua ne loquantur dolum.*)

Here another "if" appears. The moral teaching is taken verbatim from Psalm 33/34:14-16. A homily by PsChrysostom says: "The divine word calls . . . 'Who is the human being who wants life? . . . As with one voice you [pl.] answer the question of the God-man with 'I do.' But whoever wants to live, is to hear the precept . . . If you want to see life and find good days, restrain your tongue from evil."[55]

We may be surprised that the tongue is mentioned first, and this negatively in the sense that we have to guard our mouth from saying evil and the lips from falsehood (biblical parallelism). The ancients, however, were entirely convinced of the importance of the tongue. We recall James 3:5-8: "the tongue is a small member of the body and yet has great pretensions. Consider how small a fire can set a huge forest ablaze. The tongue is also a fire. It exists among our members as a world full of malice, defiling the whole body and setting the entire course of our lives on fire . . . no human being can tame the tongue. It is a restless evil." We can also make the connection with the importance of silence in RB (RB 6; 7.56-61; 4.51-56): the lips are not to speak falsehood or deceit. Hildemar (37) understands deceit either as something evil or double-faced. Commenting on verse 17b, Smaragdus (84) points to Psalm 11/12:4: "May the Lord cut off all deceiving lips." While the Prologue mentions the deceit on the lips, according to 4.24, deceit can also be kept in the heart.

---

53. Cf. Vogüé, *IV*, 52f.

54. Cf. Cetedoc I.

55. Cf. G. Morin, "Etude sur une série de discours d'un évêque de Naples du 6ᵉ siècle," *RBén* 11 (1894): 393. With regard to the Latin word *prohibe*, in this verse Smaragdus says: "that is withhold, restrain, coerce and repress. From every evil, that means from every form of slander, evil speech, murmuring, derision, vituperation, unjust reprimand, from lying words and idle speech and such like" (83).

An interesting saying of the fathers is connected with the following verse: "The brothers bring a parchment to Abbot Abraham and ask him to write a long text. But he writes only the one verse of Psalm 33/34:15, 'Avoid evil and do good, seek peace and pursue it.' The brothers say: 'Please write the entire psalm.' But he answers: 'When you will have conformed your entire life to the precept of this one verse, then I will write another text down for you.'"[56]

V. 17c: turn away from evil and do good. (*deverte a malo et fac bonum.*)

This sentence is placed in the center of this paragraph as its nucleus. It has a binary form with a negative and a positive part: turn away from—turn toward. This corresponds to the two baptismal promises: renunciation of the devil—acceptance of Christ. We may think of the teaching about the two ways. The prophet Jeremiah too was to root out and to build up (Jer 1:10). The general teaching of the monastic fathers was: first the weeds must be pulled out, then we can sow the good. Smaragdus comments on this verse as follows (84): "For many do good, but do not refrain from evil. During the day they keep a fast, and during the night they commit adultery; they give alms to the poor and receive plunder from the poor; . . . and to put it briefly, they do not cease to do in public what is right, and in secret what is wrong. . . . But there is another kind of person—and especially of monk—who turns away from evil and yet performs no good at all. He has left behind earthly toil in the world, and in the monastery follows idle pursuits."[57]

Perhaps this nucleus appears to be trite; yet in the monastic life according to RB we certainly have to deal to the very end with avoiding and turning aside from the evil in us and reach out more and more toward the good in our actions, not just in our meditations. According to RB 4 we might circumscribe evil with "anger, deceit, injustice, swearing, pride, various addictions, hate, envy, arrogance" and the good, for instance, with "love of

56. *Apophthegmata* X, 67 quoted according to: *Collection arménienne systématique. Vie des saints Pères* (Venice, 1855). Latin trans. L. Leloir, *CSCO (Corpus scriptorum Orientalium)* (Louvain, 1974), 41.

57. It is interesting to note that Dorotheus of Gaza also comments on this passage in *Instr* 4.50f., here translated here from the French: "through the fear of God he leads the soul . . . to turn away from evil and thus arouses her to rise all the way to the good . . . once one has succeeded in no longer doing evil and . . . in moving away from it, one does the good naturally. . . . The prophet adds the words: 'Seek peace and pursue it.' (51) In the attacks and counterattacks of this fight with the enemy he does what is good . . . when he is given help from God and has begun to be used to the good, then he begins to savor rest and peace ever more. . . . Is there any greater happiness than a soul that has arrived at this stage? She then enjoys the condition of being a son [of God] (Matt 5:9)."

God and neighbor, reverence, discipline, doing good, truth, trust, vigilance, openness, equanimity, chastity." We will never be done with these. During our entire life we will pray: *Kyrie eleison,* "Lord, have mercy, have mercy on me, a sinner" (cf. RB 7). It is, however, also certain what we are not able to uproot all the weeds before the good can begin to grow; rather, we need to do good deeds even while the evil is still present, and to practice love in the hope that love will slowly choke evil (cf. RB 72.2).

V. 17d: Seek peace and pursue it. (*inquire pacem et sequere eam.*)

This is the counterpart to the evil of the tongue and its deceits; at the same time, it is a positive intensification. Seeking peace, pursuing it, following it! We are asked, "What are you seeking?" We may have various answers that perhaps remain on the level of having good days and a comfortable life, or focus only on ourselves. Prologue 17, however, indicates a transcendence toward others and ultimately to God. Pursue God, chase after him, that is, energetically. "Benedict did not write a treatise on peace; rather, he created peace. Our lack of peace is caused by the fact that we do not seek God alone and have not fully accepted how God wants us to be his even in the very depths of our being. God loves me just the way I am."[58]

"Seeking" and "peace" are two key words for monastic life. The seeking of peace is related to the seeking of God (58.7) and points to the dynamics of the entire life, stretching toward the "true life" which is God (Christ) and in whom we will also find peace. Monastic life is clearly an expression of loving God with our whole heart and whole strength (cf. 4.1-2) which will become concrete in the seeking of God's kingdom (2.35) as well as in the eagerness for the *opus Dei,* in obedience and service in the community (58.7). In all this we concretely pursue peace.

Benedict does not say that we reach peace but rather pursue it. This will depend on taking at least small steps in this direction. In daily life this may mean to try again and again to contribute to understanding, respect, and reconciliation, to see the positive aspects of life, to emphasize that which builds up (cf. for instance Benedict's own way of proceeding in 34.3-5), and to pray time and again for the love of Christ so that we may again return to peace in our relationship with another (cf. 4.73; 4.25). As Hildemar (38) shows, peace among people is the fruit of "giving glory to God." Our seeking certainly is an answer to God's seeking us (cf. 7.27 and 27.8-9).[59] Thus, the beginning of this section spoke of the Lord seeking his worker (Prol 14).

58. Huerre, 20.
59. See Böckmann, *Perspectives,* 120–21.

Peace can mean not only peace in the community but also peace and tranquillity in our heart, satisfaction of the entire person, inner freedom, and *hesychia*. In the course of his Rule, Benedict will place more emphasis on the social component of peace, though the importance of inner peace is never disavowed. Does peace also mean Christ? Patristic tradition provides a basis for such an interpretation. PsJerome says in his explanation of this psalm: " 'Seek peace and pursue it.' . . . This is Christ for he himself is our peace."[60] Augustine says: " 'Where shall I pursue peace?' Where he preceded us. For the Lord is our peace, he was raised and ascended into heaven. Seek peace and follow him! . . . When you will be raised . . . you will embrace peace."[61] We need to follow Christ, to enter into his life all the way to the end, to the cross and his exaltation (Phil 3:8f.). It is certain that we cannot serve peace without imitating Christ by walking this paradoxical way of salvation (cf. the nucleus of the Prologue "to walk in his ways," v. 21).[62]

V. 18: And when you do this, my eyes are upon you and my ears [turned] to your prayers, and before you invoke me, I will say to you: "Here I am." (*Et cum haec feceritis, oculi mei super vos et aures meae ad preces vestras, et antequam me invocetis, dicam nobis: Ecce adsum.*)

Here follows the Lord's great promise that by far surpasses our actions and our seeking. I prefer to understand the word "when" in the temporal sense, not as a condition ("if"), although the differences are minimal.[63] It may seem strange that good actions appear first and only then God bestows his attention to us. Yet the same verse also says: "Before you invoke me." A Rule will certainly put emphasis on good actions that are an echo of God's Word in the Bible which RM 1.76 quotes: "Return to me . . . and I will return to you" (Zech 1:3). Whoever avoids evil, does what is good, and pursues peace will experience that God anticipates their prayers.[64] Let's not forget that good actions are made possible only by God's anticipating us. Throughout RB the necessity of grace is emphasized.

---

60. *In Ps.* 33

61. Augustine, *In Ps.* 33.2.19. Here too *sequi* is synonymous with *imitare*. Cf. Basil *In Ps.* 33.9 (v. 13), 10 (v. 15).

62. This corresponds to the fact that in the Rule the verb *sequi* is modified by its connection with the imitation of Christ (Prol 7; 4.10; cf. also obedience in 3.7-8 and 5.8).

63. Cf. Hanslik, 370.

64. Vogüé, *IV*, 51f.: *Convertimini ad me et ego convertar ad vos* (RM 1.76) [translated from the French]: "sought by the divine call, a person's 'conversion' in turn calls for the 'conversion' of God, that is, for the gift of his grace (RM 1.77-81). Here the Master looks at the gift of divine grace. . . . Whoever does what is good will have his prayer heard immediately, or even anticipated by God."

My eyes are upon you and my ears [turned] to your prayers. It is interesting that here too the eyes are mentioned first and then the ears, just as was the case when speaking of the human being in Prologue 9. Our open eyes may see God's eyes over us, our listening ears may find God's ears open to our prayers. We could say that God is "all eyes and ears" for us. Solomon prays: "My God, may your eyes be open and your ears attentive to the prayer of this place" (2 Chr 6:40). And as RM emphasizes, Psalm 33/34:16 says, "The LORD has eyes for the just." Benedict, however, does not describe his hearers as just because he is very much aware of the sinfulness and decadence of his monks. For Hildemar (40), this means that God bestows his divine mercy on us or the gift of the Holy Spirit. Smaragdus (86) quotes Psalm 32/33:18: "The eyes of the Lord are upon those who fear and revere him."

God's eyes are a particular topic in the first step of humility (7.10-30) and in chapter 19 where God's omnipresence is stressed. God's ears are open to our prayers. And Psalm 129/130:2 pleads: "Let your ears be attentive to the prayer of your servant." Eyes and ears also remind us of the mosaics of Christ in the apses of old churches. Probably the two components were not as separate for RM and RB as they are for us. Both are signs of God's turning to us: he is open to us, is entirely there for us, entirely oriented toward us. The authors of both Rules change the psalm verse by quoting it in the first person singular. Thus they turn the psalm into a personal dialogue between God and a human being. The form, however, might also have been influenced by Isaiah.

And before you invoke me, I will say to you: "Here I am." This is God's wonderful way of anticipating us. The expression is not found as such in Psalm 33/34 where we read in verse 16: "The Lord has eyes for the just and ears for their cry." Rather, two quotes from Isaiah are combined and connected with the psalm. Isaiah 58:8: "Then you shall call, and the Lord will answer, you shall cry for help, and he will say: Here I am." And in addition, we have Isaiah 65:24: "Before they call, I will answer; while they are yet speaking, I will hearken to them." These words contain something that is wonderfully freeing and shows the great unmerited love of our God. If God is so much for us, who can be against us? (Rom 8:31)

Here I am (Ecce adsum) is a circumscription of God's name (cf. Exod 3:14). "I am here for all of you, for you personally." It is an enormous declaration that our two Rules base squarely on Sacred Scripture! This recalls God's epiphany in the bush in the desert. God says this to us before we invoke him; he has known us before we were born. His love anticipates us. "I will say to you": we will probably not hear this with our bodily ears but rather with our inner senses, and thus we can speak here of an experience of God (cf. the word "sweet" [*dulcius*] in Prol 19). In its full meaning we will only hear it at the end of time; this was true for the "God-with-us," Emanuel (Matt 1:23), and it is true for each one of us personally. At times we too can intensely experience the presence of our personal God. The one who speaks these words is Christ, the Lord who is "with us until the end of the age" (Matt 28:20).

Of course we should reply to this "Here I am" with our own "here I am" that comes from our deepest heart. The Prologue tries to encourage this response. Again we are directed to the center: to walk in his ways with the Gospel as our guide (Prol 21; also Prol 3: to fight for Christ, the true King; and Prol 7: to follow him into glory).

V. 19: What could be sweeter, dearest brothers, than this voice of the Lord inviting us? (*Quid dulcius nobis ab hac voce Dominis invitantis nos, fratres carissimi?*)

The preceding verse is followed by an exclamation: see how good the Lord is! He is inviting us, he is not forcing us, he is enticing us so as to gift us with true, eternal life. Benedict now uses for the first time in his Rule the word "brothers," which he will repeat again and again, and here he even adds an emphatic "dearest" brothers, an adjective that is not found in RM. We may ask, who is meant here? The entire Prologue is directed to newcomers who are not yet called brothers. The explicit designation as brother occurs only after the rite of profession at the altar (58.23); yet apparently this also occurs within the community of brothers who, by each new beginning of a candidate, are reminded that they, too, are again at the beginning, are renewing their vocation, and are deepening their personal response to God. In a similar way, we may experience the Prologue with each reading anew as a call in our spiritual life.

The Lord inviting us is an image of God's love or, in other words, of God's hospitality. The word "sweet" can be an allusion to Psalm 33/34:9: "Taste and see how good the Lord is." If the word "sweet" might have been spoiled for us by maudlin lyrics, studies of German mystical authors can help us to grasp its meaning more deeply.[65] Since early times the word "sweetness" has been associated in German entirely with God. The word describes the ways in which God reaches out to woo a human being and how this human being recognizes him, answers him, and lives in him. The one who is allowed to taste "God's sweetness," is guaranteed to have life, earthly life, and, at the same time, the "totally other" life. God is the food for adults, and what they receive from God is always divine, is always sweet (cf. 1 Pet 2:3). Whoever is

---

65. Here I am following Schuth, "Süsse;" see also F. Posset, "Sweetness," who says that the sweetness points to Christ and especially to salvation.

enlightened "tastes the heavenly gift . . . the good word of God" (Heb 6:4), and having experienced this "sweetness" is to pass it on. In the course of time, the word "to sweeten" obtains the meaning of "to bless," and "to relieve," for "sweet" is what leads to salvation.

The human person who has opened him/herself to God responds by following God, incarnating in him/herself the life of Jesus who was the incarnated sweetness of God. God and the human person who is filled by him transform misery by touching it. Whatever is commanded is bitter; only when it is accepted, incorporated, and tasted as a gift of God—just as it is, without calculation—only then it will be transformed (cf. Exod 15:23-25). Because the cross of Christ comes from God, we can experience in it God's sweetness. Through the cross the bitterness of our old existence is transformed into divine sweetness.

V. 20: See, in his kindness the Lord shows us the way of life. (*Ecce pietate sua demonstrat nobis Dominus viam vitae.*)

Once again there is an emphatic *ecce*.[66] The word has an energetic force: see this opportunity! Now we want to act accordingly. Similarly, Benedict confronts the postulant with the decision: "This [*Ecce*] is the law under which you want to serve." Of course, this is a response to the "*Ecce adsum*—Here I am" of Prologue 18. The Lord, the one who is here, shows us the way of life or the way to life. The invitation began with the words: "Who desires life?" Now the kindness (*pietas*) of God is explicitly mentioned.[67] In the Prologue God is described twice as a "loving father/Lord" (Prol 1 and 38). The Latin word for "loving" (*pius*) does not mean pious/devout but rather benevolent, kind, loving, and merciful. God not only invites but also shows his inviting nature and—as will be shown in verse 21—even leads the way. And he himself is the way (John 14:6).

At the end, let us return once more to the beginning of this section and to the question: "Who desires life? If you desire true life, then. . . ." Now we would say more precisely: "then, follow the invitations of the Lord, follow in his way"! It is the way of Christ himself, as it is also recognizable in Prologue 21. This also sheds light on Prologue 17 (and later the explanation of Ps 14 [15]): These instructions show the way of life, the way guided by the Gospel, the way of Christ, and they help us to let Christ become incarnate

---

66. In RB *Ecce* occurs only in two other places: at the end of RB 4, "These, then, are the tools" (*Ecce haec sunt instrumenta*, 4.75), and in the initiation to the novitiate: "Here is the law under which you want to serve" (*Ecce lex sub qua militare vis*, 58.10).

67. *Pietas* as noun occurs only here in RB, it is a *hapax legomenon*.

in us. He stands at the beginning and the end of the way, and he himself is the way just as he himself is also the life.

After this section the nucleus of the Prologue follows logically which, in its way, summarizes the entire Prologue.

PROLOGUE 21-22

We come to the center of the Prologue which forms the nucleus of a chiasm (cf. schema 2–3). We could say that these two verses summarize the Prologue, and this is especially true for verse 21. It is remarkable to what extent the vocabulary of the way prevails here: "guidance, go forward on his ways, run, arrive there." Several expressions cluster around "him" and his kingdom: "guidance of the Gospel, his ways, he who called us into his kingdom, see him, in the tent of his kingdom." It is the Lord, Christ, his ways, his kingdom or his royal tent. Christ is also the one who began with us and called us. In contrast to other sections of the Prologue, it is noteworthy that in verse 21 the walking toward the goal is described only with positive expressions. Verse 22 takes up some points of the preceding verse and thus strengthens certain concepts.

> 21 Therefore, having girt our loins with faith and the practice of *good works*,
> Let us *go forward* on his ways
> under the guidance of the Gospel
> so that we may be made worthy
> to see him who called us into his *kingdom*.
> 22 If we wish to dwell in the tent of his *kingdom*,
> we will not arrive there
> unless we *run* there by *doing good works*.

This small schema shows that actually only three ideas are repeated here (italicized), namely, the final goal—though with different expressions—the good works; in addition, the running, going forward (*currere, pergere*) is emphasized in both verses. Verse 22 also provides the transition to the following section describing the way to the tent (*tabernaculum*). While verse 21 speaks of seeing (*eum videre*), verse 22 speaks of dwelling which is an important concept in the following section.[68]

Verse 21 has a very ingenious form and can be represented as a small chiasm:[69]

---

68. Many editions place v. 22 into the next section, e.g., Vogüé, Holzherr, SÄK, Lentini, RB 1980, Kardong, Colombás, and Quartiroli.

69. This particular translation tries to imitate the word order and syntax of the Latin original.

A Therefore, having girt (*succinctis ergo*)

  B with faith (*fide*)

    C and the practice of good works our loins (*observantia bonorum actuum lumbis nostris*)

      D under the guidance of the Gospel

        let us go forward on his ways (*per ducatum evangelii pergamus itinera eius*)

    C' so that we will be made worthy (*ut mereamur*)

  B' him, who called us into his kingdom (*eum qui nos vocavit in regnum suum*)

A' to see (*videre*).

The beginning of girding our loins (A) is contrasted at the end with the goal of seeing (A'). Faith (B) is born from listening and is connected with the call and being called (B'), and the good works (C) are connected with our becoming worthy (C'). This shows even more clearly that the expression "under the guide of the Gospel go forward on his ways" is the core of this verse and the entire Prologue.

With regard to the grammar, it is surprising that past, present, and future occur in this single sentence: he called us (*vocavit*), and the absolute ablative *succinctis . . . lumbis nostris* can indicate a direct past; the main verb is in the present "let us go forward," and the future is expressed in the final clause "so that we will be made worthy to see him." In this regard, too, verse 21 summarizes the Prologue.

Who is acting here? It seems that we are. But the relative clause says, "he called us." His act of grace precedes everything, and only then are we getting ready to set out on the way. The expression "we will be made worthy" (*mereamur*) indicates again that this is the doing of the Lord, not solely a result of our actions and our efforts. Verse 22 then puts the emphasis on our actions in correspondence with the tenor of this admonition.

We can read Prologue 21 slowly and in doing so set up a narrative sequence:

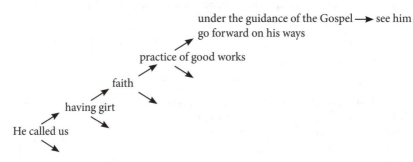

A new line begins wherever something is decided in one way or another. The Lord's call is followed by our girding the loins and getting ready. Here we may consult the entire Prologue and ask how things might proceed differently: a contrary possibility might be sleeping (Prol 8). After having girt the loins it is not self-evident that a person's first decision would consist in relying on faith; one could also rely on oneself; yet here the person trusts the call. The second expression follows right away: the practice of good works. Faith and good works are equally necessary, faith is to bring forth its fruit in good works. The reverse would be a listening that is not followed by doing good works; thus we could think that we would want to go forward on our own, under our own control. Yet here the (personified) Gospel offers guidance, and the person accepts this guidance against his/her self-will (*voluntas propria*) that perhaps is still powerful. Finally there is the marvelous promise: to see him. This or a similar narrative sequence might mirror our own life and remind us of specific pivotal points at which we made decisions. On our way we will again and again face new and even more profound decisions.

V. 21: Having girt . . . our loins. (*succinctis ergo . . . lumbis nostris.*)

This biblical image recalls Exodus, e.g., Exodus 12:11, where God commands the Israelites to eat the paschal lamb "with your loins girt." Girding oneself, however, is not only connected with readiness but also with fighting, as is shown in Ephesians 6:14-17 on which verse 21 is based: "So stand fast with your loins girded in truth, clothed with righteousness as a breastplate and your feet shod[70] in readiness for the gospel of peace. In all circumstances, hold faith as a shield to quench all [the] flaming arrows of the evil one. And take the helmet of salvation and the sword of the Spirit which is the word of God." This biblical text influenced the first half of verse 21 with the concepts of being girt, Gospel, and faith. Getting ready for a fight corresponds to the entire Prologue, as already Prologue 3 says: "you are taking up . . . the weapons of obedience," or later in Prologue 40: "Our hearts and bodies are to be prepared for the battle of holy obedience." It is significant that this battle is described twice as obedience, while the battle against demons is rarely visible, especially in Prologue 28.

With faith and the practice of good works (fide vel observantia bonorum actuum). The Latin word *observantia* connotes attending to rules or precepts. We may understand the "observance of good works" in the sense that doing good works is a practice that has become a habit that is lovingly kept (Latin *observare*). Faith and works form a pair. It seems that faith is deliberately set

70. This biblical quote has led to the following variant in RB manuscripts: *calciatis in preparatione Evangelii pacis pedibus* (shoe your feet with the boots of the Gospel of peace), manuscript group OVS, cf. Hanslik, 5; for description of the OVS mss see n103.

down as its first link, thus pointing even more clearly to baptism. Yet good works must necessarily follow, and thus Paul praises a "faith which is working through love" (Gal 5:6). How could faith here be further described? Prologue 49 (Benedict's own addition) speaks of progress "in monastic life and faith" (*conversationis et fidei*) while here monastic life is characterized as a life based in faith.[71] Faith means entering into the call of the Lord (cf. B and B' in v. 21) and expresses trust in this Lord who is calling us and whom we follow out of love.

Let us go forward on his ways under the guidance of the Gospel (per ducatum evangelii pergamus itinera eius). The human person is seen as someone who needs guidance; the Gospel here is personified. As is evident in the entire Prologue, the reference is not to one of the four evangelists but rather to Scripture as a whole, which has its center in the person of Christ. In practice this also means guidance through the psalms as the Prologue demonstrates. Moreover, the entire Prologue shows Sacred Scripture as a very active person.

The Latin verb *pergere* may still contain an echo of an adventurous beginning. As in the verb *pervenire*, the prefix *per-* indicates an energetic striking out toward a goal. Who is the person in whose ways we walk? It is clear that this is the same person who called us and whom we will see in his kingdom, namely, Christ. We might be surprised by the fact that the plural is used for the ways (*itinera*). Is not Christ's way only one? Besides reasons of rhythm, we can point out that in the Christian (monastic) community there is a variety of "ways" on which to follow Christ. What is required is that we follow in his footsteps (cf. 1 Pet 2:21) entrusting ourselves to his guidance, each person in his or her own ways. Here we also need to consider that Christ goes ahead and thus has paved the way. In a vast steppe, for instance, we are most grateful when someone has already cleared the way with a machete. Or in deep snow, it is easier to proceed when someone went ahead and left tracks or cleared the path by shoveling the snow. The expression to "go forward on his ways" may have a similar resonance: this is not a superficial imitation of a guide who is positioned in a certain spot and gives us directions; rather Christ himself went ahead, he is a guide who walks with us. In this way we can risk to strike out on these ways.

Again we see the pattern of the way that permeates the entire Prologue. We follow Christ into glory (Prol 7), run as long as we have the light of life (Prol 13), we want to run doing good works (Prol 22), truly want to reach the goal (Prol 42), and run while we still have time (Prol 44); finally, we run with the indescribable sweetness of love (Prol 49). The way may seem narrow at the outset (Prol 47f.), yet then the heart expands (Prol 49). The way of Christ is described as the way of life (Prol 20) or the way to the tent or the mountain (Prol 24), yet also as the way of the commandments or the way of salvation (Prol 48, 49). It is an intensive way within the Christian way that begins in baptism.

71. See Böckmann, *Perspectives*, 40. For *fides*, see Borias, "Foi," 249–59; Kurichianil, "Progress," 70–86, 8–15.

So that we may be made worthy to see him who called us into his kingdom (ut mereamur eum, qui nos vocavit in regnum suum videre).[72] The underlying biblical text is 1 Thessalonians 2:12 that speaks of God who called us into his kingdom and glory (*vocavit in suum regnum*). The Prologue emphasizes again and again that we are to have this "kingdom" before our eyes as an eschatological goal, or in other words, as our final vocation (*telos*). We desire to follow him "into glory" (Prol 7), desire to reach eternal life (Prol 17; cf. 44) and the tent of his kingdom (Prol 22; cf. 39), and eventually to be participants in his kingdom (*regno eius . . . consortes*, Prol 50).

Linderbauer is convinced that the liturgical formula *mereamur* must be translated as "to be made worthy."[73] This directs us to God's gift of grace; yet even so we are to muster all our energies. Being engaged with all our strengths as if everything depended on us, yet with the faith that everything is also done by him!

We will be allowed to see him (eum videre). This is a marvelous promise for which we long. It is a seeing and an experiencing of "what eye has not seen and ear has not heard . . . what God has prepared for those who love him" (1 Cor 2:9, RB 4.77). Certainly this is supreme bliss and unity. At times in our earthly life we will see it in a flash when the Lord tells us "here I am" (Prol 18) or when we are able to run on his way with an expanded heart and the inexpressible sweetness of love (Prol 49).

V. 22: If we wish to dwell in the tent of his kingdom, we will not arrive there unless we run there by doing good works. (*In cuius regni tabernaculo si volumus habitare, nisi illuc bonis actibus curritur, minime pervenitur.*)

The image of the kingdom changes into the "tent of the kingdom" as a transition to the next psalm explanation. We wish to dwell: this points again to the energy inherent in human beings, in their will. It is, however, not a matter of diminishing, or even destroying, this will, rather the will needs to be transformed or strengthened.

We run while doing good works, and thus running is, as it were, the doing of good works. Symbolically, we envision hands and feet at the same time. Without such activity, we will not arrive at our goal (*minime pervenitur*). Here the stronger verb *pervenire* (instead of *pergere*) is used, which will be taken up again in Prologue 44, where it has the same urgent tone; it will also be used at the end of the Rule (73.4, 9; cf. also 7.5, 67).

72. There are several Latin variants of this phrase: *ut mereamur eum, qui nos vocavit, in regno suo videre* (Codex O) "to see him in his kingdom." These variants connect seeing him with the kingdom. This is, however, not a substantial contradiction. According to 1 Thess 2:12 we can assume that *vocavit nos in regnum suum* is the more original version which does appear in most of the manuscripts.

73. Linderbauer, 131; cf. Lentini, 20; Puzicha, 57; Quartiroli, 11.

The entire human person, with heart and body, with loins, hands, and feet, with eyes and ears, is thus called to set out on the way as a response to the call. He or she runs, strikes out under the guidance of the "good" Lord who already went ahead, who guides us and, at the same time, desires to grace us with seeing him in eternity. Augustine said, "It was too little for God to make his Son into a signpost; he made him into the way itself so that he will guide you in your walking while he himself strides along in his own strength."[74]

PROLOGUE 23-35

After the core of the Prologue challenged us to walk on God's ways under the guidance of the Gospel and to run vigorously toward the goal, Psalm 14/15 is now being used to describe this way in more detail than was the case in the previous explanation of Psalm 33/34 (Prol 14-20).

This section is titled "Who is the human person who is privileged to dwell in the tent?" and this person is being described. The first psalm explanation had a similar beginning: "Who is the human person?" yet then proceeded to listing the conditions "if, when." These are two different ways of guiding the reader or hearer, yet both have the same function, that is, to be a practical motivation to do what is suggested. It is a surprise to note that the entire section basically consists of just three sentences: the question to the Lord (v. 23), his answer (vv. 24-34, with many relative clauses),[75] and the conclusion (v. 35). The description of the human person practically comprises only one main clause: "Let us hear the Lord" (*audiamus Dominum*). This distinguishes this section from the remaining Prologue but corresponds to the Latin text of Psalm 14. What might be expressed by this syntactical structure? Perhaps the fact that all these descriptions form a unit and are indispensable on the way to the tent.

It was possible to use Psalm 14/15 just as Psalm 33/34 in baptismal catechesis since they deal with the conditions for entering the tent and concretely for entering the church. This also is the reason for their christological interpretation. The holy mountain now is Christ, the way is the royal way (*via regia*) to the royal tent. Christ himself is standard and measure. He himself fulfilled the psalm and thus preceded us on this way. It is also significant that the psalm contains ten instructions which can be seen as parallels to the Ten Commandments, and even more to the commandments of the new covenant:

---

74. Augustine, *In Ps.* 109.2

75. One may disagree about the syntactical structure. Here the connection is seen in the relative pronoun *qui* = who, and further in *sicut* = just as (31), *et* (32) and *unde* = whence (33) as an indication that this is a single sentence. This is more pronounced in Benedict's text than in the one of RM which begins new sentences in Ths 29 with *ergo* and Ths 33 with *Respondit*.

the Sermon on the Mount.[76] The oldest commentary, the one by Smaragdus, clearly stands in the tradition of christological psalm explanation: "The guidance of the Gospel, that is also the guidance of Christ . . . the Lord's very deeds and his most sacred words are called gospels, which bring those who follow them by straight paths to the heavenly kingdom" (89). He then further explains this by pointing to the call to follow Christ in Matthew 19:28, Mark 10:21, and Matthew 16:24, as well as Matthew 11:28 and 1 Peter 2:21.

Ps 14 according to the *Psalterium romanum*	RB [in brackets important variants of RM]
	Prol 23 But let us ask the Lord with the prophet, saying to him:
Ps 14: 1 Lord, who will dwell in your tent or who will rest on your holy mountain?	Lord, who will dwell in your tent or who will rest on your holy mountain?
	24 After this question, brothers, let us hear the Lord answering and showing us the way to this tent
2 Who walks without stain and acts in justice	25 saying: who walks without stain and acts in justice,
3 who speaks truth in his heart and who did not practice deceit with his tongue	26 who speaks truth in his heart and did not practice deceit with his tongue,
nor did anything evil to his neighbor	27 who did not do anything evil to his neighbor,
and did not bear insult to his neighbor.	who did not bear insult to his neighbor.
4 Annihilated is the evil one in his eyes,	28 who drove the malicious devil, suggesting something to him, together with his suggestions away from the sight of his heart, reduced him to nothing and took his little thoughts and shattered them against Christ,
but he honors those who fear God.	29 who fear (pl.) the Lord and do not . . . become proud.
	30 they praise the Lord . . .
[taking oaths, lending, bribing]	[taking oaths, lending, bribing]
6 Who does this will never be shaken.	33 who hears my words and does them . . . built his house on rock [will never be shaken].

76. For sources and secondary studies see Egli, *Der 14. Psalm*, esp. 65, 101–3.

This psalm is well suited for portraying the dialogue of the human person with Scripture as it was already done with Psalm 33/34 in Prologue 14-20. In this psalm we have spoken words, that is, they are uttered by us as a question (v. 23), while from the other side there is an answer that contains demands and conditions and, at the end, a promise. After the first verse, both Rules insert a verse that intensifies the impression of a live dialogue: "Brothers, after this question, let us listen to the Lord!" The Lord answers and shows us the way.

In contrast to RM, Benedict used the relative pronoun "who" ten times (in the singular and once in the plural); with this he presumably wants to point to the fundamental law of the Ten Commandments in a way that is similar to what Cassiodor does in his explanation of Psalm 14. The evil one (*malignus*) who is counted for nothing now becomes the devil (*diabolus*).[77] Both Rules expand this with a quote from Psalm 136/137:9: "Happy those who seize your little children and smash them against a rock." This is the only allegorical interpretation that we find in RB. The little children are the little thoughts, the rock is understood to be Christ. In Psalm 14/15:4b, those fearing God are the direct object of the verb "to honor"; here they are the subject: those fearing God are now the monks. The verb "honor" (in Latin *magnificat, glorificat*) also becomes a plural in verse 30 and now refers to the monks.[78] RB follows RM by inserting an explanation regarding those who fear God.

Faithful to the psalm, the Master kept the demands from Psalm 14/15:4-5 about taking oaths and lending money but puts them in the mouth of the Lord, Christ—apparently alluding to the Sermon on the Mount. Benedict omitted these verses, probably because he felt that they did not apply to monks. In a monastery one is not to take oaths at all (RB 4.27); the monks have no money, and thus bribes cannot be accepted. The Master, however, is closer to the baptismal catechesis. The last verse of the psalm, "Who does this will never be shaken," is also found in Ths 31f., together with the end of the Sermon on the Mount ("Everyone who listens to these words of mine and acts on them . . ."). RB and RM explicitly refer to the Lord in the Gospel. Psalm 14/15 and the Sermon on the Mount thus are seen together and are intertwined with each other through the deliberate use of key words. Benedict

---

77. In many passages of RB the Latin word for devil, *diabolus*, is written *diabulus*.

78. Thus this paragraph transitions from the singular to the plural until v. 31 and returns to the singular with the quote from Paul. The question whether the psalm variant *glorificare* has influenced Ths 28 and v. 32 in RB can be left open. With regard to *magnificent* see Egli, 58; with regard to the christological interpretation, see Böckmann, "*Regula Benedicti*," 623f.

also closes the psalm explanation with the last sentence of the Sermon on the Mount, yet in comparison with RM, he simplified the text.

Our authors freely combine psalms, the Sermon on the Mount, and words from Paul; in all of them it is Christ who speaks to them. We ask the Lord (Christ) "with the prophet," that is, the psalmist. This entire section is a meditation on Sacred Scripture with Christ as its pivotal point: Christ, the mountain toward which we are going; Christ the rock against which we shatter evil; and Christ the rock on which we can build. Moreover, Christ walks ahead. We are walking on his ways, which he cleared, and he leads holding us by the hand. The section shows how Benedict concretely understands the term "under the guidance of the gospel."

To a large extent this explanation of Psalm 14/15 is identical with the previous one (Prol 14-20), at times even in individual expressions, though here the aspects of evil and of grace are more developed. Just like the earlier explanation, this one has as its title Prologue 21-22: the way to life or to the tent as an imitation of Christ in faith and good works. The guidance of the Gospel is concretely also guidance by the psalms, yet always in connection with all of Sacred Scripture.

It seems to me that this section, too, is structured as a chiasm which can be presented in the following manner:[79]

A 23 But let us ask the **Lord** with the prophet saying:

Lord, who will dwell in your tent, or who will rest on your holy mountain?

24 After this question, brothers, let us listen to the **Lord** answering and showing us the way to this tent:

    B 25 *who* walks without stain   and acts in justice,

    26   *who* speaks truth in his heart,

    who did not practice deceit with his tongue,

    27 *who* did not do anything evil to his neighbor,

    who did not listen to slander against his neighbor,

        C 28 *who* drove the malicious devil,

                making some suggestions to him, together with his suggestions

                    away from the sight of his heart,

                    reduced him to nothing,

              took his still little thoughts

          and shattered them against Christ,

---

79. The pronoun *who* is italicized (ten times), the name **Lord** is given in bold (also ten times).

B' 29   [those] *who* fear the **Lord**

and do not become proud about their good practice,

but rather know that they cannot do the good in them

on their own,   but that it is done by the **Lord**,

                                       30 they praise the **Lord**

                                       working in them,

                                       saying with the prophet:

Not to us, not to us, **Lord**,   but to your name give glory;

31 just so the Apostle Paul did not attribute

his preaching to himself   saying: by the grace of God

                                       I am what I am;

                                       32 and again he says:

                                       Who boasts, is to boast

                                       in the **Lord**;

A' 33 thus says the **Lord** in the Gospel:

who[ever] listens to my words and does them,

I will compare to a wise man

who built his house on a rock;

34 the floods came, the winds blew

and beat against the house, yet it did not fall

because it was built on a rock.

35 Fulfilling this the **Lord** expects

that every day we are to respond with deeds to his holy admonitions.

A (23-24) and A' (33-35) contain our dialogue with the Lord or his dialogue with us (first in the psalm, then in the Gospel), these verses speak of the mountain and the rock, of the tent and the house, of dwelling and building, and also contain the word "listen" (*audire*). B (25-27) and B' (29-32) are part of the psalm explanation. B contains six imperatives: four are negatively expressed, two positively while B', which continues with the relative pronoun, has ten instructions: four negative and six positive ones. Thus B' is outdoing B. I see C (28) as the center: evil is unmasked and even the little thoughts are to be shattered on Christ.

V. 23: But let us ask the Lord with the prophet saying: Lord, who will dwell in your tent, or who will rest on your holy mountain? (*Sed interrogemus cum Propheta Dominum dicentes ei: Domine, quis habitabit in tabernaculo tuo aut quis requiescat in monte sancto tuo?* [*Ps 14:1*])

Clearly the psalm is addressed to Christ, a way of addressing that is often found in RB.[80] In the psalmist who is designated as prophet Benedict first sees David but he also interprets the psalm as a prophetic expression regarding Christ.[81] Sacred Scripture is not only God's words to us, and we are not only its hearers; but also, in a second step, we are to make God's word our own and let the words of Scripture arise out of our hearts as question, as prayer, as expressions of our own. Those who read Sacred Scripture also have a better sense of how we can speak to God. The words of Scripture are, as it were, vehicles for the dialogue between God and us.

Lord, who will dwell in your tent? Using the psalm we direct the question to Christ. The twice repeated interrogative pronoun "who?" (*quis*) has its correspondence in the relative pronoun "who" (*qui*) that is repeated ten times in the following verses. The Latin word *tabernaculum* for tent (which occurs only in the Prologue) symbolizes the constant presence of God to human beings, a God who accompanies them since a tent can be taken down and pitched again. But the psalm goes even further by indicating that human beings also may live in the tent with the Lord. In RB, however, we do not find a spiritual, interiorized interpretation as in RM Thp 16-18: "rather may God himself sanctify it in the good deeds of his sons, so that as Father and Lord he may make his dwelling in our souls and send the Holy Spirit to live in us, giving help to our hearts by his regard and ever keeping watch over them by his presence." RM also uses the word "tent" in Scripture quotes, both for human life and for the monastery: "We have entered his tent [dwelling], we have worshiped in the place where his feet stood" (Ps 132:7; RM 57.20 and 66.6). Whether the tent is interpreted in an interiorized manner or an eschatological one, as seems to be the case in RB, it always indicates the presence of God, his dwelling with us and our dwelling with him, and in this respect it contains a mystical element.

"Dwelling" (*habitare*) is an age-old, primitive human desire, certainly for the Israelites during their wanderings but also for Christians and monks on their pilgrimage. John's disciples ask Jesus, "'Rabbi, where are you staying?' . . . and they stayed with him" (John 1:38f.). During our wanderings, moments of intense encounters with the beloved Lord will occur again and again;

---

80. It is "the voice of the Church [directed] to Christ;" cf. Fischer, "Psalmenfröm-migkeit," 25, 31; 64, 75.

81. Ambrose, *In Ps.* 1.9.

already here on earth we may be given a few such experiences, yet full bliss awaits us in the eternal glory toward which we are traveling. In the preceding verse (v. 22), our authors presented dwelling as an eschatological reality: "If we desire to dwell there, then . . .," whereas they see it as a description of monastic life in the summarizing final admonition in verse 39.

Or who will rest on your holy mountain? In most manuscripts (RB, RM, *Psalterium Romanum*) this rest is a future promise.[82] The tent, which can be taken along on the journey, is seen here together with the immovable holy mountain, presumably Mount Zion in Jerusalem. There we will not only dwell but also find rest. The authors of our Rules may have thought of Matthew 11:29: "and you will find rest for yourselves." In patristic exegesis, both mountain and tent are symbols for Christ. Smaragdus points to the mountain, which is the goal of peoples' pilgrimage in Isaiah 2, and says that the mountain itself is understood as "our Lord Jesus Christ himself" (92).

Tent and mountain are also symbols of the Lord's hospitality. We are at home with the Lord, are allowed to dwell with him, to see him, to find rest with him. In the Prologue this is primarily a good of the end time, but this does not exclude that it may be experienced in some ways even now. Benedict combines dwelling and remaining with dynamic movement. Jerome and Cassiodorus see it as significant that the tent is mentioned first, the mountain second. The pilgrimage comes first, the era of the church, while the dwelling comes only later.[83]

V. 24: After this question, brothers, let us listen to the Lord answering and showing us the way to this tent saying . . . (*Post hanc interrogationem, fratres, audiamus dominum respondentem et ostendentem nobis viam ipsius tabernaculi dicens . . .*)[84]

In keeping with the question, listening again is important. Those who are addressed are called "brothers" (in v. 19, even "dearest brothers"), a term that appears once more in verse 39, which shows great similarity to verse 24: "Since we have thus asked the Lord, brothers, about the one dwelling in his tent, we have

82. Cf. Matt 11:29: *Invenietis requiem animabus vestris.* The Latin edition of SÄK reads *requiescat* as do Hanslik and the manuscripts of the OVS group (cf. n103) while Vogüé has *requiescat.* RM has the same variants. Presumably the quote is from the *Psalterium Romanum* which reads *requiescet* though with *requiescat* as variant in some manuscripts. It is, however, also possible that in the sixth century, the future tense was seen as a present tense which led to an exchange of the verb forms.

83. PsJerome, *In Ps.* 14: *Non prius in monte, et postea in tabernaculo, sed prius in tabernaculo, et ita in monte. Tabernaculum non est firma domus . . . sed est domus incerta.* Cf. Cassiodorus, *In Ps.*14.1

84. The present participle "saying" (*dicens*) is part of biblical language and according to Linderbauer, 133, also characteristic of late Latin.

heard the precepts for dwelling there." The Lord hears our questions—even our deepest ones—and answers them. And not only this but he also shows the way, and according to Prologue 21 he even goes ahead, or according to Prologue 35, he himself fulfills all the instructions and thus in a twofold manner functions as a signpost. The royal way (*via regia*) is made concrete in Psalm 14/15.

Again, life's nature as a way, a journey, is emphasized, but now it is no longer termed "the way of life," but "the way to the tent." This also implies that dwelling in the tent is seen as true life. In contrast to RM, Benedict omits the phrase that the Lord speaks *contra nos*—"against us" (Ths 20).[85] Apparently he does not want to understand Christ's words in the psalm as a threat against us but rather as help.

In Prologue 25, the ethical instructions begin in the form of describing those human beings who are allowed to come to the mountain and will be admitted to the tent.

Vv. 25-27: Who walks without stain and acts in justice, who speaks truth in his heart, who did not practice deceit with his tongue, who did not do anything evil to his neighbor, who did not listen to slander against his neighbor. (*Qui ingreditur sine macula et operatur iustitiam; qui loquitur veritatem in corde suo; qui non egit dolum in lingua sua; qui non fecit proximo suo malum; qui opprobrium non accepit adversus proximum suum.*)

The three verses contain six solid ways of practical conduct, four of which are formulated in the negative, two in the affirmative. In formulating these instructions, Benedict used the relative pronoun "who" five times, which may be seen as half of the Ten Commandments (RM has this pronoun six times). Everything here has a direct bearing on living with others.

Who walks without stain and acts in justice. "Without stain" recalls purity of heart (*puritas cordis*, cf. RB 49.2; 20.2-4) as well as the beatitude in Matthew 5:8: "Blessed are the clean of heart for they will see God," or Psalm 118/119:1: "Happy those whose way is blameless." And RB 7.18 says, "Then I will be without stain before him if I guard myself against my evil" (Ps 17/18:24).

Benedict creates a stronger connection between the first and the second part of verse 25 by joining them through "and" (RM has "who"). It is of no use when people only avoid evil, they also must do good. Smaragdus describes justice as "fairness and rectitude. But because justice consists of works and of faith, that man fully does justice who believes rightly and exercises the whole of himself in good works" (93). According to Scripture God's saving justice

85. This expression "against us" is in the Latin text of RM but not in the English translation.

finds its human response in *iustitia,* in practicing love of God and neighbor. Christ himself came in order "to fulfill all righteousness" (Matt 3:15, *implere omnem iustitiam*). The teaching of the abbot is to permeate the community like a "leaven of divine justice" (2.5), and he is not to hide God's justice in his heart (2.9; cf. also 2.14, 19, 35). The chapter about the abbot in particular likes to use this word in connection with human justice which is to model itself after divine justice.[86] In RB, justice appears almost exclusively in quotes from, or allusions to, Scripture. In view of the gifts of God and Christ, we may ask ourselves today what mistakes against justice and peace ought to be avoided in our modern world and what positive steps we could take in the right direction.

Who speaks truth in his heart, who did not practice deceit with his tongue. The two parts of the sentence belong together, and just like in the psalm they form a pair beginning with "who." As in the explanation of Psalm 33/34, the tongue appears early. It is significant that after justice, the emphasis is on truth or veracity. According to the Latin Bible, *veritas* could also be translated as reliability. Without truth and reliability there is no justice! In the Bible both concepts often occur together; they are mutually dependent. This is also mirrored in the fact that in the first psalm explanation, peace is the crowning of the moral instructions. Thus we have three expressions: truth, justice, and peace! Truth occurs in a similar vein in 4.28: "to speak the truth in your heart and with your mouth." This is also the concern of the Prologue, namely, first to purify our innermost heart so that no untruth will proceed from it.

Immediately afterward we read that one "did not do" [practice] deceit. The Latin verb *egit* indicates the past tense, in speaking people were careful to avoid deceit and therefore are now able to speak the truth. We could say that this has become an attitude.[87] Again there is a similar text in RB 4: The tool "Do not keep deceit in your heart" (4.24 *dolum in corde non tenere*) is followed by "do not give a false peace" (4.25 *pacem falsem non dare*). Hilary referred to Romans 10:10: "For with the heart one believes in accordance with justice, and with the mouth one confesses for salvation."[88] Christ modeled all this for us because he only announces what he has heard from the Father (John 15:15).

Who did not do anything evil to his neighbor, who did not listen to slander against his neighbor. These two sentences relate to the neighbor in the singular, both contain the word "not," and are expressed in the past tense. Who is this

---

86. See Kardong, *"Justitia."* The three virtues of justice, truth, and peace (Prol 17) recall the three pillars of a good human and Christian community.

87. The *Psalterium Romanum* has three verbs in the present tense: *ingreditur, operatur, loquitur,* actual actions; then uses the past tense with regard to the person: *egit, fecit, accepit* followed by the passive form *deductus est.*

88. Cf. Hilary, *In Ps.* 14.4; Rom 10:10 is translated literally from the Latin Vulgate: *Corde enim creditur at iustitiam; ore autem confession fit ad salutem.*

neighbor? So we could ask with the Gospel and receive the answer: it is the one who has to rely on me, whom I can help (cf. Luke 10:29-37). In RB 4.2 Benedict states that we are to love our neighbor as ourselves. The expression "not do anything evil to him" may remind us of Tobit 4:15: "Do to no one what you yourself dislike" (cf. RB 4.9; 61.14; 70.7), or of its positive form in Matthew 7:12: "Do to others whatever you would have them do to you." There are innumerable possibilities to do something bad (or good) to my neighbor at my side, especially when we live in close proximity to each other. The past tense of the verb may again indicate that this has become a stable attitude.

Not to listen to slander (*opprobrium*) against another. Concretely this means any bad talk, slander, insult, and everything that results in shame. Many translations say that one is not to slander or insult another. Presumably the main point here is that one is not to accept, not to lend one's ear to such talk (*accipere* = accept). This keeps others from continuing to speak badly about a person and we ourselves do not do anything evil to the person. Sometimes we do not stoop to voice such slander ourselves, yet we might listen with hidden pleasure when others say such things about our neighbor, and thus might even take pride in our innocence and our feeling that this would be beneath us. Yet for Benedict it seems important not even to listen to such talk and to make sure that not-listening becomes our basic attitude. These admonitions are easy to apply to the monastic community, where we are always each other's neighbor (and very close ones at that).

These practical instructions of the psalm explanation (B) have a corresponding part in verses 29-32 (B'). In Prologue 28, the nucleus, all the evil is being unmasked, and this verse is significant for both section B and B'.

V. 28: who drove the malicious devil, making some suggestions to him, together with his suggestions away from the sight of his heart, and reduced him to nothing, and took his still little thoughts and shattered them against Christ. (*qui malignum diabulum aliqua suadentem sibi cum ipsa suasione sua a conspectibus cordis suo respuens deduxit ad nihilum et parvulos cogitatos eius tenuit et adlisit ad Christum.*)[89]

This sentence begins and ends with the two antagonists: the malicious devil and Christ. Where the devil emerges in person, as it were, the presence of

---

89. Someone tried to see the word *diabolus* = devil as a marginal gloss, yet all manuscripts have this word, which also corresponds to the patristic explanations of Ps 14. The Latin word *cogitatos* belongs to the fourth declension but is used here in the second (acc. pl). RM and RB interpret the "evil" in Ps 14 as the "malicious devil" who needs to be reduced to nothing by driving away his thoughts from the face (of the heart) and shattering them on the rock of Christ.

Christ also appears as he does not leave us alone with our opponent. Toward the middle part of the sentence, the devil's whispered suggestions (*suadere, suasio*) are mentioned twice, they are also called "little thoughts" (*parvuli cogitati* [sic]). In the center of the sentence we find the expressions of driving away and annihilating all these suggestions. Thus we could write the sentence in the following manner:

> Who drove the malicious devil,
>> making some suggestions to him, together with his suggestions
>>> away from the sight of his heart,
>>> and reduced him to nothing
>> and took his still little thoughts and
> shattered them against Christ.

This is a contest against *the* evil one who is at the center of every temptation and vice. An important part of monastic life is the struggle against demons, and thus Benedict describes the hermits as those "who learned to fight against the devil; . . . with their own hand and arm they fight against the vices of flesh and thought" (1.4-5). Antony of the Desert is the prototype for this fight against demons.[90] The desert is the place for fighting against vices; Christ brings salvation, he is the rock. In the cenobitic community we can train for such fights.

Benedict presents a spirituality of the heart. The devil's suggestions are perceived in the heart. Perhaps we find here a trace of a martyr's spirituality, possibly there is also a connection to the "acts of a struggling heart" (RM 10.12-13, *actus militiae cordis*). Benedict has only a few allusions to the devil: we learn to fight against him in community (1.4), "the devil is not to be given an opening" (54.4), and Benedict also attributes the desire to run away after having made profession to the "suggestion of the devil" (58.28). He sees the devil's presence not as often as the Master.[91] Might we assume that Benedict is more aware of Christ's victory over the devil?

"Suggestions" are mentioned here, that is, a gentle persuasion which, in a positive sense, is demanded of the abbot (2.31 *alium suasionibus*; cf. 40.6; 61.9). The devil wants to get close to the heart. He attacks the center of a person very gently so that, at the beginning, we may not notice it or even see the attack as something good. At the end of this verse the suggestions are called "little thoughts," which recall the expression *logismoi* of the Des-

---

90. Cf. e.g., *VitAnt* 9–10.
91. See e.g., Kardong, "Devil," and Leloir, "Diavolo."

ert Fathers. They were convinced that the temptations slip into us through thoughts and begin as thoughts which then grow stronger when they find fertile soil. Benedict uses the expressions for "thought" (*cogitatio* and *cogitatus*) mainly in a negative sense which confirms the opinion that he saw in them the temptations (*logismoi*, cf. 7.14-18).

The monk tosses all this away from his eyes, from his face, from the sight of his heart. Perhaps Benedict recalled the expression from Ephesians 1:18, "may the eyes of your hearts be enlightened." Just as the heart has an ear (Prol 1), so does it have eyes; and perhaps we may consider that it is important first to see and clearly perceive the temptations before doing something about them.

At this point the allegorical interpretation of Psalm 136/137:9 which is incorporated into Psalm 14/15 bears fruit. The Latin text reads: *beatus qui tenebit et allidet parvulos tuos ad petram*: "Happy the one who will seize and smash your [little] children on the rock." Our Rules interpret the little ones or little children as the thoughts which were just born and are still small. A quote from Cassian provides a helpful description:

> We must keep a careful lookout for . . . the beginnings of evil thoughts by which the devil attempts to creep into our soul. . . . It behooves us as well to destroy the sinners in our land—namely our fleshly feelings—on the morning of their birth, as they emerge, and, while they are still young, to dash the children of Babylon against the rock. Unless they are killed at a very tender age they will, with our acquiescence, rise up to our harm as stronger adults, and they will certainly not be overcome without great pain and effort (*Inst* 6.13.1-2).

Almost all the Fathers agree that the rock is Christ.[92] Commenting on this verse Smaragdus said: "Therefore for the devil to be brought to naught is for the monk to achieve maturity" (95).

The Prologue does not say how this smashing is actually done, but we may recall the fifth step of humility where the evil thoughts that creep into the hearts are laid open (7.44). RB 4.50 is equally clear: "To smash the bad thoughts which come into your heart, smash them against Christ and reveal them to a spiritual elder." Benedict added this last remark to what he found in RM 3.56.[93] The thoughts always want to enter the heart, the person's center.

---

92. For the patristic explanation see Egli, 61–64; Origen, *In Num* 20:2: "The soul gives birth to the little ones of Babylon which are our evil thoughts. Although the little child in us has not yet done anything evil, we are not to show any compassion, but must dash it immediately against the rock, Christ. . . . When they are still small, we can easily grab them." Similarly Jerome, *Ep* 22.6; Augustine, *In Ps.* 136.21 calls the little ones the evil desires that were just born. Cf. also Hilary, *In Ps.* 136.14; Ambrose, *De Paenit.* 2.106.

93. The Latin verb in 4.50 is *patefacere* = to lay open, reveal; in 7.44 the idea is expressed negatively: *non celaverit* = are not kept hidden. Cf. Ambrose, *De paenit.* 2.106; *In Ps* 136.9.

As they creep in and arrive there, the impulse to destroy them immediately must also begin there. This occurs, for instance, when they are disclosed to a spiritual elder (in Latin *senior*). It is good that Christ, the rock, provides us with help so that we can examine without fear everything creeping into us, then seize it and smash it on him. Other concrete possibilities are: saying an ejaculatory prayer, especially psalm prayers and the Jesus prayer, opening and reading the Bible, or simply gazing on Christ. All this requires vigilance over ourselves.

At this point in the psalm explanation a longer section (B') about grace and good works is inserted. Here other actions are mentioned (cf. above 48) which we are to do (six) or not to do (four). The list of the good actions is longer: may we understand this in the sense that the good will prevail after the evil thoughts were shattered on Christ? The negative actions do not deal with evil actions per se (since these verses speak of good behavior, good things, of a sermon etc.), but consideration is given to what we do with them and to the attitude in which we do them. The focus is on different virtues or vices, namely, the pride of being conceited about the good in us, and in contrast, humility in which all the good in us is attributed to God.

This reminds us of the classic doctrine about virtues and vices. First the focus is on overcoming our fundamental sin: verses 25-27 list evil, deceit, and slander. Once we have overcome these evils and are practicing what is good, i.e., justice and truth, then vanity and pride raise their ugly heads, taking advantage of everything, even of virtues. And these last vices are particularly difficult to overcome. We can see the connection in verse 28, where the devil suggests "you are really good, you are practicing all the good things, speaking the truth and doing justice; you have advanced very far already." At this point everything may go awry.

In considering the schema (47–48) we see very clearly that the worm can creep even into our good behavior, our good actions, the salutary sermon. On the left side in verse 28 we have expressions such as to be proud, to do things on our own, to ascribe things to ourselves and give glory to ourselves. This is all very human and cannot be quickly caught and uprooted. The devil has very clever ways of attacking us. Thus the weight of the good actions must be greater (cf. the six expressions on the right side): the good is done by the Lord, he is acting in us, we give glory to his name, all we are comes through the Lord's grace, and thus we boast in the Lord. These are six variants of the same topic. It is significant that here the **Lord** (printed in bold) occurs more often than in verses 25-27, namely, seven times. It is necessary to hold fast onto him, yet he also acts with greater power.

The good is not denied, but the verse continues in a different vein: We boast in the Lord and acknowledge "by the grace of God I am what I am;" we believe that all the good in us comes from the Lord and that the Lord works in us. Thus everything serves to glorify the Lord. As remedies of pride, the text mentions to be aware of God's grace and to give all glory, honor, and praise to the Lord. We can compare this with the fifth step of humility, which in its center has the phrase: "Confess to the Lord for he is good, his mercy endures forever" (7.46). Praising the Lord means: of myself I am nothing—every good in me comes from him (cf. also 4.42). All this is also an important foundation for the doctrine on prayer. Everything always points toward the Lord, and it seems to me that in the spiritual life, progress is made when we live in such a way that it cannot be explained without God.

The prepositions in the section are interesting: the good in them (*in se [bona]*)—not from them (*non a se*)—by the Lord (*a Domino*)—the Lord in them (*in se Dominum*)—in the Lord (*in Domino*). With regard to the "in" we note that it refers to the Lord, Christ, working *in* us and to us boasting *in* the Lord.

This section is expressed to a great extent in antitheses:

to become proud (*elatio*)	to fear the Lord (*timentes Dominum*)
to do the good on our own (*bona a se posse*)	
to give us the glory (*Gloria nobis*)	to give glory to God (*Gloria Domino*)
attribute to ourselves (*sibi inputare*)	to give glory to the Lord who works in us (*operantem in se Dominum magnificant*)

V. 29: [Those] who fear the Lord and do not become proud about their good practice, but rather know that they cannot do the good in them on their own, but that it is done by the Lord. (*Qui timentes Dominum de bona observantia sua non se reddunt elatos, sed ipsa in se bona non a se posse, sed a domino fieri existimantes.*)

This is the second time that the fear of the Lord is mentioned in the Prologue. While in the first part it has as its content avoiding evil and doing good (Prol 17; 12), we can now say, whoever fears the Lord does what is good and attributes it to God, all praise is given to him. Or expressed negatively: we do not place ourselves above others nor ascribe the good to ourselves. In the Latin word *elatus* we have a graphic image of a person who wants to rise above the crowd, in this case because of his or her good observance of the commandments, his or her good life (*bona observantia*). This is the attitude of the Pharisee in Luke 18:9-14. The good "in them" is, however, done "by the Lord"; it is in us but is done, effected, by the Lord. In a similar manner

Prologue 6 says "with his good gifts that he implanted in us." Here the text takes a further step: we are to acknowledge that the good is done by the Lord aware of the biblical word "without me you can do nothing" (John 15:5). We cannot do the good on our own.[94]

V. 30: They praise the Lord working in them, saying with the prophet: Not to us, not to us, Lord, but to your name give glory. (*Operantem in se Dominum magnificant illud cum propheta dicentes: non nobis, Domine, non nobis, sed nomini tuo da gloriam* [Ps 113:9].)

I would like to call this passage the "Magnificat" of Benedict's Rule: "My soul proclaims the greatness of the Lord; my spirit rejoices in God, my Savior. . . . The Mighty One has done great things for me" (Luke 1:46-47, 49). Benedict's expression here is simpler and perhaps more radical than the one in RM if we translate *operantem in se magis Dominum magnificent* as "they are to praise the Lord who is working more in them" (Ths 26).[95]

The Lord acts in us. It is characteristic that this does not describe God's presence in us as such. Benedict does not want to write either a theology or a Christology; rather, as a practical man, he is interested in the fact that the Lord works in us, that we are to let him work in us, and acknowledge his working in us. In 4.42f. we read, "To attribute some good you might see in yourself, to God, not to yourself; yet to know always that evil is done by yourself and attributed to yourself." In this way everything becomes an occasion for praising the greatness and the power of God. We are allowed to accept, receive God's working in us, even in our prayer. Might we even see the two expressions "the good in us" (v. 29 *bona in se*) and "God working in us" (*operantem in se Dominum*) together and say: At the end it is not the good (*bonum, bona,* neutral gender) but the good Lord (*bonus,* masculine gender) that is in us?

Saying with the prophet: Not to us, not to us, Lord, but to your name give glory. Once more the human person speaks with the prophet (the psalm). RB contains several psalm verses that are suitable as ejaculatory prayers. This is one of them that may well be used against temptations of thoughts and vanity. Herwegen sees here the culmination of the three tasks: "In truth and love the monk stands within the community, and through his inner struggle against evil his personality enters into Christ; in this growing union with Christ he gives God alone the glory."[96]

94. In *Inst* 12.17.1, Cassian says: "I am not able to do anything by myself" (*nihil a semetipso se posse facere*), cf. also *Conf.* 13.12.1.
95. The sentence, however, might also be translated as "rather they are to praise the Lord."
96. Herwegen, 36.

V. 31: Just so the Apostle Paul did not attribute his preaching to himself saying: "by the grace of God I am what I am." (*Sicut nec Paulus Apostolus de praedicatione sua sibi aliquid inputavit dicens: Gratia Dei sum id quod sum.*)

Here Benedict, together with RM, names the apostle Paul directly; normally he says simply "apostle," which designates Paul almost as a matter of course (with one exception in 58.1, where "apostle" refers to John). Paul talks about how much he has worked but adds: "By the grace of God I am what I am, and his grace to me has not been ineffective. Indeed, I have toiled harder than all of them; not I, however, but the grace of God that is with me" (1 Cor 15:10). He speaks highly of himself, yet at the same time says that everything is to be attributed to grace. This shows a healthy sense of self-esteem: I am worthy, I have done much, but everything I am is due to the grace and love of God. We do not praise God when we say that we have not accomplished anything and have no worth. While Benedict here speaks about Paul's preaching and evangelization, he certainly does not want to limit his statement to this function, rather it seems significant that Paul in his preaching is also a model for Benedict and his monks. Hand in hand with this goes the admonition that we are not to receive the grace of God in vain but rather serve in and with it (2 Cor 6:1). This has also consequences for our prayer: faith and recognition that God is at work both in our life and our prayer, however it may go!

V. 32: And again he says: "Who boasts, is to boast in the Lord." (*Et iterum ipse dicit: Qui gloriatur, in Domine glorietur.* [2 Cor 10:17]).

Benedict here changes a Scripture quote from RM that says: "If there is to be boasting, it is not for me to do it" (2 Cor 12:1; Ths 28). To be sure, the Apostle speaks highly of himself, but he does so with regard to his weaknesses. Benedict chooses this other Scripture quote from the same letter to the Corinthians. Perhaps he wanted to prevent a misunderstanding that one was not allowed to speak highly of oneself at all. We are allowed to see the good in ourselves and to acknowledge it but then must go a step farther and give God praise and glory for it. The expression "in the Lord" (*in Domino*) reminds us of Paul's expression "in Christ." He is present in us and acts in us though we are already basically embraced by him and live in him. "Remain in me, and I will remain in you" (John 15:4).

Verses 33-35 (A') belong together and with verses 23-24 (A) form the inclusion of this entire section. There is a slight shift in the images: the focus is no longer on the tent and the mountain but on the house on the rock. The house belongs to the Lord and the Lord himself is the rock. Thus we have altogether three different views, as it were, of Christ the rock:

The rock, the mountain toward which we go—our goal;
the rock against we can smash everything that is evil;
the rock on which we can build.

Thus we could say: Christ as the rock before us, below us, and with us.

V. 33: Thus says the Lord in the Gospel: who[ever] listens to my words and does them, I will compare to a wise man who built his house on a rock. (*Unde et Dominus in evangelio ait: Qui audit verba mea haec et facit ea, similabo eum viro sapienti, qui aedificavit domum suam super petram* [Matt 7:24].)

The psalm explanation is brought to its end by quoting the conclusion of the Sermon on the Mount. Already RM had combined it with the last verse of Psalm 14/15:5: "whoever acts like this will never be shaken." In Matthew 7:24 we read, "Everyone who listens to these words of mine and acts on them . . ." The expression "these words of mine" not only identifies the Sermon on the Mount in the Prologue but also designates the preceding words of the psalm and of Paul as words of Christ and acting according to them as fulfilling the law of the new covenant. Now it is fully evident that the preceding was in fact a dialogue between Christ and the monk. In a certain sense the Sermon on the Mount, too, was a Prologue for Christ's teaching ministry. Verses 33-34 are probably designed to call to mind the entire Sermon on the Mount.

The connecting word *unde* = whence, from which, is not a fortunate choice but is a clear proof that RM existed prior to RB because in RM this conclusion is preceded by explicit quotes from the psalm, including those verses that do not directly relate to monks (mentioning swearing of oaths, lending at interest and bribes).[97] The text from the gospel is slightly changed: In RM and RB Christ himself compares ("I will compare him" [*similabo*], not as in the NT "he will be compared" [*adsimilabitur*]) the listener and follower to a wise person. To build the house on a rock now means to build it on Christ. Shortly before this, Christ had been described as rock. According to Smaragdus (98), building on sand would mean building on oneself, for the human person is dust and returns to dust, but Christ is rock (cf. 1 Cor 10:4 "the rock was Christ"). We also recall 1 Corinthians 3:11: "for no one can lay a foundation other than the one that has been laid: Jesus Christ."

Monastic life is compared to building a house: "The monk is unshakably in Christ when the word of God is incarnate in him and has given him a spiritual scaffolding that is indestructible and of divine stability."[98] Hildemar (57)

---

97. Then Ths 31 continues logically: *Et subsequitur nobis Dominus in evangelio*, "and in the gospel the Lord continues saying to us."

98. Huerre, 98.

thinks that the one who builds on rock is the one who does good works out of love for Christ and has Christ as his foundation; but the one who builds on sand is the one who does anything good in order to gain human praise. We can think of the parable of the vine: "Whoever remains in me and I in him will bear much fruit because without me you can do nothing" (John 15:5).

The person who is so anchored in Christ is a wise person who knows by way of discernment what is essential, who fears the Lord, listens to the word and puts it into practice, and in everything praises God. Thus the greatest human endeavor is combined with total dependence on God! The word "wise" (*sapiens*) may also resonate with the idea that for such a person the good things are tasty, "sweet" as it were, or that such a person is able to accept "what is bitter as sweetness."[99]

V. 34: The floods came, the winds blew and beat against the house, yet it did not fall because it was built on a rock. (*Venerunt flumina, flaverunt venti et impegerunt in domum illam, et non cecidit, quia fundata erat super petram.*)

Built on Christ and firmly anchored in him, the house cannot be shaken by anything. The gospel text speaks of rain, floods, and winds. RM and RB omit the rain, but the writers of the old commentaries apparently read it into them, as the gospel text was present to them. This does, however, not cause any change in the context because the floods are probably occasioned by cloudbursts.[100] This image was not foreign to the Mediterranean region where, for security, houses and cities were firmly built on rocks. Storms and floods are symbols of all adverse, inimical powers to which we are exposed and which are beyond our control. Yet we can trust in Christ, our rock, who gives us security and protection.

V. 35: Fulfilling this the Lord expects that every day we are to respond to his holy admonitions with deeds. (*Haec conplens Dominus expectat nos cotidie his suis sanctis monitis factis nos respondere debere.*)

This verse concludes the section.[101] We can translate it in two ways: the Lord concludes, or the Lord fulfills; both translations are correct. Smaragdus, for

---

99. See the explanation of Prol 19. The close proximity of the two expressions "fear of the Lord" and "wise" is present through the entire RB, cf. e.g., 31.1-2; 66.1, 4.

100. Cf. Smaragdus (99) and Hildemar (57). The SÄK translation mentions "cloudbursts and flows of water" (instead of *flumina* = floods) and storms (*venti* = winds); Holzherr and Steidle mention "cloudbursts and storms."

101. In my opinion, this verse is not to be moved into the next section as do Vogüé, Colombás, and Quartiroli as well as RB 1980 and Kardong. *Expectat* belongs to the

instance, points to Christ, the Lord, who announced in words and fulfilled in deeds what he said. "He himself completed in himself what he commanded the dweller in the tent to fulfill" (100), he himself fulfilled the entire psalm and even surpassed it. With the conclusion from the Sermon on the Mount, Benedict desires to present the way to the tent as evangelical perfection.[102] It is very important to Benedict that all this is to be practiced every day, for the Lord also calls us every day (Prol 9), daily opens our ears, and nourishes us with his bread every day. RM said: "The Lord is silent, waiting for us" (Ths 35), which has an almost menacing ring. Benedict omits the Lord's silence and changes the verb "waiting" (*spectans*) to "expects" (*expectat*): the Lord expects something of us; he has, so to speak, expectations of us. Moreover, the verb *expectat* becomes the main verb and is no longer as in RM an accompaniment to *tacet* = is silent.

Everything we do is a response to the Lord; he himself precedes us (Prol 21, 7), we are following him. This section provides the content for the expression in the Prologue's nucleus "to go forward under the guidance of the gospel." This means to practice love of one's neighbor daily, then let the Lord himself work in us and to give praise to him in everything, to anchor ourselves ever more deeply in Christ, not to fear the ungodly powers, and to smash temptations right away against Christ. We will never be done with all this during our earthly life. To go on his ways under the guidance of the Gospel means to let ourselves be guided by all of Sacred Scripture, by the psalms, by St. Paul, by the Sermon on the Mount, and above by Christ himself.

PROLOGUE 36-39

After the explanation of Psalm 14/15 concludes with the Sermon on the Mount and its admonition to practice what was heard, we would expect that the school of the Lord's service is now presented in concrete terms. But both RM and RB insert another section (Prol 36-39) that corresponds to the introduction to the first psalm explanation of Psalm 33/34 (Prol 8-13). This introduction emphatically urged us to listen by already using a verse of this psalm, "Come, children listen to me" (v. 12). Now, after the second psalm explanation (Prol 23-35), there follows an equally emphatic admonition to translate what was heard into real action. In doing so, there is another allusion to Psalm 14/15 ("dwelling in his tent"). Both the introduction (Prol 8-13) and the conclusion of the psalm explanations (Prol 36-39) mention

---

psalm and the Sermon on the Mount, and *conplens* is an integral part of the psalm explanation. Verse 36 begins anew with a different scenario.

102. Cf. Hildemar (58).

both sides, the negative—sleep, hardening of the heart, shadows, misdeeds, death—and the positive—life.

The section of Prologue 36-39 is not designed to offer new ideas but rather to emphasize and to imprint more deeply in our minds some of the ideas already mentioned. This can be presented as another chiasm:

36 Therefore the days of our life are a gift to us as a period of grace for the correction of our mistakes,

> 37 as the Apostle says: "Do you (sg.) not know
>
> that the patience of God would lead you (sg.) to repentance?"
>
> 38 For the good Lord says:
>
> "I take no pleasure in the death of the sinner,
>
> but rather that he turn back and live."

39 Since we have thus asked the Lord, brothers,

about the one dwelling in his tent,

we have heard the precept for dwelling there,

may we fulfill the obligations of one dwelling there . . .

The sentences in the plural ("we, us") at the beginning and the end contain demands: "therefore" (*ideo*), "thus" (*ergo*). In the center there are two statements with Scripture quotes that are formulated as parallels: The "patience of God" corresponds to the "good Lord;" first repentance is mentioned, then conversion, and beyond this, life. Both quotes refer to the human person in the singular (in RM one sentence is in the plural, the other in the singular).

Verse 39 summarizes this short section as well as the preceding psalm explanation. The address "brothers" is repeated (cf. Prol 24), yet is brought into line with verse 35: there the Lord fulfilled (*complens*) what he said; here we too are to fulfill (*compleamus*) what he said. Here the concern is with admonitions and precepts and a response in deeds (*factis respondere* [35], *complere officium* [39]). Based on this we can understand why some manuscripts concluded the Prologue here. The group of the OVS texts (the so-called interpolated text) concludes thus: "If we fulfill the duties of a dweller [in the tent] we will be heirs of the kingdom of heaven."[103]

***

103. OVS group: Manuscript Oxoniensis, Veronensis and Sangallensis, 916. The most famous codex is Hatton 48, of which we have a facsimile edited by D. H. Farmer. The question of where to end the Prologue is thoroughly discussed by Zelser, "Geschichte," 724f., 749. With regard to the problem of a short or a long Prologue, cf. Roth, "Ursprung." The expression *sed si compleamus habitatoris officium* sounds harsh and unusual as end of a section, thus the redactor added: *erimus heredes regni caelorum*. Cf. Hildemar, 61f.:

V. 36: Therefore the days of our life are a gift to us as a period of grace for the correction of our mistakes. (*Ideo nobis propter emendationem malorum huius vitae dies ad indutias relaxantur.*)

Our days are lengthened by a period of grace (*dies ad indutias relaxantur*). The Latin word *indutiae* can also denote a pause or interval, though here its meaning is clearly that we are to make good use of this gift of precious time. In comparing this with Abraham's begging for Sodom and Gomorrha, Gordan states: "With Benedict the superior and patient kindness of God as well as the autonomous dignity of the human person appear in an even brighter light."[104] 2 Peter 3:9 says, "The Lord does not delay his promise . . . but he is patient with you, not wishing that any should perish but that all should come to repentance." And later the same text says: "And consider the patience of our Lord as salvation" (2 Pet 3:15).

For the correction of our mistakes. In his own addition to the Prologue Benedict talks once more about the correction of our mistakes (Prol 47: *propter emendationem vitiorum*). We are all sinners in need of purification; no one is excluded. Even with regard to the abbot, we read in the last verse of RB 2: "Thus he is cleansed of his own faults" (2.40). The time for doing this is given to us.[105] Benedict is convinced that throughout our life we will have to deal with our sins and mistakes and will never be able to feel that we have moved beyond this. Thus it is never superfluous to use the Jesus prayer: "Lord, have mercy on me, a sinner." As shown in the preceding paragraph, only the vices change as they become more subtle, more interiorized. This basic insight into human nature may not be very obvious to us, but it certainly challenges us. While the previous passages of the Prologue describe the human person as listener, worker, and brother, this description is now deepened: the person is now shown to be a sinner—yet is still called and loved by God.

V. 37: As the Apostle says: "Do you [sg.] not know that the patience of God would lead you [sg.] to repentance?" (*Dicente Apostolo: An nescis, quia patientia Dei ad paenitentiam te adducit?* [Rom 2:4])

The text of the Vulgate does not use the word *patientia* but *benignitas* = kindness. *Patientia* also translates the Greek *makrothymia* = forbearance, patience, and magnanimity of God who wants us to change our ways, to convert. In the

---

sed si compleamus habitatoris officium subaudiendum est (is to be understood as): *erimus haeredes regni caelorum.*

104. Cf. Gordan.

105. Here Benedict omits the word "daily" (*cotidie*) of RM (Ths 35) which he probably saw as superfluous.

Latin text of our Rules, *patientia* and *poenitentia* have a similar meaning, and it seems that both authors want to emphasize the connection between these two realities. God's patience is the ultimate sheltering basis for our repentance, making repentance possible and leading us to it. On the way to the correction of our mistakes (*emendatio*, v. 36) and conversion (*conversio*, v. 38), we find repentance, and with it recognizing and repenting of our guilt. Then conversion can follow: entrusting ourselves entirely to God and being guided by him alone.

V. 38: For the good Lord says: "I do not want the death of the sinner, but that he turn back and live." (*Nam pius Dominus dicit: "Nolo mortem peccatoris, sed convertatur et vivat,"* [Ezek 33:11].)

In Ezekiel 33:11 God says: "I take no pleasure in the death of the wicked man, but rather in the wicked man's conversion that he may live." And similarly in Ezekiel 18:23: "Do I indeed derive any pleasure from the death of the wicked? says the Lord GOD. Do I not rather rejoice when he turns from his evil way that he may live?" RM and RB add a characteristic adjective "the good Lord" (*pius Dominus*) which recalls God's kindness (*benignitas*) of Romans 2:4. In waiting for us, God shows his kindness, even his love.

What matters here is not only the conversion per se but also that conversion is the way to life—indeed, to a full and true life. Thus this verse refers back to the promise with its alluring appeal: "Who desires life?" (Prol 14). Jesus came that "they might have life and have it more abundantly" (John 10:10). We can recall Deuteronomy 30:15-19: "I have today set before you life and prosperity, death and doom. If you obey the commandments of the LORD, your God . . . loving him and walking in his ways . . . , you will live. . . . I have set before you life and death, the blessing and the curse. Choose life, then, that you and your descendants will live." In the Prologue the perspective of life is fundamental, and this explains why the kindness of the Lord is mentioned three times. Life has to do with love; and where are we loved more fully and totally than by God himself?

V. 39: Therefore as we have asked the Lord, brothers, about the one dwelling in his tent, we have heard the precept for dwelling there, but only if we fulfill the obligations of one dwelling there. (*Cum ergo interrogassemus Dominum, fratres, de habitatore tabernaculi eius, audivimus habitandi praeceptum; sed si compleamus habitatoris officium.*)

This sentence beginning with "therefore" (*ergo*) concludes the second part of the Prologue (beginning with v. 23), which focuses on dwelling in God's tent and the way to this tent. Listening and fulfilling in practice are the two steps that permeate the entire Prologue. Smargdus (102) says that we have really heard the voice of the Good Shepherd if we fulfill in practice what we heard. We recall the beginning of the Prologue: "Listen . . . and put it into practice!" Verse 39 mentions dwelling three times: the one dwelling [dweller], dwelling [there], the one dwelling [dweller] (*habitator, habitandi, habitator*). Apparently this is already preparing the transition to the dwelling in the school of the Lord's service, in the monastery.

Looking back on this section, we are struck by the image of the Lord as a good God and by the ways in which he speaks, guides us, and wants us to live. On our part it is important to know and recognize this—"do you not know?" (Prol 37)—and then to mend our ways, to repent, to turn our life around. This is the perspective of chapter 7 of the Rule. In all this we are given the promise of true life—thus the last word of the quote in Prologue 38 is "live" (*vivat*).

PROLOGUE 40-50

Once RM and RB concluded the psalm explanations with an urgent appeal to conversion, they could have immediately proceeded to describe the school of the Lord's service in concrete terms. Yet once again they summarize the entire Prologue in a new and even more urgent section (connected again by "therefore" [*ergo*]): "Therefore we must run."

This section has many similarities with the beginning of the Prologue (1-7):

40 hearts	1 ear of the heart
battle of obedience	3 serve, weapons of obedience
(*oboedientiae . . . militanda*)	(*militaturus, oboedientiae arma*)
precepts (*praecepta*)	1 precepts (*praecepta*)
41 pray for the help of grace	4 most earnest prayer
(*rogemus . . . gratiae auditorium*)	(*oratio instantissima*)
42 punishments of hell	7 eternal punishment
(*gehennae poenas*)	(*perpetuam . . . poenam*)
42 to eternal life	7 to glory
(*ad vitam perpetuam*)	(*ad gloriam*)

The concluding verse 44 can also be compared with Prologue 13, which concludes the section 8-13: "Run while you have the light of life so that the darkness of death may not seize you." It can also be compared with verse 22: "If we wish to dwell in the tent of his kingdom, we will not arrive there unless we run there by doing good works."

44 run (*currere*)	13 run, 22 unless you run (*currite, curritur*)
light of life (*lucis vitae*)	light of life (*lumen vitae*)
punishments of hell (*gehennae poenas*)	shadows of death (*tenebrae mortis*)
truly arrive (*pervenire*)	22 you will arrive (*pervenitur*)

Here is it necessary to compare the text that Benedict took from RM (Prol 40-45, 50) with the one he inserted (Prol 46-49).

At the beginning of the Prologue, Benedict joined two rather dissimilar texts, i.e., the first four verses written by himself (Prol 1-4, modelled after PsBasil) and the next three verses, taken from the Master (Prol 5-7). His own text created a balance between the text common to RM and RB. Here the situation is similar: the text that is common to both Rules (Prol 40-45, 50) has a very serious note: now we need to act, we need to do our utmost and persevere until death. If we want to escape hell, we must take part in the sufferings of Christ, and then we will also have a share in his kingdom. The verses Benedict inserted (Prol 46-49) mitigate and balance this view. His Rule does not aim at laying heavy burdens on monastics and emphasizes that in discouragement beginners should not run away. But in walking the ways of monastic life, their hearts will expand, love will take the lead (as God lives within them), and thus impels them from inside.

V. 40: Therefore, our hearts and bodies are to be prepared for the battle of holy obedience to his precepts. (*Ergo preparanda sunt corda nostra et corpora sanctae paraeceptorum oboedientiae militanda.*)

After a new "therefore" (*ergo*) there is an increase in urgency. In the Latin original the sentence is rhythmically structured: five times a word ends on an "a" (*preparanda . . . corda nostra . . . corpora . . . militanda*). We see the image of a soldier who quickly picks up his weapons, there are no half measures here. This is an energetic beginning, just as in Prologue 21 (having girt our loins) and Prologue 3. We must be ready for action. The concern here is obedience to the commandments, that is, first to Sacred Scripture, but "the precepts of the Master" are included also. "Once heart and body come together (in interior collectedness) in order to submit obediently to God's guidance, a person does not have to fear losing his or her own center even in a complex environment filled with conflicting forces."[106] Smaragdus (103) points to Romans 12:1-2: we ourselves are the sacrifice that is pleasing to God. Paul continues by admonishing us to "be transformed by the renewal of [our] mind," and thus we will discern the will of God (obedience). This is the only

---

106. Holzherr 2007, 60.

place where Benedict calls obedience "holy" (RM does this also in 90.43), and such obedience is part of the spiritual craft. This adjective is probably a further indication to what extent Benedict deliberately places obedience as the main virtue in the center of his Rule from the very beginning.

The word "battle" (in Latin the verb *militare*) includes the notions of sweat and hard work, and thus also includes the battle against our own self-will. We are sinners and need to be cleansed. Similarly Benedict describes obedience at the beginning as "labor" (Prol 2),[107] a battle which will last until we draw our last breath. And our own strength is not sufficient.

V. 41: and in what our own nature is not able to do, let us ask the Lord to help (serve) us with his grace. (*et quod minus habet in nos natura possible, rogemus Dominum, ut gratiae suae iubeat nobis adiutorium ministrare.*)

Although the goal is very encouraging and attractive, and although we desire to walk on this path with all our enthusiasm and mustering all our strengths, we sense that, in mere human terms, we are simply unable to avoid evil, do good, and follow Christ. While RB, unlike RM, does not see human nature in purely negative terms—and even says that it normally tends to be merciful (RB 37.1)—it is still weak and cannot bring about salvation on its own.[108] Romans 7:18 says: "The willing is ready at hand [in me], but doing the good is not" (*Iam velle adiacet in mihi, perficere autem non invenio*). Assuming that our translations correspond to the original meaning of this sentence, we cannot read it as a semi-Pelagian statement as some have tried to do.[109] Benedict does not say that what we can accomplish with the help of grace we could also do on the basis of our own nature, just not as well. Rather, he says that nature alone, though not degraded, is unable to accomplish it. This also corresponds to Prologue 29: "They know that they cannot do the good in them on their own, but that it is done by the Lord" (cf. also RB 4.42-43). Therefore prayer is indispensable as is shown in Prologue 4.

This verse reminds us of liturgical prayer: "And what is not possible for human weakness, give us in your mercy through your holy Spirit."[110] The Latin verb for "let us ask" is *rogemus*, which recalls the expression in litanies

---

107. For the importance *militia* had in Lérins see Kasper, "Faustus von Riez," (IV).

108. According to Lentini, 28, Quartiroli, 16, and Kardong, 21, the expression *quod minus habet in nos natura possible* is to be translated as "what is not possible" rather than "less possible."

109. Cf. Böckmann, *Perspectives*, 27, 31n42; Vagaggini, "Posizione," 77–80; also Lauer, "Gnadenbegriff," 32–34.

110. Cf. *SacrVeron* 973: *Et quod possibilitas non habet fragilitatis humanae, tuo spiritu miseratus impende.*

te rogamus, audi nos (we pray to you: hear us).[111] The authors of both Rules are shaped by the liturgy. And the word *adiutorium* = help calls up the ejaculatory prayer, "O Lord, make haste to help me" (*Deus, in adiutorium meum intende*). In RB the word *adiutorium* occurs only here and in 68.5, where human obedience seems impossible; yet the monk eventually obeys out of love for God and trusting in his help (*confidens de adiutorio Dei*).

Verse 41 prays that God may send us the help of his grace. In Latin the verb is *ministrare* = to serve, minister to: God assists us, serves us, and does so out of his abundant love. Grace here acts like a person. In a similar manner, RM says in another passage: "we must without ceasing pray to the Lord that he deign, by the protection of his assistance, to surround us with the wall of his grace."[112]

Vv. 42-44: And if fleeing the punishments of hell, we want to reach eternal life while there is still time and we are in this body and still have time to accomplish all this by the light of this life, we must run and practice that which will benefit us in eternity. (*Et si, fugientes gehennae poenas ad vitam volumus pervenire perpetuam, dum adhuc vacat et in hoc corpora sumus et haec omnia per hanc lucis vitam vacat implere, currendum et agendum est modo, quod in perpetuo nobis expediat.*)

Prologue 42-44 is a single, tripartite sentence: "if we want while—and—and—we must run." The repetition of the demonstrative pronouns—*adhuc, hoc, haec, hanc*—sounds like the crack of a whip. *Vacat*—"there is still time"—occurs twice (cf. *indutiae* in v. 36). This life (*lucis vita*) and eternity (*in perpetuo*) are set in opposition, yet eternity has two faces: a negative one (hell) and a positive one (eternal life). The verbs underline the urgency, the dynamism, and the necessity of a vigorous decision: "fleeing, want to reach, accomplish, run, practice."

Already in Prologue 7, Benedict had warned his readers about hell, and the Prologue stated several times that we want to reach life (Prol 7, 17, 21-24, 38, 50). We truly want to get there (*pervenire* in Prol 22; 7.5; 73.4, 9). The light of life (*lucis vita*, a genitive of identity) is the life in this world (cf. *lumen vitae* in Prol 13), it is a light that prepares us for a life filled with even more light—for God himself will be our light. In faith we are able to discover this

111. We may think of the old formula *Jube, domne, benedicere* (My Lord, bless me). With regard to the liturgical vocabulary, cf. *dignatus-dignari* in Prol 5 and the final formula of the Prologue in Prol 50; cf. Kasch, *Liturgisches Vokabular*, 196.

112. Thp 71: *Incessabiliter est praecandum ad dominum, ut dignetur adiutorii sui custodia muro nos suae gratiae circumdare;* and in Thp 69: *ne . . . sine suo adiutorio aliqua nos hora consistere.* Cf. also *Visio Pauli* 9, quoted according to Vogüé, RM, 325; cf. Kardong, 21.

marvelous light, enkindled by Christ, both within in us and everywhere in our world, and we can strive to let it penetrate every last corner, however dark it may be (cf. Luke 11:36).

Again the will is emphasized (*volumus*) as in Prologue 17 and 22. It is as if Benedict wanted to say: "You have a vigorous will—then act accordingly!" In the Latin text there is alliteration: *ad vitam volumus pervenire* ("we want to reach life") which is a device for easily remembering it. Now we still have a time of grace, we are in our bodies and are able to do all that is required. We recall 2 Corinthians 5:6: "So we are always courageous, although we know that while we are at home in the body we are away from the Lord." And 2 Corinthians 6:2: "In an acceptable time I have heard you, and on the day of salvation I helped you."[113] As in Prologue 13, this is based on John 12:35, though both authors have changed the walking into running and interpret the light as the light of life (cf. Prol 13).

The old baptismal catechesis directed to new Christians might have influenced this text up to Prologue 44. Yet now the monastic spirituality is to come to the fore within the baptismal spirituality. Prologue 45-50 present the school of the Lord's service, and this new section logically follows and also corresponds to Prologue 1-4 which were used as the very beginning of the Prologue. True to the genre of a Rule, a concrete way of how to translate the preceding text into daily life must now be shown. Here we may recall not only the "theme" of RM but also the Prologue of RM, which starting with basic Christian instruction eventually points at the end to the Rule itself (cf. RM Prol 22-27). In a similar way, the school of the Lord's service is now described.[114]

V. 45: Therefore we wish to establish a school of the Lord's service. (*Constituenda est ergo nobis dominici schola servitii.*)

For a better understanding of "the school of the Lord's service," a grammatical reflection and a look at Benedict's time are helpful. Grammatically, the "school" (*scola*) is accompanied by a genitive "of [the Lord's] service" (*servitii*) and this term is also qualified by an adjective *dominici*. *Scola servitii*[115] is a school for service, a school that teaches service. But how are we

---

113. Smaragdus (105) summarizes this as follows: "Let us take time and see that the Lord is sweet, and while there is time let us do good in regard to all." And later: "so we must run not with our feet but with our lives and conduct, so that we may be able to seek eagerly in this life what we know to be profitable for us forever." Cf. 1 Cor 9:24f.: *in stadio. . .omnes currunt. . . 25 Sic currite ut comprehendatis.*

114. For a detailed interpretation of Prol 45-50 see Böckmann, *Perspectives*, 33–49; thus there will be only a summary here.

115. For the following see Guevin, "*Dominici.*"

to understand *dominici servitii*? In Latin, adjectives are often used instead of a genitive of identity. Guevin points to the following expressions in RB: *dominicum praeceptum* in the sense of "the Lord's precept" (4.61), which is usually translated as "the precept of the Lord," i.e., a precept given by the Lord (an allusion to Matt 23:3); *dominicis . . . ovilibus*, the "sheepfolds of the Lord," i.e., the sheepfolds belonging to the Lord (1.8); and *oratio dominica* (13.12; 17.8), i.e., the prayer of the Lord that the Lord prayed and taught. Even without squeezing the expression, there is room to point to the service that Christ did for us. Thus we can translate: a school for service, a school where we learn the service the Lord did and where we enter into his service, into serving in the way he himself served and in which, naturally, we also serve him. This corresponds to the spirituality of RB. When Benedict speaks about the foot washing, his main concern is that we serve like Christ and serve Christ, the Lord, in another human person (cf. RB 35.9 and 53.13f.). By being obedient, we obey Christ (in the person in front of us), and obey as Christ obeyed (cf. RB 5.5-6, 13).

In his article, Studer points to schools in antiquity and the importance of reading and forming character.[116] Other authors rather emphasize that the monastic school, e.g., in Lérins, stands in opposition to the school in antiquity.[117]

V. 50: Never swerving from his instructions we want to persevere in the monastery until death, faithfully observing his teaching and sharing by patience in the sufferings of Christ, so that we may also deserve to share in his glory. (*Ut ab ispsis numquam magisterio discedentes, in eius doctrinam usque ad mortem in monasterio perseverantes, passionibus Christi per patientiam participemur, ut et regno eius mereamur esses consortes.*)

Now the school is not that of the abbot but of the teacher Christ from whose teaching we are not to deviate. Already in Prologue 12 Christ appeared as a wisdom teacher in the psalm verse: "Come . . . listen to me, I will teach you the fear of the Lord." This school is not pure joy; rather, the verse mentions that we participate through patience in the sufferings (in the plural, not in the singular as in RM). This part of the sentence is carefully structured again using alliteration as a device for remembering: *passionibus Christi per patientiam participemur*. While Sacred Scripture generally speaks about participating in Christ's sufferings (cf. Rom 8:17), the authors of our Rules think that this occurs concretely in patience—and this certainly means in everyday life. And according to our Rules, this is to be a persevering until death;

116. Studer, *Schola.*
117. Cf. Kasper, "Faustus von Riez," (III).

beyond this world, in the next life, we will be coheirs in Christ's kingdom. Two translations of the Greek word *koinonia* are used here: *participemur . . . consortes*. While later in the Rule these words are used to denote the community (RB 43.15-16), both words are used in the Prologue for our relationship to Christ which is, of course, also the root and basis for the communal life.

This final verse fits very well into the entire sequence of the Master (Ths) and also mirrors the Master's basic spiritual outlook: opposition of the time of now (with its suffering) and eternity (with its joy). By taking over this verse, Benedict also affirms this basically biblical arrangement. Yet he interrupts this literary unity by inserting the verses of Prologue 46-49.

Vv. 46-48: In this foundation we hope to set down nothing harsh, nothing burdensome. If, however, there is occasionally a little strictness, as required by reason of justice, for wiping out faults and preserving love, do not flee immediately, daunted by fear, from the way of salvation which is bound to be narrow at the beginning. (*In qua institutione nihil asperum, nihil grave, nos constituros speramus. Sed si quid paululum restrictius, dictante aequitatis ratione, propter emendationem vitiorum vel conservationem caritatis processerit, non ilico pavore perterritus refugias viam salutis quae non est nisi angusto initio incipienda.*)

Benedict feels the need to correct the school concept of the Master as well as the acceptance of an absolute dualism "now—beyond." Once more he addresses an individual newcomer and tries to offer encouragement. Fleeing was a real possibility which Benedict apparently had experienced (cf. RB 48.24; 64.19). There are reasons for using more strictness: each person has his own needs, each is to be given the necessary space and the required things, but above all we need to be cleansed of faults from the beginning to the very end of monastic life (cf. the first phase of "practical" monastic life, 62–66) and then to preserve love (second phase of "practical" monastic life), a love that is not just for the moment or only a day. Rather, love is to be preserved and to last. Therefore Benedict admonishes the newcomer to remain on this way which is "the way of salvation" for those called to monastic life and to be aware that this way is narrow, especially at the beginning. And the text does not say that later the way will be broader!

V. 49: But as we progress in the monastic life and in faith our hearts expand and with unspeakable sweetness of love we run the way of God's commandments. (*Processu vero conversationis et fidei, dilatato corde inenarrabili dilectionis dulcedine curritur via mandatorum Dei.*)

At the culmination of this section we have, as it were, a brief insight into the heart of Benedict himself: "we run with our hearts expanded" on the way of

God's commandments. Psalm 118/119:32—"I will run on the way of your commands for you open my docile heart"—helped him to harmonize the biblical text of the "sweet and light yoke" (Matt 11:29f.) with the one of the "narrow door" (Matt 7:13f.). Though the way is narrow, especially at the beginning, the heart in time will expand. Benedict expresses this almost exuberantly: we run with "unspeakable sweetness of love" (*inenarrabili dilectionis dulcedine*). But he also knows that this is not yet the final glory; it is, rather, a gift of God for us who have participated in the sufferings of Christ. Thus Benedict brings the two dimensions together: on the one hand, contrasting this world (sufferings of Christ) with the eternal world beyond, and on the other hand, the narrow beginning and the progress in the monastic life with its hallmark of an expanded heart, the sign of God's indwelling. In the midst of all the difficulties there are experiences of sweetness and indescribable joy. Benedict would not have been able to write this had he not experienced it himself.[118]

With regard to the use of the psalms and the structure of the entire Prologue, this verse, in my opinion, seems to be a rather late addition (it is also not necessary for the chiastic structure). This would coincide with the realization that the verse comes from Benedict's own experience of God which we may call mystical. At the same time, this insertion also indicates how his personal experience of God makes him more sensitive toward a weak newcomer who might be filled with fear and thus would want to flee. What is true for Benedict is also true for his Rule, namely, that spiritual depth assures the human element. Moreover, it is characteristic for Benedict that we do not run on a particular way but on the "way of God's commandments."

CONCLUSION

Looking back on the entire Prologue, we can recall to what extent this text has its original center in baptismal catechesis. We think of the topics of light and darkness or of life and death. The two ways are presented; and time and again we see behind them the impulse to choose the way to life or to the kingdom. As humans we have to renounce what is inimical and evil; we must not harden ourselves but rather listen intently to the voice of Sacred Scripture (of the Church) and then begin to practice good works in consonance with what we heard. In other words, we must actually and practically run on the way pointed out to us. And as Christ is the center of baptismal spirituality, so he is the center of the Prologue. To live a Christian life means to obey Christ, to serve and follow him under his guidance, and eventually to participate in his kingdom.

118. See also Böckmann, "Experience of God," 15; "Benedictine Mysticism."

It is within this fundamental Christian call that the call to monastic life is to be seen. Here, too, the main concern is following the "way of salvation" for the one who is called to this way of life. Monks want to risk living communally a life that is totally centered in and on Christ. The monastery is a school where Christ is the teacher, where we are never finished learning but rather persevere until death, just as Christ was obedient until death. In this school there is, however, according to Benedict, a progression from initial fear and discouragement to the "sweetness" of love.

By gathering all the statements about human persons in the Prologue we arrive at a biblical view of the human being who is son, slave, servant, and worker. Human beings may be seen as dwelling in the tent, and as wise persons they build their house on the rock of Christ. Three times those addressed are called "brothers" (in the plural). Doing so emphasizes their relationship with each other, which is certainly anchored in the vertical dimension while the human individual is essentially bound up with the community.

The Prologue speaks mainly about the heart (six times) but also about the body (twice, without devaluing it) then especially about the ears and listening (thirteen times) though also, to a lesser extent, about the eyes and seeing (twice, three times about light) and finally about the tongue and speaking (three times, and an additional six times if we also count the questions and answers). It is characteristic that listening is predominant. In connection with it obeying is strongly emphasized (five times together with listening) as well as running (twelve times) and doing, practicing (nine times) and this last element increases in importance toward the end of the Prologue. This is a holistic biblical view of the human person devoid of any philosophical dualism as it appears in the Rule of the Master, especially toward its end.[119]

Yet the Prologue is fully aware of the obstacles found on this way which lie in part in the human individuals themselves (their self-will, Prol 3), or try to enter their heart through thoughts (Prol 28). We need to amend our sins (Prol 36, 47), need repentance and conversion (Prol 37f.), must avoid evil in general (Prol 17), and especially evil words (Prol 17, 26f.) Human nature is not denigrated but, on its own, is not capable of salvation, and thus earnest prayer is necessary (Prol 4, 14). God himself has given us his good gifts, the Lord effects the good in us (Prol 6, 29f.), and what we are we are by grace (Prol 31).

This human individual is existentially dependent on the Lord and thus also on dialoguing with him. In the Prologue such a dialogue occurs concretely through Scripture which is a living person, not just a compilation of dead letters. It is astonishing how many actions are described through scriptural

119. Cf. Böckmann, "Mensch," 47–54.

quotes: speaking (seven times), awakening (once), calling (twice), admonishing (once) and indirectly: guiding (Prol 21). We can initiate a real dialogue with Scripture. Thus we could look at the Prologue as a practical *lectio divina* describing it in the following dialogue:

> "Listen, incline the ear of your heart!" Scripture shakes us up, and once we open our eyes to the divinizing light, we hear with thunder-struck ears the divine voice that daily calls us with this admonition: "Today, if you hear his voice, do not harden your heart!" And what does the voice say? "Listen, I will teach you the fear of the Lord!" The Lord seeking workers calls: "Who is the human individual who desires life?" If you hear this and answer "I do," God says to you: "If you seek true life . . . do good . . . then my eyes will be upon you and my ears are open to your prayers, and before you call me, I will say: 'Here I am.'" What is sweeter than this voice of the Lord inviting us? See, how in his goodness he is showing us the way to life! Yet let us ask the Lord with the prophet: "Lord, who will dwell in your tent?" After having asked this we listen how the Lord answers and shows us the way by saying: "Practice good deeds . . . smash all evil on the rock of Christ." Then we will say with the prophet: "Not to us give glory, O Lord!" Therefore the Lord says in the Gospel: "Whoever hears my words and practices them . . ." While we are fulfilling this the Lord waits that every day we respond to his holy admonitions with good deeds. The kind Lord says: "I do not will the death of the sinner, but that he convert and live."

We have asked the Lord about his precepts for dwelling with him and now we want to fulfill them. Let us ask the Lord that he give us the help of his grace.

According to the ancient monastic spirituality of *lectio*, we have our *ears* in Sacred Scripture. We hear the voice in the pages, and so it is here. The Bible responds to our human questions, yet it also provides us with the words for our questions and puts answers into our mouth. Scriptural words are vehicles for the existential dialogue that the human individual is to enter with his personal "*Ego–I.*" Ultimately it is a matter of incarnating the word in our life. *Lectio* leads to *action* or *conversion* but also to *oratio*, prayer (Prol 4, 41).

In the Prologue we see this dialogue with Sacred Scripture above all in the use of psalms in which Christ, the Lord, speaks directly to us who are speaking to him "with the prophet." He guides us, he instructs us about leading a good life (tropological or moral sense, cf. on Prol 17). The psalms supply us with the weapons for fighting against the enemy (ejaculatory prayers, cf. Prol 28). Lastly they may accompany us from the beginning of our spiritual journey to the stage where we make progress and experience ourselves in a deeper way as sinners, yet also feel how our heart expands (Prol 49). This last use of the psalms is typical for Benedict (not for the Master).

The psalms point to Christ, yet they are, as it were, a gathering bowl of the entire Sacred Scripture, be it of Paul, of Revelation or whatever other book.

And everywhere in the Prologue, Christ stands before us as the dominant image. Three times he is explicitly called Christ, the Lord and true King (Prol 3), Christ the rock (Prol 28), and Christ in whose sufferings we participate so as to inherit his kingdom (Prol 50). The Prologue begins and ends by mentioning his kingdom (*rex, regnum*—Prol 3, 50), and in its center (Prol 21) speaks of this kingdom where we will be allowed to see him. Yet Christ is also the father who adopted us in our baptism (Prol 7), the loving father, the kind Lord (emphasized three times in Prol 1, 20, 37). He is the image of God who, in his patience, gives us time (Prol 37f.), who speaks in Sacred Scripture and whose voice is "sweet" (Prol 19). He anticipates us with his call (Prol 21, 1, 14, 18); he stands before us as our goal (Prol 23) toward which we advance; he walks ahead of us (he fulfills, we walk on his ways, Prol 35, 21, 7); he guides and assists us (Prol 21). We may smash all that is inimical on him (Prol 28). He is also, as it were, our basis and foundation on which we can build the house of our life (Prol 33-34). Ultimately it is he who acts *in* us, and we boast *in* him (Prol 29f., 32). In everything it is the Lord, present here and now, who acts in our personal and communal history.

As we saw in the introduction, we can see the Prologue as organized in a chiasm around a central core (Prol 21-22), yet because of the many repetitions we could also represent it as a spiral.

SPIRAL with ever new beginnings (though the expressions are here greatly abbreviated):

	(1)	(2)	(3)	(4)	(5)
1-7	loving father counted among sons	listen (2x)	self-will evil deeds	obey fulfill	the Lord fulfills his good in us for glory
8-13	Sacred Scripture divinizing light	rouse	not harden	run	light of life
14-20	the Lord seeks	listen	avoid evil	practice good	my eyes upon you here I am / *adsum*
21-22	he called us	gird		walk on his ways run doing good deeds	to see him in his kingdom arrive there

23-35	(promise)	listen	without stain	do justice	the good in us is not from us
	the Lord fulfills		smash the evil	practice good deeds	praise the Lord who works in us
	shows		floods, winds	do, respond	give God the honor
					by the grace of God I am
36-39	kindness, patience leads us	listen	cleansing of sins repentance, conversion	practice respond	live
40-50	it is time light of life Lord's service	prepare school	battle flee hell cleansing of sins	obedience run, act preserve love run persevere	help of grace to eternal life expanded heart coheirs of his kingdom

Seven spirals succeed each other. They mirror how our spiritual life develops, yet not in a straight line but rather in the form of a spiral. Each spiral contains some characteristic elements, yet still differs from the others. In our life we probably discover something similar: repeatedly there are new beginnings, made possible by God's call or his grace, by his anticipating us (column 1). If we listen to it all, arise and prepare ourselves (column 2), then we need to confront evil, fight it, and convert ourselves (column 3) and continue to practice good deeds, to obey and run vigorously (column 4). Yet when we do all this, we will again and again realize that we will not be able to reach salvation by our own efforts, however great. Grace comes to our help, it is God who completes. He speaks his "here I am"—*adsum*, he acts in us (column 5), and thus enables us to inherit his kingdom (also column 5). Even the expanded heart in this life is gift of his grace. These are some basic elements of our life circles and life spirals that we find in almost every section of the Prologue, as is evident in the schema above.

Yet at the same time an attentive reading of the Prologue shows that each circle is different, just as it is in our life. At one time the anticipating action of God is dominant or our listening or the battle against evil; at another time it is the purposeful running or acting, or our depending on God who is acting and dwelling in us. Thus in Prologue 8-13 we see God's actions mainly emphasized through Scripture. This is an opportunity for us. At the beginning and the end of Prologue 14-20 God's actions are given more space. In Prologue 21-22, the battle against evil is not present because this center shows a positively shaped phase. In Prologue 23-35, the battle against demons is evident, yet the gracious divine action in the human person is also given more space. The emphasis in Prologue 40-44 lies on our actions. We could say: the Prologue describes the colorful and varied forms of life as it develops in the spiritual journey. This pattern of a spiral can give us courage with the knowledge and faith that God will always again provide us with a new beginning and will bring it all to its fulfillment.

As a conclusion, we establish a semiotic chart for the entire Prologue:

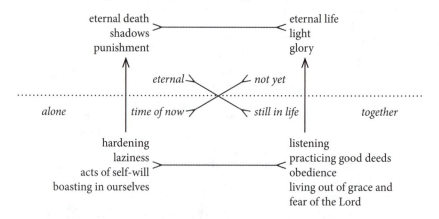

Here we see clearly the two opposite ends of human life. The upper part presents the future, the lower our earthly life. Laziness, hardening of heart, acts of self-will, and finally boasting in ourselves lead to a negative eschatological result, while the battle against all this, and further listening, practicing good deeds, and living out of grace help us to walk on the way to eternal glory. Thevenet added to the left side "alone" and to the right one "together."[120] This accords with the Rule of Benedict: "alone" regarding to myself alone, in egotism and isolation I easily fall prey to all the vices, and above all may harden in these vices. Yet the reverse is also true: All these attitudes have an isolating effect. In contrast the attitudes on the right side are conducive to community. Christ leads us together, as brothers/sisters we are responsible for one another so that we will also let him guide us together to our common goal (cf. RB 72.12).

The Prologue of the Rule has a counterpart in the epilogue (RB 73) which also underlines the dynamic nature of monastic life until we arrive at our eternal goal. Benedict precedes this epilogue with chapter 72 into which he pours his heart. This shows clearly that for him, the cenobite, the monastic way of life is a communal one, yet at the same time this way of life is always

120. Thevenet, "Essai," 78.

again a beginning. In the course of life we grow in the awareness that we always lag behind the grace given us. And as is evident in Prologue 49-50, it is essential to stay, to persevere, yet not in a static manner but rather in a dynamic "movement toward" . . . walking, running on the way with all our brothers and sisters as well as with all those who are entrusted to us.

Preliminary Remarks on
RB 1–3

For Benedict, these three chapters represent the basic constitution for the monastic community with an abbot and a Rule, and his spirituality shines through them everywhere. Let us quickly survey these chapters together with our own expectations while also casting an eye on the Rule of the Master (RM)!

RB 1 deals with different kinds of monks. In doing so, it is clear that RB is written for cenobites; and we assume that in this discussion the Rule plays a major role. RB 2 discusses how the abbot is to be and behave, and thus we mainly expect admonitions for the abbot. RB 3 talks about calling the brothers to counsel, and here the element of community seems most important to us. At important points we therefore expect statements about the Rule (RB 1), the abbot (RB 2), and the community (RB 3).

RM has only two, not three chapters: the first one deals with the kinds of monks and defines the cenobites as monks who fight under a Rule and an abbot. The chapter's last part already presents the abbot assigning him a position that is parallel to the teachers of the church. The second chapter directly discusses the abbot and has, as its last part, an addition about the counsel which is seen as an instrument of the superior. In my view the smooth transitions from one topic to the next are typical for the Master. At the end of the introductory topic, RM presents the school of the Lord's service. The students are the cenobites who serve under a Rule and an abbot (RM 1.2). The word "rule" might allude to the end of the Prologue in RM (Prol 22-27), "abbot" to the abba-father in the explanation of the Our Father (Thp).

Chapter 1 in RM has an addition about obedience (taking up the plea of the Our Father, "Thy will be done," which is already a prelude to the chapter on obedience!) and also about the Master's theology of monastic life (RM 1.76-92). Subsequently this chapter addresses the three stages of teaching: prophets, apostles, and teachers. Apostles are in charge of churches, teachers of communities, the schools of Christ. The abbot teaches the art of fighting the devil and one's self-will. It is simply logical that in RM 2 the teacher takes center stage. This chapter ends with a mention of the brothers' counsel and that the abbot is a master in the sacred art which he teaches in the workshop of the monastery. Thus the chapters about the spiritual craft follow logically, discussing it first in general, then in particular, i.e., obedience, silence, and humility.

Coming from chapters with nearly perfect structure, with smooth transitions and great coherence, we might be disappointed when reading RB. RB 1 says relatively little about the cenobites and is devoid of any kind of explicit theology or spirituality. The chapter about the abbot follows without transition. And after the chapter about the abbot, chapter 3, about the brothers' counsel, follows without any preparation. It seems that Benedict strings chapters together in a sequence which, for the most part, can be explained from the structure of RM or as a composition that follows certain key words while many internal connections and theological and spiritual explanations are lost in Benedict's text.

Yet it seems to me that Benedict pays greater attention to the composition of the individual chapters. In comparing the different structures, we find other connections: each of the three chapters has a circular structure with its own nucleus.

The center of RB 1 is the statement that the sarabaites are without a shepherd and are thus not with Christ but rather enclosed in their own sheepfolds (1.8). This is framed by remarks that they are a law to themselves and know no other law, that is, that they have not been tested by a Rule (1.6-7; 1.8b-9). First, they lack a shepherd while the cenobites serve under a Rule and an abbot, but they also lack a Rule.

The community and its unity in Christ is clearly the center in RB 2 (2.20) and this is framed by the equality of all the brothers (2.18, 20b)! Apparently this unity must be the chief concern of the abbot. At the same time, this nucleus clearly shows the basis of the community which is in Christ, and only in Christ can there be unity. Only in him is a Christian community possible at all.

It is interesting to note that in RB 3, concerning the meeting of the council, the Rule and obedience to it form the core (3.7-8), which is surrounded by exhortations to the abbot and the brothers (3.4-6; 9-11). We might expect that the chapter's core would deal with the community, but apparently Benedict sees the necessary basis for communal life and counsel in each brother's willingness to give up his desire to act according to his own pleasure and discretion and instead follows a Rule.

We can represent the connections in the following graph:

RB 1 Kinds of Monks	RB 2 Abbot	RB 3 Communal Counsel
without Rule	equality of brothers	exhortations to abbot—to brothers
shepherd	all are one in Christ	all are to follow the Rule
having their own Rule	equality of all	exhortations to brothers—to abbot

The middle line shows the following sequence: shepherd, community (in Christ), and Rule. Thus we could say: Cenobites are characterized by having a shepherd, the abbot is characterized by his concern for the entire community and its unity in Christ, and a good council meeting rests on the basis that both the community and the abbot follow the Rule.

At first this observation may look like a trivial matter, yet it does show how for Benedict the topics, and even more the realities, are interconnected: Rule, shepherd, community, equality, Christ, Rule. As negative images we have: to be one's own Rule, to follow only one's own will, and to judge according to a person's social position. Compared to RM, Benedict is also autonomous in the way he connects the main thematic points in the structure of the chapters. Benedict, too, is an artist but in a manner different from that of the Master. We could say that his way of thinking is more Semitic and circular, while that of the Master is rather linear and repetitive.

In the manuscripts of the Rule of Benedict the list of chapter titles generally follows the Prologue which is not mentioned separately. In some manuscripts, e.g., in the *textus purus*, the title of RB 1 reads: "Here the text of the Rule begins. It is called "Rule" because it guides the way of life of those who obey it." Even though this title is not found in all manuscripts, it is commensurate with the entire Rule: obedience seems to be essential.

Chapter 1

About the Kinds of Monks

CONTEMPORARY CONTEXT

When we hear this title, we may perhaps think of the present situation in the church. How many kinds of religious communities there are! Their very diversity is the "crux" of the postconciliar documents, eluding systematization. Just recall *Vita consecrata*. It first treats monastic life in the East and West, then the status of virgins, hermits, and widows, then institutes entirely directed to contemplation, active religious life, secular institutes, communities of apostolic life, and finally new forms of life consecrated to God (*VC* 6-12).[1] This diversity is by no means viewed as something negative, even though one could list a degenerate variation of each form described.

Thinking of the four familiar kinds in RB, the degenerate ones might come to mind first.[2] Sarabaites, who live together in twos and threes, doing what they consider right, remind us of cliques and factions in communities that can go astray and grow rigid. There is also a tendency in each of us not to expose ourselves to criticism and to challenging questions. The sarabaites define their monastic life along their own views, and their own interpretation is their norm. They see hardly any need to listen to the experience of others or to accept spiritual direction in order to learn from the wisdom of others. "I already know what I have to do," they might say. Thus they can build a fence around themselves and lock themselves up inside. It is easier to enter into such an enclosed area than to leave it again.

Then there is the tendency of the gyrovagues. Stasiak reminds us of the key word "to prefer nothing to the work of God," which now is changed to

---

1. *Acta Apostolicae Sedis* 87 (1996): 381–85; English translation in *Origins* 25, no. 41 (1996): 681–719.
2. Cf. Stasiak, "Four Kinds."

"prefer nothing to a journey." There are geographical journeys, on a large and on a small scale. We have, however, also gyrovagues in our churches, in the dining room, in the area of the cells, in our place of work, or even moving from one community to another. Some are gyrovagues less in an external sense but more in regard to their thoughts, wishes, and fantasies.

In regard to the two good kinds of monks in RB, we can reflect about the fact that it is also possible to overdo what is good or to do what is good for the wrong reasons. These "cenobites" are seeking community, friendship, perhaps intimacy, support, help, emotional security, and may forget that community can be truly lived only by mature persons. They might forget the importance of solitude in which a person matures. Community could be viewed as a remedy for many problems and sufferings (a kind of romanticism about community).

In pursuing the ideal of the "eremitical" life, the foremost motivation might be the seeking of solitude in the sense of withdrawal, of emigrating. They might wish to hide their own weaknesses and also avoid solidarity with others. Though keeping the same postal address, they withdraw more and more into a psychological, emotional, and spiritual hermitage. The concern is less about solitude than about isolation from the imperfections of the community. In nearly all of our communities we have such pseudo "hermits."

For this reason it is useful to read this chapter in RB again and to hold it up to ourselves like a mirror, not in order to discover the less than good traits in our surroundings, but rather to face similar tendencies within our own selves.

CONTEXT IN THE TIME OF BENEDICT

Benedict and the Master are not the first ones to furnish us with descriptions of various kinds of monks. They are part of an older tradition.

Jerome describes the kinds of monks in Egypt: There are those who live in community; the anchorites live in the desert by themselves; then there is a third kind, called *remnuoth*, a very bad and negligent kind.[3] They live in twos and threes; they do not want to depend on anyone. There is a contrast between their behavior in secret and that in public. They are hypocrites, particularly as regards poverty or sharing among themselves, fasting, and obedience. After these descriptions, Jerome continues: "Having treated of these degenerate kinds of monks, we return to the cenobites."[4] They cultivate good order, discipline, virtue, and zeal.

---

3. *Ep* 22.34f.

4. *Ep* 22.35, *His igitur quasi quibusdam pestibus exterminatis veniamus ad. . . .*: this formulation resembles that of RB 1.13. Cf. also *Ep* 125.9 and 125.13: "The hermit also can lead a degenerate life; actually the hermit ought to emerge from the school of the monastery as a fighter."

Augustine praises the hermits and also the cenobites who have come together for a holy and chaste common life; they practice prayer, reading, and love of neighbor.[5] All hearts are directed to God (*in Deum*). No one owns private property, all are helping each other. Concerning the gyrovagues he says: "So many hypocrites in monk's clothing . . . they pass through the provinces, having no assignment and no fixed residence; they never stand still or sit quietly. Some of them are selling bones of the martyrs—if only they were the bones of martyrs!—others boast of their 'tassels on the clothes and their phylacteries' (Matt 23:5). . . all are begging, asking payment for their greedy poverty and a reward for their pretended holiness."

Cassian also lists three kinds of monks:[6] The cenobites live together in community and are guided by an elder. The anchorites first were tested in community and then decided to live as hermits. Regarding the cenobites, Cassian names two types: According to the tradition of Jerusalem, the Christians first lived in community but then abandoned the ideal.[7] Yet Christians who were alive with apostolic zeal remembered the beginnings. Thus the cenobites are the first according to time and by grace. They do not wish to have control over themselves or over possessions; they work hard and hand in the proceeds of their work. According to the second tradition, that of Alexandria, a minority of Christians remained faithful to the original community. In line with their ideal, they developed a Rule for themselves.[8]

The anchorites are like flowers and fruit that emerged from the perfect cenobites.[9] They are guided by the desire for spiritual progress, for contemplation, and are not afraid of meeting the demons in direct battle. This is truly the perfection in the art of humility and self-abnegation; they achieve purity of heart.

The sarabaites are inferior and unfaithful monks.[10] Cassian compares them to weeds. They live in twos and threes and care only for themselves. Their lives are a sham. They don't bother about cenobitic discipline or obedience but desire to be praised for perfect poverty. They also do not live according to any Rule. They want to satisfy all their desires and do whatever they want at the moment.

There is a fourth type of monks who deceives themselves and others. These monks only pretend to live as hermits. They do not struggle against

---

5. Cf. *Praec* 1.1-4; *De MorEccl.* 1.31.66-68; *OpMon* 28.36.
6. *Conf.* 18.3-7; cf. *Inst.* 5.36.1; 10.6.
7. *Conf.* 18.5.
8. *Conf.* 18.6.
9. Ibid.
10. *Conf.* 18.7.

their faults, nor do they practice stability, obedience, patience, or discipline. They have yielded to *acedia*, turning into vagabonds and seeking the pleasure of their belly.[11]

Thus we already have, in fact, four types of monks in Cassian. These passages influenced Benedict and his source both in content and expression. About the gyrovagues, which seem to have been a general nuisance, other authors also have written.[12]

Before we get to the RM, it is useful to cast a glance on what Basil says concerning hermits and community (*Reg* 3). He describes a life together, experienced with soul and heart, which brings a sense of security; its model is the first Christian community of Jerusalem. Community life is placed above the other types of life for many reasons, e.g.,

- We depend on mutual help,
- love does not seek its own advantage,
- criticism from others is helpful,
- living together the commandments of love of neighbor can be put into practice,
- only as a community are we one body in Christ,
- an individual alone cannot receive all the gifts of the Spirit,
- the prayer of a community is especially valuable due to the grace given to each individual member,
- life in solitude has its dangers: for example, lack of vigilance against evil, uncritical over-estimation of self, merely theoretical rather than practical Christian living and the impossibility of living as an ecclesial community in the sense of Scripture (Acts 4:32).

This brings us to the direct source of the RB: RM 1.[13] There are four kinds of monks. The first are the cenobites, the second the hermits, the third the sarabaites, where RM has one more comment than does Benedict: "I would do better to call them still of the world, except that the tonsure of their religious intent prevents me from doing so" (1.6). At the end of their description

---

11. *Conf.* 18.7-8; also 18.23.2; *Inst.* 5.16.

12. Cf. Art. "Girovaghi" lists sources e.g., Cassiodorus, *In Ps.* 132.1; Paulinus of Nola, *Carm* 24.325-332; Isidor, *De eccl. Off.* n7 in the chapter "Monks" in book 2; Evagrius, *Sent.* 81.

13. Ms P has a different title for this chapter: *Incipit de generibus vel potus* (E: *vel ordine) vel actus et vita monachorum in coenobiis.* The text, however, is generally the same as in RM.

RM states: "And while they want to have cells, chests and various things according to their own judgment, they are unaware that they are losing their own petty souls" (1.10). Then RM describes the fourth kind, the gyrovagues, in a long satire of more than sixty verses,[14] which Benedict summarizes only briefly. With regard to the content we read: They eat and drink much, have others serve them, exploit the hospitality of their hosts and the compassion of others. When they claim to be ill and tired, saying that no place on earth is suited to their striving for perfection, when they feel called to a higher form of prayer, it is all lies and sham. They avoid discipline and work; in addition, they are cruel to their poor donkey. Their greed is great; they collect many items, but showing only the old and worn things.[15]

After the author of RM stated that he would now move on to the cenobites (1.75), an appendix follows and presents in 1.82-92 a theology of monastic life, in a parallel to the concept of church that has shepherds while monasteries have teachers. The Master is above all concerned to provide the abbot's authority with a foundation in the church and to have the self-will of the monks killed.[16] The Lord gives commands through the teacher. This last addition prepares for the following chapters about the abbot (RM 2) and about obedience (RM 7) as the requirement to submit to the will of the teacher. This school of the Lord's service is parallel to the Church of Christ, which also is to educate people.

By comparing RM and RB we can see clearly that Benedict takes for himself the very parts that RM took over from Cassian.[17]

OVERVIEW OF THE CHAPTER
DIRECT CONTEXT

When paying attention to intensive and negative expressions, we see that they are used chiefly for the sarabaites and gyrovagues. RM and RB seem to speak from experience and even seem annoyed with these kinds of monks.

14. This is perhaps a later revision. Bozzi 1, 211, sees in it a tendency of the Master to move from the abstract to the concrete. The negative model is more convincing than the positive, for the sinful person recognizes his own weakness in it and is thus led to improve himself (*castigando ridendo mores*).

15. The text of Eugippius is the same, but he omits verses 16-71 and adds to the praise of the cenobites some verses from the Prologue: RM Ths 40-46. But one can rightly assume with Vogüé, *RB-DSC*, 87, that Benedict had the full text of RM from the manuscript P 12205 in front of him.

16. The Scripture text of 1 Cor 12:28 (cf. Eph 4:11) is inverted. For RM it is important that monastic authority is firmly anchored in the church's hierarchy.

17. Cf. Vogüé, "De generibus," 185.

First, one can divide RB 1 according to the content.

- 1.1 Introduction
- 1.2 Cenobites
- 1.3-5 Hermits
- 1.6-9 Sarabaites
- 1.9-12 Gyrovagues
- 1.13 Introduction to the following, inclusion to RB 1.2

As a circular composition (chiasm) one can write the entire chapter as follows:

RB 1 About the Kinds of Monks
1 It is known that there are four kinds of monks.

A 2 The first is that of the cenobites,
that is, those who live in a monastery
and under Rule
and abbot
are serving/fighting.

B 3 Then the second kind is that of the anchorites, that is, the hermits,
those who, not in the first fervor of *conversatio*,
but by long testing in the monastery
4 sufficiently trained with the help of many others
have learned to fight against the devil,
5 and now, well trained in the ranks of the brothers
for single combat in the desert,
are able to fight confidently alone,
    without the help of another,
with their own hand and their own arm
against the sins of the flesh and thoughts
    with the help of God.

C 6 The third, and most despicable kind of monks
is that of the sarabaites,

who are not tested by any Rule, as a mistress of experience,
like gold is tested in the fiery furnace, but soft as lead,
7 still following the world in their actions,
they clearly lie to God by their tonsure.

D 8 Living in twos and threes or even alone,
without a shepherd, not in the Lord's sheepfold,
but enclosed in their own,

C' they take as their law what their cravings demand (*desideriorum voluptas*),
9 for whatever they think or want,
they call holy,
and what they dislike, they consider forbidden.

B' 10 The fourth kind of monks are the so-called gyrovagues,
who spend their whole lives wandering through various provinces,
staying as guests in different monasteries for three or four days,
11 always moving (*vagi*) and never stable,
subject to their own wills and to the cravings of their palates,
they are in every respect even worse than the sarabaites.
12 Of the most miserable way of life (*conversatio*) of all these
it is better to be silent than to speak.

A' 13 Let us bypass these, therefore, and proceed
with God's help, to write a plan for the strongest kind of monks, the
cenobites.

RB 1.2 and 1.13, A and A', are parallel, treating of the cenobites. RB 1.3-5 and 1.10-12, B and B', are matching, both dealing with the genuine and the false hermits. The terms are set as opposites.[18]

The sarabaites are in the middle. I would see 1.8a (D) as the nucleus: They have no shepherd and are fenced into their own sheepfold. This sentence is framed by C and C': 1.6-7 and 8b-9. Both parts speak of Rule and law, which

---

18. *Probatione diuturna—diversas . . . numquam stabiles contra vitia carnis vel cogitationum—propriis voluntatibus et guilae inlecebris servientes.*

are totally missing, so that they are a law unto themselves, or to say it with 1.7: They are lying to God and to the world.[19]

In looking at the entire chapter, we can see the importance of verse 8a. Saying it positively: For cenobites it is essential to have a shepherd (*pastor*). This points to chapter 2; to be in the Lord's sheepfold points to the monastery (it is specifically named in 1.2 and RB 3.1, 12).

RB 1 ABOUT THE KINDS OF MONKS (*DE GENERIBUS MONACHORUM*)[20]

Vv. 1-2: It is known that there are four kinds of monks. The first is that of the cenobites, that is, those who live in monasteries and under Rule and abbot are fighting/serving. (*Monachorum quattuor esse genera manifestum est. Primum coenobitarum, hoc est monasteriale, militans sub regula vel abate.*)

It is presupposed that the meaning of "monk" is known. But this word had already undergone a development:

- *Monachus* meaning one who lives alone for the sake of Christ,
- further, as having become "one, whole," by seeking the One.
- Finally I would like to recall Augustine: *Monachus*—all are one "in God" (*in Deum*), the many become a unity.[21] The first sentence: "It is known that there are" shows that it was not difficult, following the tradition and probably also his own experience, to list four kinds of monks, two good ones and two bad ones.

Verse 2 is the first plain description of the cenobites, for whom Benedict wants to write his Rule (cf. the inclusion at the end in 1.13). They are the ones who live in monasteries and serve under a Rule and an abbot. We could expand each term in 1.2 by adding phrases from the whole chapter, e.g.:

---

19. As contrasts we have "no Rule" and "they take as their law"; similarly they "lie" and "call holy what they dislike."

20. RM has the longer version: "The Kinds of Monks, their Drink and Conduct and Life in Monasteries." In RM's list of chapters the title reads: "Of the Four Kinds of Monks." Benedict in his list of chapters following the Prologue wrote "Of the Kinds and the Life of Monks."

21. *In Ps. 132.6: qui ergo sic vivunt in unum . . . ut sit illis, una anima et unum cor . . . recte dicitur monos, id est, unus solus.* cf. also *Praec 1.2.*

The cenobites	are trained by the help of many (1.4).
	They stand in the ranks of the brothers (1.5).
monasteriale	There they are tested daily (1.3).
	They live in the Lord's sheepfolds (1.8).
	The monastery can also be a fiery furnace (1.6).
	There they are always stable (1.11).
militans	They learn to fight against the devil (1.4)
	and against the sins of the flesh (1.5).
	They are not soft as lead (1.6)
	and do not follow the world in their actions (1.7).
regula	*Their* law is not whatever they desire (1.8).
	They have been tested by the Rule, the mistress of experience (1.6).
abbas	They live with the shepherd (1.8a).

The first kind: What is this to mean? Historically, the cenobites are not the first monks. Thus, interpretations already begin here. For this term, it is very interesting to look at the various commentaries, for they generally reflect the preference of the author or his monastery. Some, like Herwegen, read the term as meaning that the cenobites are the best kind of monks. Benedict "wishes to put them in the first place as the most valuable. For him their way of life is the ideal."[22] According to Lentini, Benedict considers the cenobites as the most reliable monks and also the most suitable for people in general.[23] Puzicha says: "It is the first form, that is, the most important, perhaps also the best."[24] We also can recall Cassian: Cenobites are the first because they first appear in history (the initial Christian community).[25] Martène in his commentary can even list twelve reasons why it is better to live in a monastery, so for example (besides those already mentioned) the freedom from cares, humility, practice of mutual love, a certain safety when one is tempted, an easier rising up from sins.[26] Benedict writes his Rule for cenobites. So they are first, according to Vogüé, because the Rule deals with them.[27] Also, the cenobites constitute

22. Herwegen, 57.
23. Lentini, 41.
24. Puzicha, 69.
25. Cassian, *Conf.* 18.5.3: "This was the most ancient kind of monks, which is first not only in time but also in grace."; cf. Martène, 247.
26. Martène, 259–62.
27. Vogüé: *Ce que dit*, 33f. One may recall 5.1, "The first step of humiliy is obedience." According to RB 7 obedience is not the first but the basic (lowest) rung on the ladder.

the majority of monks. Hermits will always be exceptions, especially among monks in the West, for whom the RB is written. Concerning the temporal sequence for individuals, Benedict thinks that experience in a community (*coenobium*) is the foundation for eremitical living.

Cenobites (*coenobitarum*, or as in RM, *coenobiotarum*). The Greek roots *koinos bios* (community life) are easily recognized. Cassian explains that they live in community.[28] Benedict uses *coenobita* only here, in this chapter, and two times at that; then in 5.12 he has *coenobium* as the place of communal life. The use of the word can be explained from his dependence on Eastern sources. The monks living in a *coenobium* want to be under an abbot and a Rule, they help each other, and there they have the consolation of many; they form a "battle front of brothers."

"Living in a monastery" (*monasteriale*, derived from *monachus*). One foreign word is being explained by means of another. Originally used for the dwelling of a hermit,[29] this word was later also used for cenobites. The monastery is a fiery furnace (*fornax*), in which a person is purified; it is also the enclosure of a shepherd, of the Lord, and is contrasted to "the various cells" (1.10) in which the gyrovagues stay successively. It is possible that this is already an allusion to stability. Belonging to a place is important to Benedict. So place and community have been named as important elements.

Under Rule and abbot (sub regula vel abate). Benedict wants to introduce the Rule even ahead of the abbot: Rule as a tradition of monastic discipline, as Cassian says.[30] For Benedict the Rule was the unbroken tradition since the time of the apostles, but already for Augustine and Caesarius it is a written document.[31] Benedict tends to call this written Rule generally a "rule" (*regula;* one exception could be the eighth degree of humility). Already RM had given great importance to the written Rule (cf. Prol 22-27). For Benedict, it is no longer only the *regula scripturarum*—seeing the Sacred Scriptures as Rule—rather he wants to offer something derived from Scripture for the communal life, as can be seen again and again. The monks are to walk "under the guidance of the Gospel" (Prol 21). In RB 1.2 it is important to emphasize the Rule because the hermits do not live according to an official Rule. The Rule is also the *experientia magistra* (1.6), the mistress/teacher of

---

28. *Conf.* 18.5; for the cenobites cf. also Justinian, *Nov.* 5.3.
29. E.g., Cassian, *Conf.* 18.9-10.
30. *Conf.* 18.5-7.
31. Vogüé, *"Sub regula."*

experience under whom one learns and is trained.[32] Those who do not follow
it, like the sarabaites, Benedict calls "not tested by any Rule." Instead, their
Rule is "their gross desire." In other words, the Rule offers testing and a sure
safeguard against the excesses of desire.

The abbot applies the Rule. But the Rule also legitimizes the abbot's office. The abbot also has to observe the Rule (cf. 3.7; 64.20). In contrast to the
sarabaites, the cenobites are "with their shepherd," (not "without one," 1.8).
To him the following long chapter is devoted (RB 2).

They fight, they serve (militans). Again there is a discussion about the
meaning of this term (as in Prol 3).[33] It seems that in RM the meaning of
fighting is still stronger, but as can be seen from the following paragraph in
RB 1, fighting is also required in the monastery. Commentators of the past
centuries strongly emphasized this element so that the monastery became a
sort of barracks, with the monk seen primarily as a soldier, and with special
emphasis on the weapons, regulations, and the battle of life. The New Testament used *militia*, especially in Paul's writings. The Christian's fighting is
not in the army of the king. The battle is against the powers of darkness (Eph
6:10-20; 1 Thess 5:8-9).

In the early church, the word *militia* was applied to the Christians' responsibility in general. Martyrdom was a special form of *militia Christi,* the
fight for Christ. In contrast to the emperor, Christ is presented as the true
king of Christians (cf. Prol 3). After the era of persecution, baptism is seen
as entering the *militia Christi.* In the fourth century, the word gradually lost
its accent of fighting and was also applied to public service. Christian life
is a battle against anti-Christian powers, a battle to acquire virtue, and service to the true king. Now we might ask whether RB primarily emphasizes
against whom or *for whom* one is fighting. It seems to me that for Benedict,
the main accent is no longer on fighting demons (as in the case of hermits,
1.4-5); rather the following of Christ takes center stage. For him the *militia*
consists above all in obedience, as he says in Prologue 3 (as well as in Prol
40). According to 58.10, it is necessary to fight / serve under the law of the
Rule or under the one king (cf. 61.10, as in Prol 3). The same *militia* = service
we take upon us makes everyone in the community equal (2.20). Benedict

---

32. The Latin *magistra* is the feminine form of *magister* = master; German has
"Meisterin" which the author uses throughout for *experientia magistra.* Even though
"mistress" in English has lost its connection with "master," it seemed important to keep
this feminine form here hoping that readers will keep its original connection to "master" in mind.

33. Böckmann, *Perspectives,* 23-25. Smaragdus quotes Job 7:1, doing military service
because "human life on earth is warfare" (116).

uses the word less frequently than RM (only in half of its occurrences does he depend on the RM).

We can think of the following terms that explain RB 1: In the community one learns "to fight against the devil and vices," here is the "battle line of the brothers," here one is "trained" well. And from the opposite images: Without struggle, the monks are soft as lead, serving the world, following the desires of self-will and their palate. Through indulging one becomes soft as lead, but in the monastery one serves Christ, fortifying the will and becoming solidly established in what is good. Obedience—community—Christ, these seem to be Benedict's three accents in this concept. In all three dimensions not only fighting but also "serving" is emphasized. Considering not only the text but also the content of the entire Rule, we can say that the word *militia*, even though it tends toward serving, does not lose the aspect of fighting entirely.

Some commentators hold that the three terms *monasteriale, regula, abbas* are used in contrast to the three other kinds of monks; this would mean that hermits are without an abbot (problematic), sarabaites without a Rule, and gyrovagues without a monastery.[34] This is, however, rather artificial, especially if further parallels are seen in the threefold promise of *stabilitas, conversatio morum,* and *oboedientia* (RB 58.17). Stability would be in contrast to the gyrovagues, fidelity to monastic life (*conversatio morum)* to the sarabaites, and obedience to the hermits. This also is very questionable. Certainly the terms are points of emphasis, but Benedict has a more unified view. He might have depended on RB 1 while drafting 58.17, but in general without stressing each part of the promise as opposed to a certain type of monk. The promise is part of cenobitic life, marked by the monastery and by the *militia* under Rule and abbot.

Vv. 3-5: Then the second kind is that of the anchorites, that is, the hermits, those who, not in the first fervor of *conversatio*, but by long testing in the monastery, sufficiently trained with the help of many others, have learned to fight against the devil, and now, well trained in the ranks of the brothers for single combat in the desert, are able, without the help of another, to fight confidently alone, with their own hand and their own arm, against the sins of the flesh and of thoughts with the help of God.[35]

These verses deal with the hermits. As seen earlier, much is also said about the cenobites, though indirectly. One can contrast communal and eremitical life:

---

34. Cf. Herwegen, 57.
35. As the English sentence, the original Latin sentence is not perfectly clear.

3 Then the second kind is that of the anchorites, that

is, the hermits, those who, not in the first fervor of *conversatio,*

but by long testing in the monastery 4 through

the help of many others, have learned

now well trained in the ranks of the brothers

to fight against the devil 5 and

for single combat in the desert, are able, without

the help of another, to fight confidently alone, with

their own hand and arm, against the sins of the flesh

and of thoughts with the help of God.

On the left is stated what they had in the coenobium. On the right is what happens now in the desert. This is high praise for the cenobites! And in the desert, first fervor is not enough, as the devil is present, against whom one has to fight, and this with his own hand and his own arm against the vices of flesh and of thoughts. But all this is only is possible "with the help of God." It is interesting to note to what extent the hermits are described in the vocabulary of fighting (in Latin, three times *pugna* = combat, or *pugnare* = to fight, two times *contra* = against), and in the radical opposition of God versus devil. The main battle fields are flesh and thoughts (*caro, cogitationes*).

V. 3: Then the second kind is that of the anchorites, that is, the hermits, those who, not in the first fervor of *conversatio*, but by long testing in the monastery . . . (*Deinde secundum genus est anchoritarum, id est, heremitarum, horum qui non conversationis fervor novicio, sed monasterii probatione diuturna . . .*)

Anchorites is derived from *anachoreo*, to withdraw, which Benedict explains with another Greek word: hermits. It derives from *heremos*, the desert. Both words again show the origin of monasticism in the Orient. In general Benedict follows RM.[36]

36. Deviations are noted under the individual concepts.

Not in the first fervor of conversatio (*non conversationis fervore novicio*): this is not a criticism of a beginner's fervor, which is necessary but needs testing and is part of the tradition. *Novicius* is an adjective, describing "fervor," just as in 58.23 it describes a new brother in *frater novicius*. In the sayings of the Fathers, there are stories of young monks who immediately, in their eagerness, wanted to live alone. One saying is especially memorable: "If you see a young monk who willfully wants to rise up to heaven, grab his foot and toss him down to earth, for otherwise it will be of no use to him."[37]

The word *conversatio* occurs here for the second time in the Rule (cf. Prol 49—*processu conversationis et fidei*). Here it denotes monastic life in general. In 73.1 we read of the beginning of monastic life (*initium conversationis* through the little Rule, 73.1, cf. 73.8) and then of a *perfectio conversationis*, completeness of monastic life (73.2). In chapter 1, does this mean that cenobites generally have only an initial zeal and hermits have its "completeness" (*perfectio*)? It seems to me that in 1.3-5, Benedict is speaking of those who move out. They should not be beginners in community life. For these exceptional persons, solitude may be the "completeness of monastic life," yet Benedict shows in his Rule that progress is also possible in the community. It seems that youthful zeal, in Benedict's mind, becomes more fervent in the course of common life until it is the "most ardent zeal" (*ferventissimo amore*) of RB 72.3. There is a holy *conversatio*, a holy monastic life (RB 21.1), and also a "most miserable" one (*miserrima conversatio*, 1.12).[38]

Long testing in the monastery (*probatione diuturna monasterii*)—in the community in the sameness of each day. This does not mean, of course, that the monastery is only a testing for hermits, and the community only a "school" for preparing hermits. I think there is no danger that too many will leave a community for the single combat. Benedict himself had stated with RM that one perseveres in the monastery until death (RB Prol 50). This is the normal course. Benedict, however, allows for special vocations. The word *probare, probatio* occurs only four times in the Rule. It means testing newcomers for their ability, earnestness, and patience, and whether they are motivated by the right spirit (58.2, 11). The difficulties of community life (cf. the fourth degree of humility) are seen as God's testing, by which the character becomes strong like silver in the fiery furnace (7.40). The *Regula Magistri* frequently mentions testing, which may, in addition to other factors, reveal that the Master was an author who was suspicious. The testing

---

37. *VitPat* 5.10.111; cf. also 5.10.110.

38. As in other places, Benedict changes here RM's *conversio* into *conversatio*; the word *conversatio* also occurs in Cassian in the passage about the cenobites (*Conf.* 18.4).

in both Rules is *diuturna*, which can be translated as either long in duration or a daily, frequent testing.

Vv. 4-5: sufficiently trained with the help of many others, they have learned to fight against the devil, and now, well trained in the ranks of the brothers for single combat in the desert, are able, without the help of another, to fight confidently alone, with their own hand and their own arm, against the sins of the flesh and of thoughts with the help of God. (*qui didicerunt contra diabulum multorum solacio iam docti pugnare, et bene extructi fraterna ex acie ad singularem pugnam heremi, securi iam sine consolatio alterius, sola manu vel brachio contra vitia carnis vel cogitationum, Deo auxiliante, pugnare sufficiunt.*)

Trained by the help of many (*multorum solacio docti*). What might this mean? Does it mean that in case of discouragement or sadness we could receive consolation from many? This is certainly included. *Solacium* in the larger sense, however, also implies help and support, so that the other person can learn, become self-reliant, and not remain dependent. Support also in the fight against the devil—this is meant to happen in the monastery. Later there is mention of the *consolatio alterius*, the consolation by another person, by a confrere, or of his loving help.[39]

Fight (*pugna*, see also 1.5: *pugnare*). These are the only three times that the root of this word is used by Benedict, whereas RM continues to use it later (e.g., 82.2; 94.5).[40] But in a text of his own, Benedict also had talked of weapons (of obedience, Prol 3). If the hermits are such fighters, we must add that they have learned how to fight while in the monastery. The contrast is therefore not between a quiet life and fighting but between fighting in community and fighting alone (as is seen more clearly in RM). Benedict speaks of hermits with respect. But he is not concerned here about motivating people for one or the other form of life. This is not a question of choice. Rather, he wants to introduce his Rule for community life and therefore distinguishes it from others: his Rule is not written for hermits. Cassian had emphasized an additional difference: The cenobites are practicing a "purifying asceticism," while the hermits are in constant union with God. In this sense, the life of an anchorite would rank higher than community life, but it proceeds from it. This view differs from Basil's.[41]

---

39. According to Hildemar (77): *cum vulneratur aut percutietur a diabolo, adjuvatur a fratribus, i.e. oratione, consolatione atque exhortatione.*

40. RM further has synonyms such as *agon* = rivalry (92.72), and *certamen* = vying with each other (70.1).

41. Cf. Basil, *Reg* 3; Vogüé, *Ce que dit*, 34–35; Holzherr 2007, 73.

Devil (diabolus)[42] from its Greek root means one who throws things into confusion. This *diabolus* occurs very often in RM (forty-three times) but only a few times in RB: The little ones of the *diabolus* one should dash against Christ (Prol 28). RB 58.28 deals with the devil's suggestions to which one might yield. No occasion should be given to the devil in the monastery (54.4). This is not much compared to RM. But Benedict does not deny the reality of the devil. It would be a smart tactic of the devil to conceal himself, so that his existence would not be treated as important. Benedict, however, is not as preoccupied as the Master with the presence of the devil; he is more relaxed.

Well trained (bene extructi; RM: *instructi).* The word can be used of a building which is being erected, of the stones that are put in layers, and also of the training, the educational or spiritual formation one receives.[43] A good formation, a solid foundation also seems important for a potential hermit.

Well trained in the ranks of the brothers for single combat in the desert, they are able to fight confidently, alone, without the help of another (fraterna ex acie ad singularem pugnam heremi, securi iam sine consolatione alterius). The term "line/rank of battle" (*acies*) does not mean uniformity,[44] but safety and support of the others, so that the monks can be *se-curi*, without worry, when facing the devil. The monastery trains monks to be self-reliant, to stand on their own, free from false dependence and attachments.[45] The fight in the desert is termed *singularis*. This can mean single combat but also an extraordinary, special fight. We may translate the word differently according to one's own attitude toward hermits.

With their own hand and their own arm to fight against the sins of the flesh and of thoughts. The devil now becomes concrete as the vices of the flesh. "Flesh" presumably includes whatever relates to the lower and sinful human being (among others, negatively oriented sexuality and lusts); the temptations are to be dashed against Christ (Prol 28). In RB *caro* = flesh is always used in the biblical sense of a sinful and weak human being.[46]

Thoughts generally designate the undisciplined inclinations of the mind.[47] In RB the word *cogitatio (logismos)* is almost always used in the negative sense. In the first part we find it nine times, always in close connection with

---

42. See Kardong, "Devil"; "Demonic"; also Gertler, "Herausgefordert."

43. *Instruere* seems to be used more frequently. Whether Benedict employed alliteration *et . . . extructi . . . ex acie . . .* is a legitimate question.

44. Cf. Lentini, 43.

45. According to Linderbauer 152, *sufficiunt* would mean: to be strong enough, be capable.

46. Cf. Böckmann, "Der Mensch," 41f.

47. Cf. Lentini, 44; art. "Logismos" in *DS, DIP.* Smaragdus says that "the vices are at first in one's thinking, and afterwards come forth in one's action" (118).

RM, finally one more time in RB 65.5. The discernment of spirits is important for the spiritual life in order to prevent evil attitudes. Certainly Evagrius and Cassian have influenced this part. Here it is clear that the meaning is sins/vices of the mind.

Hand and arm are not suitable weapons against temptations and the devil. Perhaps this is the very paradox that leads to the next phrase, "with God's help" (*Deo auxiliante*). Our own weapons are never sufficient for the fight against the evil one, so that we might feel safe.

With God's help (*Deo auxiliante*). The necessity of grace is emphasized more in RB than in RM. The master here just used the expression to fight "with God and with the spirit" (RM 1.5). This probably means God and the spirit (one's own) are fighting together. The spirit joins God's side, or God's light enters through the human spirit and enables a person. Also, the master used *repugnare* instead of *pugnare*. I tend to agree with the *Lexica* that *repugnare* is even stronger and indicates fighting "against." Cassian had used the word about ten times, usually in regard to the fight of "flesh and spirit" (*caro et spiritus*), or the law of the members of the body that fights against the law of the spirit.[48]

Benedict is more general. *Auxilium* is derived from *augere*—to increase, to cause to grow; this is what God's help does in us, so that we can say: "By the grace of God I am what I am" (1 Cor 15:10, Prol 31). "With the help of God" also reflects the end of the chapter, "with the Lord's help (*adiuvante Domino*, 1.13). Note that for the hermits, the word is *Deus*, but for the cenobites *Dominus*! This corresponds to 73.8-9 where "the help of the Lord" (*Domino adiuvante*) applies to the beginning, the little Rule, or the writing of the Rule, but "under God's protection" (*Deo protegente*) is used for the ascent to the heights. I think we might cautiously conclude that for the cenobites, being centered in Christ is particularly important. Presumably, as the monk progresses, Christ will lead him more and more to God, to the Father, or the Trinity. Thus Benedict does give a very small, almost hesitant view of that which Cassian had described with *contemplatio* and similar terms.[49]

Looking back, we can see how positively Benedict saw the monastery where there is testing (*probatio*), help, support (*solacium, consolatio*), and training in the rank of others (*fraterna acie*). No negative word is said about the cenobites; but also no exuberant praise is given to hermits either; there is simply a very basic description so that everyone who reads it will certainly

48. The Vulgate translation of Rom 7:53 uses *repugnare*.

49. Cassian *Conf.* 1.10.5 equates *caritas Dei* with the *contemplatio . . . divinarum rerum . . .* and the purity of heart; this is the culmination of the spiritual progress; cf. also *Conf.* 3.7.8 referring to 1 Cor 13 and *Conf.* 11.7.6.

admire the hermits yet will carefully consider whether they dare to take this step.

Vv. 6-7: The third, and most despicable kind of monks is that of the sarabaites, who are not tested by any Rule, as a mistress of experience, like gold is tested in the fiery furnace, but are soft as lead, still following the world in their actions, and so clearly lie to God by their tonsure. (*Tertium vero monachorum taeterrimum genus est sarabaitarum, qui nulla regula adprobati, experientia magistra, sicut aurum fornacis, sed in plumbi natura molliti, adhuc operibus servantes saeculo fidem, mentiri Deo per tonsuram noscuntur.*)

The sarabaites are described in 1.6-9. Benedict generally follows RM but omits one comment: "I would do better to call them still of the world [lay persons], except that the tonsure of their religious intent prevents me from doing so" (RM 1.6). Words and ideas are the Master's (also taken up in Eugippius). Why did Benedict omit this sentence? I think he avoids the negative description of lay persons, just as he does in the remaining chapters of his Rule. As a whole, RM is closer to Cassian, even though he has organized the materials according to his own ideas. These two sources help us get a better idea of what "lying to God" (*mentiri Deo*) really means. For Cassian, Ananias and Saphira are the image of the sarabaites,[50] yet in RB the biblical basis is barely discernible.

In addition, Benedict omits a comment of RM at the end: "And while they want to have cells, chests, and various things according to their own judgment, they are unaware that they are losing their own petty souls" (RM 1.10). Here it is clearer that the sarabaites live not only according to their own desires and self-will but also from private possessions. Moreover, it becomes more evident that their life itself is a lie: They want to look good but are really bad.

RM also adds the false hermits to the sarabaites and thus makes an inclusion to the hermits. RM 1.11-12: "Likewise there are those who, recently converted, in unrestrained fervor think that the desert is a place of repose. Giving no thought to the devil's lying in wait for them, untrained but confident, they go forth to single combat with him, doubtlessly only to fall victim to the jaws of the experienced wolf." The Master takes up the words of the hermits but in the reversed sense. They don't want to fight, they don't know the devil, they are going into the fight "not well trained," but they feel "sure"

---

50. *Conf.* 18.7.1-2; Acts 5:3-4, "why did you lie to the holy Spirit . . . you have lied not to human beings but to God."

of themselves. Their zeal is not just a beginner's enthusiasm but is intemperate (*immoderatus*).[51] The false hermits, however, are not named as a fourth kind as in Cassian. RM integrates the false hermits with the sarabaites, for he wants to add the gyrovagues as a new kind. Benedict also has said with the master about the sarabaites that they live "in twos and threes or alone." This means, they might also live alone.

The most despicable kind (*taeterrimum genus*). The word *taeterrimus* occurs once more in a similar form with the gyrovagues: "even worse than the sarabaites" (*deteriores sarabaitis*). *Teter* by itself already means ugly, detestable, terrible. The superlative form here indicates the emotional aggravation of both authors.

Sarabaitae. Jerome had called them *remnuoth* (living alone, dispersed, in cells). Perhaps they were monks in the city, who settled near basilicas and did not break off their relations with the world, or simply monks who did not want to live in their monasteries.[52]

Not tested by any Rule (*nulla regula adprobati*). Expressed negatively, this corresponds to the *probatio,* the testing in verse 3, which the monastery provides. The Rule guarantees direction, provides legitimization, and furthers authenticity. This is precisely lacking in the sarabaites.

The Rule, mistress of experience. Here Benedict has made what seems like a slight external change, yet a more profound one on meaning. RM says that "tested by no Rule and the master in experience" (*nulla regula adprobati et experientia magistro* [1.6]). By using the "and" he has placed the master (not magistra—mistress) on the same level as the Rule. This is reflected in RB and RM 1.2: "under Rule and abbot." Cassian had written that the sarabaites do not accept "any Rule of sound healthy discretion" (*sanae discretionis regulam*).[53]

---

51. A juxtaposition may be helpful:

true hermits	false hermits
non fervore novicio	*fervore immoderato*
pugna	*putant quietem, . . . tranquilitas*
contra diabolum . . . iam docti pugnare	*singularem cum eo pugnam indocti*
securi	*securi*
contra . . . pugnare	*lupi faucibus occursuri*

52. Vogüé points out that the Coptic word means "separated from monasteries"; cf. *Ce que dit*, 36; Steidle, 63.

53. *Conf.* 18.7.3.

So, what is the exact meaning of the term? Translations of RM and RB show different versions:

a. *adprobati: regula et magistro(a) (in experientia),* so Bozzi I;
b. *adprobati: regula et experientia* (which is a teacher), according to Linderbauer: "They are tested neither by a Rule, which would provide support, nor by experience as mistress of an ascetical life" (153); Holzherr: "tested neither by a Rule nor by experience as a mistress," (68); Frank: "tested under no Rule and also under no experience as a mistress" (RM 1.6, 89).
c. *adprobati regula: experientia magistra* "tested by the Rule, which is a mistress in experience" according to Lentini (45), Kardong (39), and Vogüé I (439); that is, they interpret *experientia* as an ablative of *magistra*, the Rule; they take it as a term for the Rule, which because of its experience is a mistress, or a teacher in experience, or the Rule with its experience as mistress.

We have, therefore:

a. parallelism of : *regula* and magister (RM)
b.   "   : *regula* and *experientia* (mistress)
c. an expression : *regula* as *experientia magistra*

I accept the third translation. It is of interest that this verse shows many variants in the RB manuscripts. Some add *et* or *vel*: that is, Rule and experience, others say *experientia magistri* (the experience of the Master), still others have *magistro* (Rule and master, as in RM).[54]

The Master is logical, for in contrast to the cenobites, who serve under Rule and abbot, the sarabaites are not proven by the Rule nor by the Master in experience (the abbot). Thus, Rule and master are set face to face. Both test the monks (also according to Eugippius). RM does not have the feminine form of master—*magistra*—but only the masculine one—*magistro.* In this case, Benedict follows more closely Cassian, who also speaks of the Rule as a mistress.[55] In 3.7, Benedict once more calls the Rule a mistress.

---

54. Cf. Hanslik, 29. Hildemar (79) thinks "*magistra* can also refer to the Rule and experience."

55. Not in *Conf.* 18, but in *Conf.* 19.7: *utramque perfectionem lungo usu ac magistra experientia consecutus*—"with experience as his teacher"; *Conf.* 12.4: *experientiae magisterio*—"the school of experience"; *Conf.* 12.16: *experientia docente*—"with experience as our teacher"; also *Conf.* 3.7.4.

Regula / Rule can mean a written rule or simply a disciplined life, otherwise one would have to condemn all forms of monastic life prior to the development of written rules, making them, as it were, types of the sarabaitic life. The Rule, one might say, arising from experience, leads the monks through crises and tests (fourth degree of humility) to spiritual experiences that are also open to experiencing God. The Rule as a mistress of experience not only teaches the mind but also introduces the monks to reality (cf. 2.5, 12) through the common life in obedience (in contrast to the sarabaites [1.8]). This Rule, a teacher in experience, is at the same time a very small Rule for beginners (73.8). The community does not smother the élan of the individual monk toward the heights.

As gold is tried in the fiery furnace. This recalls other Scripture texts: "as gold in the melting furnace has he tried them" (Wis 3:6). Our authors acknowledge that community living, with its Rule and regulations, also has the purifying power of fire (cf. Prov 27:21).[56] Precious metals were cast into the fire together with molten lead in order to separate the silver from its impurities, which collected at the bottom of the melting pot together with the oxidized lead. The image is used in a similar manner for the fourth degree of humility: "You have tested us God, as silver is tested in the fire" (RB 7.40; RM 10.57). Cenobites are like silver or gold, sarabaites like lead.

Soft as lead (sed in plumbi natura molliti)—these are the false monks, not shiny and precious metal, but soft, indulgent, without a backbone. They have no recognizable strong identity; others don't know what to think of them. They indulge in everything they like.

Still faithful to the world in their actions (adhuc operibus servantes saeculo fidem). *Saeculum* here designates the world as opposed to monastic life. Concretely, one may think of possessions, comfort, and having one's own way. Deliberately the text says: in their actions, that is, not in their words. The emphasis is on the contrast between the appearance of monastic life on the one hand and the necessary renunciations on the other; on their beautiful words about monastic life and the tonsure on the one hand, and their real lifestyle on the other. In the phrase "still faithful to the world" (*servantes fidem*), *fides* does not mean faith but rather loyalty and dependability. Together with the verb *servare*, it means keeping a promise or remaining loyal. In the life of these monks there has been no conversion, though they pretend there was.

---

56. Cf. Sir 2:5 "For in the fire gold is tested, and worthy men in the crucible of humiliation." Cf. Cassian, *Conf.* 6.11.2; and 7.25.2 refers to Isa 1:25: "I will refine your dross in the furnace removing all your alloy." Smaragdus says about this text: "The one has received the brightness of gold and goes up to heaven to reign with Christ; the other, become soft as lead, goes down to the netherworld to be tortured with the devil" (120).

They clearly lie to God by their tonsure. The tonsure (meaning originally to cut the hair short) was always meant to indicate a firm belonging to God, and for the monks in particular, it meant a renunciation of the vanity of the world.[57] Note that the tonsure is mentioned in the RB only here (one would expect it in RB 58; RM mentions it several times). In this point the aspect of lying is explicitly introduced. Lying to God is dreadful. It occurs in the Bible, for example in Acts 5:3 (Ananias and Saphira—the ancestors of the dreadful sarabaites, according to Cassian).[58]

V. 8a: In twos or threes, or even alone, without a shepherd, not in the sheepfolds of the Lord but enclosed in their own, they take as their law what they desire. (*Qui bini aut terni aut certe singuli sine pastore, non dominicis sed suis inclusi ovilibus, pro lege eis est desideriorum voluntas.*)

In twos or threes or even alone: already Jerome had said that of the *remnuoth* (cf. p. 103); one also finds it in Cassian.[59] RM and RB also write of sarabaites who live by themselves.[60] In mentioning the sarabaites, RB combines those living in small groups and those living alone. The expression "or even alone" seems like an appendix. As already mentioned, at the end Benedict omits the phrase about their belongings (RM 1.10).

Without a shepherd, not in the Lord's sheepfold, but enclosed in their own. In Cassian this reads: "they live in cells by twos and threes, not content to be governed by the care and judgment of an abba" (*Conf.* 18.7.4.). The shepherd and his enclosure, that is, the stable of the sheep, recall the speech about shepherds in John's Gospel (John 10:1-30). The sarabaites are enclosed, whereas the cenobites are free. The sarabaites are also without a shepherd, that is, without an abbot. We may recall the contrary description of cenobites in the nucleus of RB 5.12—that they desire to have an abbot over them. For our two authors, a truly monastic community is not conceivable without a superior, even though there is a difference in their perspectives and descriptions. Here the emphasis is on the insight that no shepherd is leading the individual sarabaites out of their enclosure; they are locked into themselves. The door is not just closed—they are firmly locked in. The sheepfolds of the Lord are the property of Christ. In their own folds are those who follow their

---

57. Cf. Lentini, 47.

58. Cf. for example, Vulgate Pss 17:46; 77:36; 80:16. Regarding Ananias and Saphira, cf. *Conf.* 18.7.1. Smaragdus explains the lie thus: "he keeps faith with the world because he does not separate himself from it" (120) and compares the sarabaites to wolves in sheep's clothing (121, cf. Matt 7:15f.).

59. *Conf.* 18.7.4.

60. Cf. *solitarie sedere*, *Conf.* 18.8.1.

own desires and self-will. The good folds, in which the cenobites are living, are the sheepfolds of the Lord (*dominici*), that is, Christ.[61] This means that the pastor-abbot always is obliged to keep the sheep directed to Christ and his fold.

Considering that this verse is the nucleus of RB 1, we can see how important it is to live in obedience. The verse also states indirectly that the cenobites are in the sheepfold of Christ and have placed themselves under Christ, the good shepherd. The abbot is his representative. Their fold is open, as one may say, so that the shepherd can lead them to freedom. But in this fold there also is protection from danger (in contrast to RM 1.12). The sarabaites, however, are exposed to danger, locked in, turned in on themselves, they cannot escape from themselves. This "being enclosed" is in contrast to the next verse, for a superficial assumption is that someone who can do anything he wishes is free.

Vv. 8b-9: They take as their law what their cravings demand for whatever they think or want, they call holy; and what they dislike, they consider forbidden. (*Pro lege eis est desideriorum voluptas cum quidquid putaverint vel elegerint, hoc dicunt sanctum. Et quod noluerint, hoc putant non licere.*)[62]

They do not accept the law of the Rule but instead have a law of their own that enslaves them. Here we are reminded of Romans 6.15-19. The lusts of their desires (as in Ms A of RB)! We can read the word "desires" (*desideriorum voluptas*) as a *genitivus epexegeticus* in which both words reinforce each other. The sarabaites obey their lusts (cf. RB 5.12). These are sensual pleasures, the delights of love, sexual delights, etc. *Desiderium* is used here in the sense of evil desire. In the Rule it is used several times in the expression *desideria carnis* (RB 4.59; 7.12-13). The sarabaites are driven by lusts and desires and are enslaved by them. They are their own self-made law which enslaves them. The phrase is evidently a parallel to verse 6, that they are not tested by a Rule. According to Cassian, we can say: It is not the "Rule of sound discretion."[63] But there is worse to come.

When there is no desire for truth, there remains only concealment or an inversion of values, the lie. They "canonize all their lusts."[64] Their desire

---

61. The adjective *dominicus* represents a subjective genitive, similar to the term *oratio dominica*, the Lord's Prayer.

62. From the manuscripts it is difficult to decide whether the word is *voluntas* = will or *voluptas* = pleasure; Hanslik has *voluptas*, while Vogüé in his edition has *voluntas*. That they declare as holy what they desire also occurs in Augustine, *Contra Ep Parm*, 2.13.31; *Ep* 93.10.43.

63. *sanae discretionis regula*, *Conf.* 18.3.3.

64. Cf. *Conf.* 18.3.2; Augustine, *Ep* 93.10.43; *Contra Ep Parm* 2.13.31.

is not the outcome of a discernment but rather a choice according to taste. And everything is lying and delusion. "They are monks caught in their own egoism that is framed by religion," their presumed liberty "only conceals a complete lack of religious orientation. . . . And the idea of an individualism of salvation is exposed as an existential lie.[65] And there is also a dynamic that keeps pushing a person ever further in doing just what he wants at the moment! One no longer wants to hear the whole truth and is not open to correction. The sarabaites set themselves up as the norm.[66]

Again the contrast shows clearly that the cenobites are tested by the Rule, they are gold, not soft lead, they have left the world, live according to their tonsure, are loyal to God, and stand under an abbot as their shepherd. They are in the Lord's sheepfold, subject to the law of Christ, have sacrificed their self-will, and therefore are truly free. In the monastery they get all the help needed in order to be truly monks.

RM mentions a further example of the sarabaites' lie and the contrast to true monastic profession: they own things, such as cells, small cabinets and some personal effects. And then the Master, almost sadly, adds: doing so, "they are losing their own petty souls" (1.10, *perdunt suas animellas*). Benedict omitted the line concerning monastic poverty; perhaps he thought this was already contained in RB 1.9: "whatever they desire and choose, they call holy."

Vv. 10-11: The fourth kind of monks are the so-called gyrovagues, who spend their whole lives wandering through various provinces, staying as guests in different monasteries for three or four days, always moving and never stable [*vagi*], subject to their own wills and to the cravings of their palates, they are in every respect even worse than the sarabaites. (*Quartum vero genus est monachorum quod nominatur girovagum, qui tota vita sua per diversas provincias ternis aut quaternis diebus per diversorum cellas hospitantur, semper vagi et numquam stabiles, et propriis voluntatibus et guilae inlecebris servientes, et per omnia deteriores sarabaitis.*)

In two verses Benedict summarizes the long satire of the RM. As Vogüé has shown, Benedict knew Manuscript P (that is, also the chapter in its long form). RM had stated at the beginning of this description in 1.13: "The fourth kind of monks one should not even mention. Much rather would I keep silence than say anything about such people." An evident contradiction

65. Holzherr 2007, 75.
66. It is interesting to list the verbs that describe the Sarabaites: "closed-in, demand, think, desire, not want." In commenting on this verse, Smaragdus says that "he pleases himself in all his deeds and has no one else to test his work" (122).

to his long descriptions! Benedict keeps the beginning (RB 1.10) but then finds inspiration for verse 11 in Augustine or Cassian (cf. below) and adds at the end that it is better to be silent than to speak about their miserable way of life (1.12). He applies his comment to both gyrovagues and sarabaites.[67] Both kinds of monks are servants of their self-will.

Gyrovagues. RM probably created this word from the Greek (*gyros*: circle, but already Latinized) and from the Latin (*vagus*: unstable, restless). Actually a very high ascetical ideal stands in the background: homelessness for the sake of Christ. It implied a total separation from the world, from family, from the homeland, from possessions, and interiorly, a separation from cares, from attachment to goods, from one's own wishes and pleasures, from thoughts and many words, from sins, and finally from pride and even from one's own ego. This ideal also implied perpetual silence. But it seems that high ideals easily degenerate when a person has no structures or rules. There were special kinds of monks who always wanted to keep wandering, living as beggars and sleeping without a roof over their heads. Some lived on herbs only. We know about them chiefly from their opponents who attacked them during their decadence, for it certainly was not easy to live up to such a high ideal.[68] They were hard to control.[69] Later some of these aspects were revived in Irish monasticism with its ideal: *pro evangelio peregrinare*, for the sake of God and the Gospel to set out and never return to the homeland.[70]

The two verses contain various contrasts:

Time	Place
their entire life	through various provinces
for three or four days	in different monasteries
always	never
moving	stable

Their entire life (*tota vita sua*). The exaggeration shows an upset author. *In various provinces . . . in various monasteries (cells)* (*per diversas provincias . . . per diversorum cellas*). The words mean various but also many. Province means district, region, and at times even country. Benedict thinks that for the habits one should take materials that are easily obtained in the

67. The Latin expression in 1.12 *omnium—quorum* links the two kinds.
68. Cf. e.g., Augustine, *In Ps.* 132.3: "they wander . . . and nowhere have a home." Cassian, *Inst* 10.6: "unstable and fickle" with "a slothful mind"; also Evagrius, *Sent* 80, 81.
69. Justinian, *Nov.* 5.7.
70. *Vita Columbani* 1.5: "having lived for many years in a monastery, he began to desire to travel mindful of the Lord's command to Abraham."

province (55.7), or he mentions an unknown monk who arrives from far distant lands (*de longinquis provinciis*—61.1). According to classical Latin, a province would be a land outside the Roman Empire. In the present verse, it would mean in any case that the gyrovagues roam about far and wide. *Cella* originally meant the dwelling place of a hermit, but it can also designate a monastery of cenobites or a part of the monastery.[71] RM 78–79 reveals the extremely suspicious attitude of the Master in receiving guests (potential parasites). If they were like those described in his long satire on the gyrovagues, one can more readily understand his negative attitude in regard to hospitality. His monastery evidently was directly suffering from this nuisance.

Three or four days. As older texts illustrate, it was often the custom to put the guests to work after the third or fourth day. The master was strict and allowed the guests two free days, with work from the third day onward (e.g., RM 78.5-6). He thus wants to prevent monks from becoming parasites, especially gyrovagues.

Ever moving and never stable. Stabilitas is an essential element for Benedict and also for RM. The vice of *acedia* causes a feeling of horror for a place. Cassian and others describe this vice,[72] which makes a person feel driven from place to place. The satire of the RM 1.74 draws a vivid picture: "Always on the go from place to place, they don't know where they will next be a nuisance and, to top it all, they do not know where they will be buried." The master also describes gluttony as a typical vice of instability, because during their first two days as guests they receive good meals. They try to arouse pity in their hosts because of their—as they say—long and strenuous travels to various holy places.

Serving their self-will and the cravings of their palate. In the *Vitae Patrum* we find a similar-sounding sentence, that when we live in community, we may not serve our self-will.[73] The gyrovagues are enslaved. To be a servant of Christ makes a person free, but the gyrovagues forge their own chains. Their yearning for good food urges them on, according to RM, to exploit other people's love of neighbor shamelessly. They force "the poor host out of sympathy for their long journey to use up his whole scanty means in cooking and serving them food" (RM 1.38), and they often omit the praying of the Psalms "because of their preoccupation with their gluttonous travels" (1.63). One can sense the Master's disgust for them. They are totally degenerate, no longer having even a trace of *ascesis*, discipline and moderation. Hildemar (83) points out that from gluttony, other vices develop.

---

71. Cf. Blaise, *Dictionnaire*, 142.
72. For example, *Inst.* 10.5-6.
73. *VitPatr.* 5.14.10.

In every respect even worse than the sarabaites. This is the conclusion. Benedict already had called the sarabaites "most detestable" (*deterrimum / taeterrimum*, 1.6). Here he gives a superlative of the superlative, omitting the lengthy descriptions of the Master (1.13-74). Hildemar (84) says that the sarabaites at least live from the work of their hands, whereas the gyrovagues are lazy.

V. 12: It is better to keep silent about the most miserable way of life [*conversatio*] of all these than to talk about it. (*De quorum omnium horum miserrima conversatione melius est silere quam loqui.*)

And Benedict does just that, while the Master had described this plague at great length in sixty verses. "All these" links gyrovagues and sarabaites. The word for keeping quiet (*silere*) can also mean to hold the hand over the mouth. From what is said so far, one might conclude that, like the Master, Benedict had experienced such kinds of monks. RB 53, however, about hospitality, makes no allusion to them.

V. 13: Let us bypass these, therefore, and proceed, with God's help, to provide a Rule for the cenobites, the strongest kind of monks. (*His ergo omissis, ad coenobitarum fortissimum genus disponendum, adiuvante Domino, veniamus.*)

To give a Rule (*disponendum*) is an almost legal term; it resembles Prologue 45 in setting up (*constituenda est*) the school of the Lord's service. The adjective *fortissimus* occurs only one other time, in Prologue 3, "with the very strong weapons of obedience." RM 1.75 simply calls the cenobites "great" (*magnum*), while Benedict says *fortissimum*. Should we translate: the most important kind? Lentini thinks "the best." In Latin the word can mean large or good. Certainly the cenobites are the most widespread and numerous type of monks.[74] And the cenobitic way is a good and secure base for monastic life. Nevertheless, it also requires strength of character (as contrasted with sarabaites and gyrovagues). RM had added, "whose service and probation are the will of God" (RM 1.75: *cuius militia vel probatio voluntas est Dei*). Here he emphasized once again the fighting and testing in community.

With the Lord's help (*adiuvante Domino*). With the help of the Lord, that is Christ, Benedict wants to write his Rule, which one fulfills with the help of Christ (*adiuvante Christo*, 73.8). This comment is a new addition to the RM. He is very conscious of his smallness while the Master seems quite sure that the Lord is speaking through his mouth as RM introduces each chapter with the phrase: "The Lord has replied through the Master."

---

74. Cf. Lentini, 51, so also Puzicha, 74, cf. also comments on v. 2.

One can understand that God's help is needed for describing the heights of monastic life, but Benedict has a humble view of his Rule. Not even the least thing can he do without the Lord's (Christ's) help. Perhaps he deliberately used God (*Deus*) when speaking of the hermits, and *Dominus* (Christ) when he deals with the cenobites. This is similar to chapter 73. At the beginning, the person of Christ is basic; he will lead us on to God, the Trinity, for this is his desire (cf. 7.67-70).

LOOKING BACK

1. Community life—eremitical life:[75]
Cassian says that community life developed from the first Christian community. Viewing it from history, one will agree with Vogüé that community life arose from the disciples being gathered around a master. Vogüé has shown often enough that the law of a circle of disciples also applied to monasticism: followers will gather around a charismatic personality (cf. for example Lérins). This moves the emphasis to fraternal relations. The disciples become brothers.

Subsequently, principles evolve from the tradition: that one—referring to the individual monk—should first be a cenobite; then, after being tested in the brotherhood, one can move out into the desert to fight the demons. In general, the following characteristics are named for eremitical life: unceasing prayer, purity of heart, *apatheia*, contemplation. Normally this type of life entails more hardships.

There were, however, hermits who returned to the monastery because there they could better practice humility and obedience (for the purpose of eliminating self-will).[76] In addition, there are forms of monasticism in which eremitical and cenobitical life are combined (e.g., the lauras in Lérins: hermitages situated around a main monastery).

It seems that community life is seen as less demanding but as more secure. Benedict sharpens the community aspect by a common oratory (elsewhere, the cell was the place of prayer) and common dormitory. By comparison with the East, cenobitic monasticism expanded more strongly in the West.

2. This chapter sets forth four important aspects of community life:

2.1 The *monastery* or the "sheepfold" is a physical and a spiritual location, the monks are living in stability (both physically and spiritually) in contrast to the gyrovagues.

75. Cf. Vogüé. "School/Ecole."
76. Cf. Cassian, *Conf.* 19.2-6.

2.2 *Militia*—community life also entails struggle, but it is fighting in common. The monks are not soft as lead. The fight is certainly also directed against the devil but more directly against self-will, moodiness, and temptations! When everything is allowed, one becomes enslaved (like the sarabaites).

2.3. Under the *Rule* which is already a written Rule. It takes its direction from the Bible (Prol 21), refers to sound tradition, develops from experience; it is a mistress by experience while the sarabaites have no Rule, or are making up their own. The true law, however, sets a person free (Gal 4–5).

2.4. Under the *abbot* as spiritual leader, as shepherd, who is in contact with each one and vouches for the community, who guarantees the vitality of the Rule and is at the same time subject to it; he also adapts the Rule to circumstances.

3. Eremitical life is not declared as higher; Benedict speaks of it with esteem. He does not want to offer a deep theological statement, for the aim of a Rule is simply to provide structure, to create a framework for community living (without specifying all the details); the Rule also is not a treatise of spirituality, much less a theology of monastic life.

4. It seems important that the help of Christ is mentioned. In the course of the Rule this Christo-centric aspect will become ever clearer.

5. Concerning the hermeneutics of this chapter, one must see it together with RB 72–73. Benedict stresses community life but keeps the door open for the progress of individuals. In the entire Rule he shows respect for the action of grace in each person.

Chapter 2

How the Abbot Should Be
(*Qualis debeat abbas esse*)

CONTEMPORARY CONTEXT

Whereas in the society of past times, governance in religious orders was considered a position of honor, often given to members of the nobility, and meetings with superiors were marked by many ceremonies (signs of respect) so that the superior was placed at some distance from the subjects, today we often find it difficult to even find persons who are willing to serve as superiors. Terrence Kardong quotes a sociologist's comment about younger members: "They do not want to lead; they do not want to follow. All they want is interesting work and satisfying emotional relationships that are characterized by friendliness, sympathy, understanding and generosity."[1] Many of our communities are infected by individualism, and this prevents a climate in which a sense of responsibility for the whole can develop. On the other hand, the demands are greater than before with regard to supportive serving, communication, and the necessity to be a person who is able to represent the group and with whom members can identify. For younger superiors it is difficult to find their own style. Much is said about training and ongoing formation in "leadership."[2]

Within the Benedictine Confederation, many styles of leadership exist, as for example, abbesses who in a motherly way want to take care of everything themselves and in whose communities nearly everything depends on them. Since some of them, however, have great authority, they are often given unquestioning obedience; yet there are also communities that function

---

1. Cf. Terrence Kardong, "Abbot," 53.
2. This introduction is simply designed to stimulate readers to reflect about our current situation before reading the chapter.

without superiors. There is even the phenomenon of superiors departing from the community after their term of office ends—perhaps they have had too many negative experiences? In practice, very few superiors are elected for life today. For this very reason, more members than before must today face the possibility of being entrusted with such a burden. Once I was told that people would describe the succession of superiors as: hero—Nero—zero.

We might think that a chapter about the abbot would address only those who hold this office; yet chapter RB 2 can also provide important guidelines for religious who share the responsibility for others in any other form.

At a meeting of AIM (June 15, 1996, in Singeverga, Portugal) Armand Veilleux gave an important presentation about superiors and new foundations in the monastic world. He spoke from his own experience and distinguished between abbots of the cenobitic tradition and abbots of the semi-eremitical tradition. The abbot of cenobites is concerned with a good community atmosphere, places great value on communication, and motivates monks to live according to the specific tradition whose identity he confirms; his teaching is as objective as possible and unites the brothers in their common search and discernment. He provides pastoral care to each one but always within the horizon of the whole community. He supports diverse forms of leadership and of responsibility within the community, is open to subsidiarity, and tries to foster the growth of members who eventually can take his place. This facilitates succession when he retires from office.

Yet the other form, that of the semi-eremitical abbot, seems to occur more frequently. The abbot stands before his community (he asks his community; the abbot and his community send greetings). He identifies the Rule with his own person, tends to regard strong characters as threats to himself, and tries to control everything. Often he favors certain brothers, but generally he does not identify anyone that might replace him. Veilleux asks why this second form is so widespread and lists several reasons: In some new communities the founding superior is very important and venerated; often he is a strong personality. The study of RB (here Veilleux refers to de Vogüé) can firmly establish such a form of leadership.

But in respect to RB we ask ourselves whether the abbot is primarily the spiritual father of the individual monk or rather the leader of the community. The first certainly applies of Benedict's immediate source (RM), the second to the Rule of Augustine, whose influence grew during the time Benedict was writing his Rule (RB 2 is more closely connected to RM, RB 64 to Augustine).

THE ABBOT IN THE CENOBITICAL TRADITION

According to *Pachomius*, the abbot's great task is to strengthen the community; he fosters fraternal relationships, for example, by catechesis, by explaining of the Word of God, by correcting faults. Pachomius already realized that power can be abused, and so he makes sure that the superiors of a house are accountable to their higher superior.[3]

Basil sees the superior as a servant of the Word;[4] there is a special chapter about the leader who serves each member and also corrects faults, but he is also a servant of Christ, the servant of everyone and, ready to follow his model, is willing to give his life for the community.[5] The later, longer Rules develop the image of the superior. He is the eye of the community, attends to the souls of the brothers, and has internalized the Lord's commandments; he is gentle and humble of heart (Matt 11:29).[6]

Augustine speaks first of the community, then, toward the end of his Rule, of the superior, who serves with love and ought to cast himself at the feet of the brothers, who is to strive above all to be useful rather than trying to be the first. He strives to be loved rather than feared.[7]

Caesarius of Arles mentions an abbess—*abbatissa*—and a prioress. The abbess or "mother" is concerned about all the sisters and tries to promote love and discretion in the community. Both superiors encourage those who fail and support the weak.[8]

In RM, the abbot is primarily the spiritual guide. He directs the individual monks and teaches them the spiritual art, which consists above all in fighting the devil and his temptations in order to become spiritual persons themselves. The superior is also the one who makes sure that the monk does not follow his own will. The superior's commands are deliberately set against it; this is seen by the master as the necessary torture, like those inflicted in a prison. For the monks desire to become martyrs, and this *agere contra*—going against—is the main means of torture. On the whole, this model of abbot and community resembles a pyramid. The mutual relationships among the brothers do not seem important. As becomes clear in the final chapters, the Master even thinks that the office of abbot is a goal to strive for and would be a good motive to inspire all the brothers in outdoing each other in monastic discipline (cf. e.g., 92.51-53).

The uniqueness of Benedict can be seen more clearly by comparing RM with what Benedict omits, adds, and changes. In the parts he omitted RM had talked about the abbot as being both father and mother, and the monks

---

3. E.g., *Praeclud.* 2. For Pachomius himself, the title *abbas* is used; cf. Art. "Abbas," 23.
4. *Reg* 12.
5. *Reg* 15.
6. *Regfus* 25; 43; cf. also 44-46.
7. *Praec* 7.
8. *RegVg* 35.4-6. Cf. also Vogüé, "Introduction à la Règle des Vierges," 88f.

as sons (family analogy). Toward the end, he expressed his conviction that at the Last Judgment, all accountability falls on the abbot since the disciples only had obeyed whether the command was good or bad. In his own texts, Benedict adds his concern about the rank among the monks (which distinguishes him from RM, where the ranks of the brothers keep getting changed), that the abbot is to correct faults right at the start, and finally, that in difficult situations, he should not be unduly concerned with the scant property of the monastery but rather should keep in mind that his priority must be the care of souls (cf. detailed exegesis).

This can be shown in the following chart, where the first column shows the text of the Master (+M) which is not used by Benedict; the middle column (BM) shows in brief form the material common to both; the third column (+B, plus Benedict) indicates the material added by Benedict:

+M 02	BM 02	+B 02
	1-10 Introduction: Abbot, doctor, pastor	
	11-15 Twofold teaching	
21 Abbot like God	16-22 Equal love for all	18-19 Exceptions in the rank
	23-29 Teaching adapted to characters	
26-31 Humility		26-29 Correct faults immediately (Eli)
Obey the head, Abbot as father/mother Monks as sons	30 always remember what he is	
	37 To be accountable	
		31-36 guide souls according to their nature in difficult situations: priority of the spiritual, trust
35-38 all responsibility lies with the abbot		
	39-40 Be accountable for the sheep, he himself is cleansed of faults	

OVERVIEW OF RB 2

The chapter can be divided up as follows, with only the central section (C—C') written out:

A 1-10 Introduction: The abbot as *Abbas*, teacher and pastor/shepherd—
  eschatological view.
  B 11-15 twofold teaching (*duplex doctrina*)—at the end: account to
    be given (Bible).
    C 16 Let him make no distinction of persons in the monastery.
      D 17 One is not to be loved more than another,
        E except he find someone better in good actions and obedience.
          F 18 One who enters the monastery as a slave
          is not to be outranked by a freeborn one,
          (unless there is another good reason.
          19 If the abbot considers it right
          for reasons of justice,
          he may change the rank as he sees fit.
          For the rest, each one is to keep his rightful place.[9])
            G 20 For, whether slave or free,
            we are all one in Christ
            and bear, under the one Lord
            the same burden of service,
          F' for with God there is no respect of persons.
        E' 21 Only then do we distinguish ourselves in his sight
        when we surpass others in good works and humility.
      D' 22 Therefore the abbot is to show equal love to all
    C' and according to their merits, is to apply the same rules to
      everyone.
  B' 23-30 Teaching, adapted to diverse characters—at the end: account
    to be given (Bible).
A' Conclusion: Guiding souls—above all accountability and judgment.

The concern for the community in Christ despite all diversity forms the center, the core of the chapter on the abbot. Only in verses 20-21 the pronoun "we" is used. In my opinion this may show that the abbot also is included.

---

9. In parentheses is the material Benedict may have added later.

This core certainly expresses one of the chief concerns of Benedict. From this we can already surmise that Benedict himself (by his structure of the chapter which is different from RM) desires a cenobitical abbot rather than a semi-eremitical one.

Title: Qualities of the Abbot (*Qualis debeat esse abbas*)

The title of this chapter is very similar to the title of RB 31 on the cellarer (*qualis debeat esse cellararius monasterii*). Perhaps this is a subtle indication that these two officials have much in common.[10]

RB 2.1-10: THE SUPERIOR AS ABBOT, TEACHER, AND PASTOR

This part can be subdivided into three shorter paragraphs that could have the following headings:

1-3 Abbot (*abbas*)
4-6 Teaching (*doctrina*), teacher
7-10 Shepherd (*pastor*)

Each of the three parts ends with a short word of Scripture or with an outlook to the Final Judgment (the last also mentions its consequence). In the first short part there is a strong reference to Christ; in the second, the key word is "teach" or "teaching" (*docere, doctrina*); in the third the characteristic words are: "flock, sheep" (*grex*, or *oves*: 3x), shepherd (*pastor*: 3x) and also the qualities of concern and zeal (*cura, diligentia*). For each subdivision, there is one verb of knowing, of remembering (*meminere, memor, scire*, vv. 1, 6, 7).

Vv. 1-3: The abbot, who is worthy to govern a monastery, must always consider what he is called and must make the name of superior a reality by his deeds. For he is believed to take the place of Christ in the monastery; as he is addressed by his name, as the apostle says: "You have received the Spirit that makes you sons, and in which we call out: 'Abba, father!'"

This passage has a classical structure: first the general main clause, then the first reason with "for" (*enim*), and a second, a biblical reason introduced by "as" (*quando*). The biblical quotation forms the climax. One can certainly say that these three verses are like the "musical key" for the image of the abbot in the Rule.

---

10. RB 31 is most similar to the second chapter about the abbot: RB 64.7-22.

**V. 1: The abbot, who is worthy to govern a monastery, must always con-
sider what he is called and must make the name of superior a reality by
his deeds. (*Abbas qui praeesse dignus est monasterio, semper meminere
debet quod dicitur et nomen maioris factis implere.*)**

Abbas (cf. also Egyptian monasticism) is a person who by his word generates
another, as Paul says that he became a father by the Gospel (1 Cor 4:15; cf.
also Phlm 10).[11] The *Abbas* has wisdom from experience, the gift of discerning spirits, and is able to pass on the right word of God as a guideline. The
term *abbas* was first used for hermits and semihermits; later it was also used
for the superior of communities. In the West it was replaced by *pater*, father.
RM uses *abbas* more frequently than *pater*, which has the same meaning.
In 63.13 Benedict says: "The abbot, however, since in faith he is believed
to hold the place of Christ, is to be addressed as 'Lord' and 'abbot,' not by
his own claim, but out of reverence and love for Christ." When the abbot
is called "father of the monastery" (*pater monasterii*) in RB 33.5, we might
recall the discussion between Herwegen and other experts on the Rule and
ask ourselves: "Does the abbot resemble the '*paterfamilias*' of the Romans?"
By the sixth century, the Roman *paterfamilias* chiefly continued to live on
in people's memory—not in reality (cf. also comment on 2.7). In general, we
distance ourselves today from this comparison and place the word *abbas* in
the biblical context and that of the Desert Fathers. He should be a spiritual
giver of life who fosters life by his teaching as well as by his spiritual guidance
in the ambit of the community. This also implies that he so promotes the life
of the others that they might even surpass him. The task of being a father
is shared with others, for example the *senpectae* (27.2-3) and the "spiritual
fathers" (*seniores spirituales*, 46.5). The power of the superior is given limits in
the Rule. Above all, RB brings the abbot face to face with his accountability
to the judge.

He is worthy (*dignus est*): this is a favorite expression of Benedict, which
he generally uses when talking of officials, such as the abbot, dean, priest,
and prior.[12]

To govern a monastery (*praeesse . . . monasterio*). The word *praeesse* is
mostly used in close connection with RM;[13] it signifies: to be in front, to
preside over a matter, to administer, but also to give a good example and to
give commands. This is, however, surpassed by the expression in 64.8: "to
provide rather than preside" (*oportere prodesse magis quam praeesse*), which
is found in the second chapter on the abbot and is derived from Augustine.

11. Cf. Art. "Abbas"; see also "Abbot," 322–29; 332–43.
12. Cf. RB 21.6; 62.1; 63.14; 64.5; 65.20.
13. Once in connection with Basil, *Reg* 68.2.

He must always consider (semper meminere debet). Meminere, and in addition *semper*—this is characteristic for the abbot (cf. conclusion). The abbot especially must be a man who is thinking, considering, and consciously living in the presence of God. The word is mostly used in connection with the Final Judgment or with Holy Scripture.

To make the name of a superior a reality by his deeds (nomen maioris factis implere). There is a discussion about what "the name of a superior" means. Later we read that his name is abbot. In general, *nomen maioris* is assumed to be a genitive of possession.[14] The admonition to make this real by deeds appears more clearly in the later emphasis on the "twofold teaching" (e.g., in 2.11-15).

V. 2a: For he is believed to take the place of Christ in the monastery. (*Christi enim agree vices in monasterio creditur.*) In RM the expressions *vices Dei*[15] and *vices agree* are used in reference to Christ (RM 2.2). These expressions are common in RM and seem to be derived from church language. Vogüé here refers to Cyprian, who uses it concerning the bishop and draws from this expression the power, tasks, and responsibility of the bishop.[16] *Vices Dei agentes* is said to refer to rulers, but *vices Christi agunt* refers chiefly to bishops. The *doctores* represent the apostles.[17] The abbot represents Christ or God. One could say with F. Ruppert: The abbot is "only the representative."[18]

Verse 2.2 needs to be considered together with 63.13: "The abbot, however, since in faith he is believed to hold the place of Christ, is to be addressed as 'Lord' and 'abbot,' not by his own claim but out of reverence and love for Christ" (*Abbas autem, quia vices Christi creditor agere, Dominus et abbas vocetur*);—Benedict said this in a text that is proper to him. In addition, this statement is moved to the center of the second part of RB 63 (63.10-18); it is not just said casually somewhere. The abbot represents Christ in

---

14. a. Herwegen, Lentini, and Bozzi, 1, emphasize the contrast: the sociojuridical concept of *maior* and the spiritual-holy one of *Abbas*.

b. RM uses *maior* more than thirty times; the *seniores, senes,* occur rarely.

c. Masai-Manning believe *maior* is the real name, whereas *Abbas* is a title: thus *Abbas maior*. But this cannot be maintained. *Nomen maioris*: The name of the *maior* is Abbas, or the title of the *maior* is Abbas. Cf. Vogüé, "Recherches," 275–76; "Abbot," 44.

15. E.g., RM 7.64; it is also said of the dean, the bishop, the priest and the deacon in 11.9-10.

16. Cf. Vogüé, *Ce que dit*, 40. *Vicem* (no nominative exists) signifies in the wider sense: place, role, office, in the place of, like.

17. Regarding the following see details in Vogüé, *Communauté*, 120–28; cf. also "Abbot," 47–48.

18. Cf. Fidelis Ruppert, "Nur Stellvertreter."

the community that has both older and younger members; he stands for the oneness of the community. In RM, a Scripture text is added as a reason: "He who hears you, hears me" (Luke 10:16) which is used eight times in RM.[19]

V. 2b: for he is addressed by his name. (*quando ipsius vocatur pronomine.*)

He is addressed with Christ's "pronomen"[20] (not *praenomen* = first name). *Maior* is the general name in RM which is used for all superiors, also ecclesiastical ones, in this case for abbots and also for deans. *Maior* is a synonym for *Abbas*, yet is more general, indicating someone with authority. What the abbot must do in his actions is not primarily understood from the word *maior*, to be in charge, in authority, a superior; rather, it points ahead to the next verses: that as abbot he represents Christ (cf. *enim* in v. 2a).

To take the place of Christ (*vices agere*)—he acts in dependence on another, in the intention of the other, he must continually align himself with the other. The text does not say directly: He is Christ, but he acts in Christ's name, in his place. Here we surely must also consider that Christ comes in the sick and in the poor as well. What is done to them, is done to Christ; again, a type of action is described.[21] It is interesting to note that this phrase does not occur in the chapter on obedience but in the admonition to the abbot. For Benedict, the requirement of obedience never directly implies the conviction that the one issuing always has the correct insight. Rather the contrary might be true! And he immediately adds exhortations to verse 2.22. The abbot is to teach according to what he commands. Also in 63.14: "He must so conduct himself that he is deserving of the honor." Christ actually is the one to whom love and reverence are given. He is the father of the house to whom the sheep belong (2.7). The abbot is not the real lord of the house but points to Christ and mediates his demands. In addition, we must consider Benedict's numerous warnings not to abuse the abbot's office, which is at great risk of being compromised. For our own time, in which holding the abbot's office is so difficult, we miss seeing a word of encouragement.

He is believed (*creditur*). The word *creditur* might not have the strong meaning which was assigned to it—especially in the Congregation of Beuron and its dependent monasteries—by an oral tradition as one of the weightiest words of the Rule. It probably is not used in the sense of theological faith but rather as denoting "one considers him to be," as Vogüé expresses it in

---

19. RM 1.89; 7.6, 68; 10.51; 11.11; 12.6; 57.16; 89.20.
20. Regarding *pronomen*, cf. Vogüé, "Abbot," 43–46.
21. Cf. RB 53.1; 36.2-3; Ruppert, "Stellvertreter," 107–10, 118.

his translation: "he appears as the representative of Christ."[22] In his deep, yet one-sided view, Herwegen states:

> The fundamental principle for the sacred position of the abbot in the Rule thus is inherent in the analogy of "taking the place of Christ" (*Christi vices agree*) to the salvific action of Christ. . . . All the distribution of graces to the monastic family proceeds mediately and immediately from the abbot. For this reason he is consecrated and engenders by his monastic consecration his spiritual descendants. Therefore, all actions in the monastery are to proceed from him and without him nothing is to be done. Whatever is done without his permission and thus is not touched by his spirit, is "presumption and vain pride."[23]

In this interpretation, proper to Herwegen, the abbas is seen as pneumatic figure.

Benedict does not want to present a theology, thus he immediately adds the admonition about what the abbot should do (cf. also 63.13-14). He starts with the concrete situation, provides the christological basis, and then promptly returns to acting within a situation. Benedict is not concerned with either theology or Christology but with the need to have a good abbot for the community, one who acts like Christ.

V. 3: As the apostle says: "You have received the Spirit that makes you sons, and in which we call out: 'Abba, father!'" (*Dicente Apostolo: Accepistis spiritum adoptionis filiorum, in quo clamamus: Abba, Pater!* [Rom 8:15])

Abbot—Christ! The image of the Father—Christ expresses a threefold meaning for the abbot:

a. The father transmits life. Christ has brought us to birth, to a new life. Paul also says that through the Word he brings the Corinthians to life (1 Cor 4:15). To transmit the living word of God and thus to awaken life—this is one task of the abbot, and in 2.4 he is immediately told that he may not teach anything that is outside the Word of God, so that the teaching of divine justice may grow in the hearts of the brothers. Besides, he is not only to teach with words but also to transmit the Gospel by living according to it. Fostering life also implies that the monk might eventually surpass his master.[24] Here we might recall the key sentence of the second chapter on the abbot in 64.13: "Let him remember that the bent reed must not be broken." He should, rather, raise up, so that life can unfold again and must be ready to give his life for the brothers.

---

22. Vogüé, II, 441, in French: "il apparaît comme le représentant du Christ."
23. Herwegen, 69.
24. Casey, *Strangers*, talks of "generativity," 127; cf. also 128–31.

b. The father should enable the community, in all its diversity, to be "one in Christ,"—as the nucleus of this chapter says: "all are one in Christ" (*omnes in Christo unum*, 2.20). This is ensured by the person in authority acting like a father.

c. The father is to show equal love to all (*aequalis caritas*, 2.22; also 2.16f.), a thought that is stated before and after the nucleus of the chapter. No favoritism, but rather giving all the same love as they need it! He loves the brothers while hating the sin (64.11). The abbot is not simply an organizer and manager. Like a father, he holds all the brothers dear in his heart.

Does the family analogy continue? Compared to RM, Benedict is much more cautious. He does not call the brothers "sons" (except in one Scripture quotation, 2.29). Often he also changes the term "disciple" of RM into "brother." For Benedict the important relationship is neither that of master–disciples nor of father–sons but rather abbot–brothers. They are not the sons of the abbot but sons of Christ, and this requires a different attitude on the abbot's part. It seems that Benedict's model for his community is primarily the *koinonia* and fraternity of the first Christians rather than the Roman family. (This is a criticism of Herwegen's view.) Thus Benedict also omits the phrase from RM 2.31 that refers to the abbot as father and mother.

An abbot who is truly as he is described in 2.1-2 can also be loved (63.13-14; 72.10), whereas in RM he is feared (cf. RM 7.64; 11.6). It is a sincere and humble love (72.10). Yet this type of love also is not possible without Christ. Thus 72.11 immediately states: "To prefer nothing whatsoever to Christ."

In summary, we can say that the title of abbot as father has the following meanings: transmitting life by word and example, readiness to lay down his life, giving equal love to all; and by living in this manner, the abbot is the guarantor of unity.

The abbot is father like Christ. We find it strange that Benedict does not see God as Father but rather Christ as father. This expression follows a long patristic tradition. In the Spirit we recognize Christ as our father, who has given us new life, and we can cry out to him: *Abba*. We are his sons, children, and servants. Later in 2.7, Benedict says that the father of the household (Christ) might not find enough profit in the sheep. The Master had gone a step further: "So we no longer seek Adam . . . as our father, but in the voice of the Lord [= Christ] inviting us (Th 24, Matt 11:28-30). Even the Our Father is addressed to Christ (cf. Thp 8-9). We can recall the Gospel where Jesus calls his disciples "children"[25] and thus indirectly calls himself their father. Many church fathers also refer to Isaiah 9:6, which says: "A son is given us . . . he will be called . . . Father-Forever." Peifer provides an

---

25. E.g., Mark 10:24 or John 13:33; 14:8; 21:5.

extensive documentation of various authors of the first centuries who call Christ father.[26] Finally, Augustine can be cited as an example of the Latin church fathers: "He showed his fatherly attitude towards us when he said: 'I [Christ] will not leave you orphans'—John 14:18."[27] This concept of Christ as father is based on his interior union with us, as well as on the typology of the new Adam. Christ has given us the new life. He has redeemed us from sin by his death and resurrection and has given us a birth to new life, divine life, which he himself nourishes and helps to grow. In a trinitarian sense we could say that God-Father is the first person, but in the outward action (the economy of salvation), one can also be theologically correct in calling Christ father.

Christological interpretation of Romans 8:15.[28] A text of the Byzantine liturgy paraphrasing the *Nunc Dimittis* says: "Lord, redeem us also from our follies and grant us your forgiveness and free us from the shame of our sins, so that you may fill our hearts with your holy Spirit and we will call to you: Father, our Father. Make us sons of your father" (allusion to Rom 8:15). Peifer also draws attention to Diadochus of Photice:[29] "The soul is full of grace . . . and calls out: 'Lord, Jesus,' just as a mother teaches her child to say father by repeating the word until the child . . . calls out to the father, even in sleep . . . (Rom 8:26)." Thus the *Abbas*, the father of the letter to the Romans, is seen as equivalent to the Lord Jesus. According to 1 Corinthians 12:3, no one can say "Lord Jesus" without divine grace.

Colombás is critical of this exegesis;[30] however, one cannot omit it when interpreting ancient texts. The tradition and Bible belong together. The biblical interpreters bring out the literal meaning, which probably will diverge from RB 2.3, but there is no doubt that Romans 8:15 was indeed interpreted in this sense for some time. I would like to respect the exegesis and its history.

The theological basis of the abbot's office is now followed by the first consequence regarding his teaching:

Vv. 4-6: Therefore the abbot is not to teach or determine or command anything that is outside the Lord's commandments, rather his commands and his teaching ought to permeate the hearts of the disciples like a leaven of divine justice; let the abbot always keep in mind that both his teaching and

26. Cf. Claude Peifer, "Use," 16–18, with references to Clement of Rome, Origen, Justin Martyr, and Evagrius Ponticus. Cf. also Vogüé, "Fatherhood."

27. Cf. *In Joh.* 75.1.

28. See Balthasar Fischer, "Benedikts Interpretation"; Peifer, "Use," 18–20; Puzicha with additional references.

29. *Cent,* chap. 61 b, 120–21.

30. Colombás, "El Abad," 95–104.

the obedience of his disciples will be examined in the terrible judgment of God. (*Ideoque abbas nihil extra praeceptum domini quod sit debeat aut docere aut constituere vel iubere, sed iussio eius vel doctrina fermentum divinae iustitiae in discipulorum mentibus conspargatur, memor semper abbas, quia doctrinae suae vel discipulorum oboedientiae, utrarumque rerum, in tremendo iudicio Dei facienda erit discussio.*)

This small passage speaks of the abbot and the disciples; his commands are referred to and his teaching (as noun or verb) is mentioned three times. An additional new concept is the judgment of God, which will evaluate two things: his teaching and the obedience of the monks. If the leaven of divine justice permeates the disciples, they will be obedient. But if the abbot sows his own words (contrary to the Gospel), he will be summoned for judgment. These are two intensive texts: teach *nothing* that is outside the Lord's commandments (2.4), and he must *always* remember (2.6). The important point is that he must only transmit the life-giving word of God's will and must be always mindful of it. Here the term *discipulus*—disciple—occurs for the first time (it occurs frequently in RM). The abbot is presented as the teacher, although the word as such (*doctor*—teacher) is not mentioned. Being a teacher is the first consequence of the abbot being a father. Certainly, the abbot can delegate many things, but he bears final responsibility (which is part of today's problematic situation). He knows better what the community needs, how each member is doing.

Nothing that is outside the Lord's command (*nihil extra praeceptum Domini*). *Extra* here denotes "contrary to," but it can also imply "outside." Nothing that evades the teaching of Christ, that is, no personal whims, no special theological opinions, no private revelations, but only the Lord's teaching! John 15:12 and 1 Timothy 1:5 show clearly that "the Lord's command" ultimately is his love. The example of Christ also applies to teaching. The revelation of the mysteries of God, the good news of the mystery of his love, is the strongest incentive for our actions. The word "obedience" also sheds light on the content of teaching: Not only uplifting conferences but also pointing out the right way, as further sections of this chapter will show. Words addressed to individuals or to the community with its diversity! The concern is not with theory but with the practical acquiring of virtues that realize and incarnate the Gospel.[31] Both RM and RB seem to depend on Basil: "He (the superior) must be filled with the fear of saying or commanding nothing which goes against the will of God, but instead what is clearly expressed in the Sacred Scriptures, lest he become a false witness or a robber of the

---

31. Cf. *Schola* above regarding Prol 45.

temple by introducing something that is alien to the Lord's teaching."³² In this verse RB points to the spiritual foundation of the monastic community. The abbot may "not give specific orders in a certain case nor personal orders to an individual which are not inspired by the spirit of Christ."³³ This presupposes intensive study, especially *Lectio Divina*; it is an incentive to the abbot not only to live according to Holy Scripture but also to take time for *Lectio Divina*! One must also remember that in Benedict's time the basis of faith often still had to be taught in the community, a situation which, however, can occur again in our time.

He is not to teach (docere) or determine (constituere) or command (iubere) anything. Constituere means setting up obligatory norms, giving orders, in individual cases arranging and thus requiring obedience. The office of teaching not only consists in giving general norms but also requires watching over good order in community living; it is directed to practical matters, it is teaching wisdom. *Iubere* as well as *docere* can apply to the community and individual cases in the sense that the superior conveys to a person the word which he needs, or challenges him, to act well, assigning something to him that is for his good or can also correct him.

V. 5: rather his commands and his teaching ought to permeate the hearts of the disciples like a leaven of divine justice.

His commands and his teaching . . . like a leaven of divine justice (iussio eius vel doctrina fermentum divinae iustitiae). Justice (*iustitia*) is the foundation of life in community, it means a beneficial, salutary order. God's justice is his action, by which he creates the right, useful order, it is his salvific work, which requires, however, that the people cooperate. Leaven/sourdough (*fermentum*—cf. Matt 13:33) means that it might be a small quantity, but highly effective, and that leaven, like the reign of God, aims at a person's transformation. To use another image, it is like a seed that should bear fruit in the hearts. This takes time but also requires the conviction of faith that the Word of God is effective and will eventually succeed (cf. Heb 4:12).

To permeate the hearts of the disciples (in discipulorum mentibus conspargatur), that is, their interior. Benedict uses the word *mens* only in close connection with RM.³⁴ It is probably best rendered as "heart." This is the first use of the word "disciple," which in RB occurs only thirteen times, whereas "brother" is used about 102 times, as is "monk" (*monachus*). One may say that

32. *Reg* 15.1f.
33. Herwegen, 70; also Giurisato, "Regola," 98–100.
34. It is used only one more time in 19.7: that our *mens* be in harmony with our voice in the liturgy). Cf. Böckmann, "Mensch," 43f.

"disciple" is not one of Benedict's favorite terms, mostly because it belongs to the school vocabulary.

V. 6: Let the abbot always keep in mind that both his teaching and the obedience of his disciples will be examined in the terrible judgment of God. (*memor semper abbas, quia doctrinae suae vel discipulorum oboedientiae, utrarumque rerum, in tremendo iudicio Dei facienda erit discussio.*)

We can easily see that the abbot will be held accountable for his teaching (by word and action), but it seems more difficult to accept that he is also responsible for the obedience of the disciples. His teaching aims at obedience; he must require obedience but must also make it possible. If he requires too much of someone, it is his fault; but he may also fail to challenge someone to greater progress, to grow beyond himself. He is responsible to see that the disciples do not slacken in their following Christ by obedience.[35]

In the terrible judgment of God (*in tremendo iudicio Dei*). RM uses here the term "judgment of the Lord" (*Christi—Domini*). Later RB 2.9 also uses *iudicium Domini* once. The father has entrusted the judgment to the son. As in other places, Benedict might have wanted to moderate the christocentrism he considers too strong in RM. Sometimes one gets this impression. Benedict has a slight tendency to assign the judgment (generally) to God.[36]

Vv. 7-10: And the abbot must know that the shepherd will be blamed whenever the father of the house does not find much profit in the sheep. On the other hand, when he has given all possible solicitude to a restless and disobedient flock and has applied all care towards their unhealthy conduct, their pastor, exonerated in the Lord's judgment, may say to the Lord with the prophet: "Your justice I have not kept hidden in my heart, your fidelity and your salvation I have proclaimed; but they, scorning me, have despised me"; then, at last, the all-powerful death will overpower the sheep who disobeyed his care. (*sciatque abbas culpae pastoris incumbere quidquid in ovibus paterfamilias utilitatis minus poterit invenire. Tantundem iterum erit ut, si inquieto vel inoboedienti gregi pastoris omnis diligentia adtributa et morbidis earum actibus universa fueri exhibita, pastor eorum in iudicio Domini absolutus dicat cum propheta Domino: iustitiam tuam non abscondi in corde meo, veritatem tuam et salutare tuum dixi; ipsi autem contemnentes spreverunt me, et tunc demum inoboedientibus curae suae ovibus poena sit eis praevalens mors.*)

35. Yet RB 5.9 also states how the disciple promptly "puts into practice" the Abbot's command.

36. Cf. 3.11; 55.22; 63.3; 65.22.

We can write this in two columns: the left speaks about the shepherd and what he does, the right about the sheep and the judgment.

7 And the abbot must know that the shepherd will be blamed	whenever the father of the house does not find enough profit in the sheep.
8 On the other hand, when he has given all possible solicitude, has applied all possible care,	to a restless and disobedient flock and towards their unhealthy conduct,
9 their shepherd,	exonerated in the Lord's judgment,
may say to the Lord with the prophet:	
"Your justice I have not kept hidden in my heart, your fidelity and your salvation I have proclaimed,	but they, scorning me, have despised me." 10 Then, at last, death will overpower the sheep who disobeyed his care.

This is a hard paragraph, still explaining that the abbot is a father, teacher, and shepherd. Here he is called a "pastor" (*pastor* is the Latin word for shepherd) three times, after the word *Abbas* is used once again. Again he must know (*sciat*). His counterpart is referred to as the flock (*grex*) and sheep (*oves*—2 times). But not only in the positive sense! They can be restless and disobedient, their conduct can be bad, and they can despise the shepherd. Finally, what is wrong is once more summarized in the term "disobedient sheep" (*inoboedientes ovibus*). We can see the connection with his teaching (2.4-6) where the obedience of the disciples also was mentioned. The pastor, more strongly than the teacher, is bound firmly to the community, the flock, and must take care that all of them reach the goal together.

   This is the first time in RB that the sad reality of the community comes to light: not much profit, restless, disobedient, sick and infectious behavior, and finally, scorn! This is the way to eternal punishment. In the previous section (2.6), the abbot was reminded that he must give an account of the obedience of his disciples. Here he is told: But if they are bad, even though he proclaimed the justice of God (or as v. 5 says, the "leaven of divine justice"), he will be declared free of guilt. The office of pastor and teacher merge. The actions and words that are used for the pastor are intensively marked by "all solicitude," "all possible care" (*omnis diligentia, universa cura*)!

And the abbot must know . . . : Again Benedict appeals to knowing, and we may confidently add, knowing "in faith." The sentence follows the previous concept of judgment. The word "profit" is now used as a synonym for obedience (cf. 2.6). The translations for *utilitatis minus* vary: *minus* can mean "little," but also "no profit" which, in my opinion, is the most probable meaning.[37] In addition, it agrees more with the general outlook of RB. Translating it as "less useful" would put an excessive strain on the abbot's responsibility, which RM generally tends to do while RB clearly does not.

Now Christ is called the father of the house (*paterfamilias*). He, and not the abbot, is the real father of the house; he is the supreme pastor, the owner of the sheep. The monastery is the "house of God," not the abbot's house. He is, however, responsible for being a good shepherd of the sheep according to Christ's example, so that they can be profitable and thereby follow Christ, the supreme shepherd. The abbot's own example certainly is important in the process. If the real father of the house is not satisfied, the shepherd is blamed. The following verses show that he will be excused only if he has applied all solicitude and diligence.

On the other hand (*tandundem iterum erit ut*). Linderbauer points to the difficult sentence structure. After investigating several passages from the Bible and other ancient literature, he arrived at this meaning: "it is enough, if . . . ; only so much is required, that . . ." The word *iterum* then means the same as *denuo*—again, on the other hand.[38] The same principle applies—that is, the pastor is accountable, but only if he hasn't done his best.

To a restless and disobedient flock (*inquieto et inoboedienti gregi*). We probably can say that the two Rules see disobedience as restlessness. *Inquietus* is used once more in 2.25, where it occurs together with *indisciplinatus*—undisciplined, not well brought up, lacking any control. The abbot is to correct such brothers sharply. This means that this is a bad kind of restlessness, possibly coupled with grumbling, presuming, or arrogance. The monks don't want to hear, to listen and obey. Therefore, they are not receptive to the loving care of the pastor.

Their unhealthy conduct (*morbidis actibus*). Normally, Benedict uses *infirmus* for "sick." He uses *morbidus* in only two places, here and in 2.28. The word is generally applied to animals, here as in 2.28 to the sheep. A sick or unhealthy conduct can infect others. *Morbus* is a disease of the whole body; this word is rarely used because it can easily be associated with death—*mors*, as it is here and in 2.10.

---

37. Cf. Lentini, 59; Holzherr 2007, 78 regarding "Missertrag," i.e., failure to yield profit.
38. Linderbauer, 164; cf. Lentini, 59; Kardong, 52f.

All possible solicitude . . . all possible care (*omnis diligentia . . . universa cura*). These intensive expressions can be compared with RB 27–28. *Diligentia* is related to *diligere*—to love; thus we have here a loving care (cf. also RB 36.7) which implies attention and conscientiousness. In 27.5 the expression "keen perception" is added (*sagacitate et industria*). Loving care (*cura*) occurs similarly in 31.9; 27.1, 5; 36.1, 6, 10; 53.15. These texts show what this care implies: concentrating on another, letting one's heart be on fire (*cor—urere*: heart—burning) is a possible etymology for *cura*, making the other person the center, doing everything to help the other. In this manner, the pastor here cares for his flock. The word *cura* is often joined with the verb *exhibere*—to apply, which may reinforce the medical aspect. The result, however, does not come automatically, as the next verses show.

Their shepherd, exonerated in the Lord's judgment (in iudicio Domini) may say to the Lord with the prophet: "Your justice I have not kept hidden in my heart, your fidelity and your salvation I have proclaimed; but they, scorning me, have despised me." The shepherd is freed of blame, exonerated (*absolutus*); or we might say, cleared of responsibility.

So he can say to the Lord with the prophet (dicat cum propheta Domino): "Your justice I have not kept hidden in my heart, your fidelity and your salvation I have proclaimed" (Ps 39:11; Isa 1:2).[39] The abbot says this with the Psalmist and the psalm is addressed to Christ, the Lord.[40] Psalm 39/40:11 is cited according to the Roman Psalter. In comparison with RM, Benedict has written the fuller text, placing "your justice"—*iustitia tua* first. Thus he uses three terms that are synonyms: justice, fidelity, and salvation (*iustitia, veritas, salutare*), which certainly accords with the Bible.

Earlier he had already mentioned divine justice, and in this chapter he will repeat it one more time: You recite "my just norms" (*enarras iustitias*—2.14). It is significant that this word occurs five times in the chapter on the abbot alone. In the Rule as a whole it is used mainly in Scripture quotations.[41] God makes us just and healthy, and this the abbot is to announce in word and deed. He must not hide it in his heart. Why would he want to hide it? Perhaps because it is also an admonition to himself; it also might not please the disciples, or might have uncomfortable consequences . . . *Veritas* here means not only truth but also fidelity and dependability. And *salutare* denotes

---

39. RM 2.9 does not mention God's justice but only God's truth.

40. This is probably the reason why Bendict here takes over *in iudicio Domini* (in the Lord's judgment) from RM and does not change it to *iudicium Dei* (the judgment of God) as he did in v. 6.

41. See Kardong, "Iustitia;" cf. also the title of RB 73, "the full observance of justice," cf. Böckmann, *Persectives,*79.

total healing, well-being, and redemption. As is seen later, these truths are promised to each individual, according to each one's capacity, as well as to the community as a whole. It should be noted that on God's part it is not the threatening but the positive promises that are named as content of the abbot's teaching.

Now, however, we see the fate that the prophets, and even Christ himself, have experienced: these instructions were not accepted. The Roman Psalter only says: "They, however, despised me" (*ipsi autem spreverunt me*). The expression "they however" calls to mind Isaiah 1:2: "I have raised sons and educated them, but they 'despised' me."[42] We sense the inappropriate response to God's loving action. The authors of our two Rules added a second word of disrespect to the Roman Psalter (*contemnere*). *Contemnentes* could be a reminder of Ezekiel 20:27: "They despised me, scorning me" (*cum sprevissent me contemnentes*, Vulgate). The words are synonyms: to scorn, reject, despise, oppose, defy. Human ingratitude in view of God's loving kindness is evident. Smaragdus vividly describes such monks: "For bad monks disdain and spurn their good abbot when they do not humbly obey his precepts, when they do not keep his salutary commands . . . but like the proud even find fault with them; when they despise what they are ordered to carry out, and shamelessly strive to do what they are not ordered; when . . . they become lazy, tepid, and even slothful, and in their deeds become both murmurers and complainers" (128f.). This is the fate of Christ that befalls the abbot. God, who through his own son expended all that is good, all care and effort on his people, did not reap gratitude but scorn and blasphemy (cf. Mark 15:29). One might wish to object that the community consists of persons who want to follow Christ more closely; but they are sinful persons, just as the first apostles and the first Christians. Benedict is a realist (cf. 2.23-30). This also shows, however, that in spite of and in everything, he trusts in divine grace and power that is at work in human powerlessness. But he is also aware of the seriousness of the situation, as the next verse shows.

V. 10: and then, at last, punishment come to the sheep who disobeyed his care, death will overpower them. (*et tunc demum inoboedientibus curae suae ovibus poena sit eis praevalens ipsa mors.*)

And then . . . at last. Not so fast! But if nothing at all has worked, it will happen (cf. the delays in the correctional code, e.g., RB 27–28). Obedience is a matter of salvation or death. This is no exaggeration. For the person

---

42. Isa 1:2: *filios enutrivi (generavi) et exaltavi, ipsi autem (reprobaverunt) spreverunt me.* (VL in parentheses).

with a true vocation, monastic life is the only possible form of a Christian life. RB 2.10 is a very radical statement about a possibly negative situation which, however, occurs only after all of a shepherd's care has been given. The monks have reacted to his care with unwillingness. The evil can act like an infectious disease,[43] for example, murmuring, private possessions, presumption in the Rule.

Disobedient to his care (inoboedientibus curae suae). One is not only disobedient to commands but also resistant to all the care of the shepherd. Do we discern here the image of Christ, the Good Shepherd, in the background? The drama of rejection continues on throughout history.

The all-powerful death (praevalens mors). The expression comes from the Old Latin Version (*VL*) of the prophet Isaiah 25:8, as well as from the version of the Roman Psalter Psalm 48/49:15:[44] "They are like sheep in the netherworld, and death pastures them." Since they did not want to have the abbot Christ as their shepherd, now death will be their shepherd. In medical vocabulary: Someone who absolutely doesn't want to let himself be healed will die.[45] The opposites here are:

justice, fidelity, salvation	the all-powerful death
on the shepherd's part:	on the part of the sheep:
care, attentiveness, intensive effort	disobedience, scorn, defiance

One more time, at the end of the whole chapter, RM and RB will talk about judgment: "Thus always fearing the future examination of the shepherd about the sheep entrusted to him, and while caring for the condition of others, he will also care for his own."

---

43. Cf. Gregory, *Dial* II.3.3-4: Vicovaro. Cf. Kardong's translation and commentary of *The Life of Saint Benedict by Gregory the Great.* The Roman numeral refers to Book II of Gregory's *Dialogues*; the Arabic numbers to the internal subdivisions as used in Vogüé's critical edition.

44. Isa 25:8 (VL and PsRom 48:15): *Sicut oves in inferno positi sunt et mors depascet eos.*

45. Here RM had explained *ipse mortis morbus*: the overpowering sickness of death. Benedict wrote instead: "the punishment is death."

VV. 11-15: THE TWOFOLD TEACHING

11 Therefore,

when one accepts the name of
     "abbot,"

he must guide his disciples

by a twofold teaching.

12 That is, he must show them

all that is good and holy | more by his actions than by
                          | words.

To the receptive disciples | he is to present the commands of
                           | the Lord by words,

to the hard of heart and the
     simpler ones,

however, | he is to show the divine
         | commands by his actions.

13 Everything, however, which he
     teaches

his disciples to avoid as harmful, | he is to show by his actions as not
                                    | to be done,

lest after preaching to others | he himself be rejected,

14 that God may not tell

the sinner later:

"Why do you recite my just
     norms

and talk about my covenant?

You yourself have hated discipline

and thrown my words behind
     you."

15 And "You saw the splinter

in your brother's eye | did not see the log in your own
                      | eye."

Once again, the paragraph can be subdivided into two smaller sections:

- vv. 11-13a: the twofold teaching in deeds and words,
- vv. 13b-15: when the abbot does not do what he preaches.

Each small section contains again three units:

To show all that is good and holy	by actions rather than by words
The commands of the Lord by words	the divine commands by example
13 what he teaches not to do	he shows by not doing it
13c Preaching to others	he himself be rejected
14 Reciting my just commands	you yourself, however . . .
15 You saw the splinter	you did not see
In your brother's eyes	the log in your own.

The first section refers three times to teaching or a synonym, and this is counterbalanced by the corresponding actions (right side). On the left are the disciples (three times) who are described in various ways. The second short section emphasizes three times the teaching or the views of the abbot on the left, and his contrary, negative conduct on the right.

RB 2.11-15 is concerned about doctrine, teaching, preaching, and explaining (*doctrina, docere, praedicare, enarrare*) but also places this in a particular setting: showing, presenting, showing, pointing out (*ostendere, proponere, mostrare, indicare*). Thus, once again it is a practical kind of teaching, addressed to the disciples! The author's attention is directed more and more, after verse 4, to the person the abbot teaches. What is the content of the teaching? All that is good and holy (*omnia bona et sancta*), and again: Commands of the Lord, divine commands, just norms, covenant (*mandata domini, divina praecepta, iustitiae meae, testamentum meum*). All these are closely tied to Sacred Scripture! Thus God also will judge what the abbot has done with God's Word. Three times he is made aware of his actions (*factis*). This implies that the abbot has done his *Lectio Divina* thoroughly so that the Word of God has been incarnated in his life and various actions.

The second section (vv. 13b-15) follows the *ne*—so that something will not happen. This is followed by three examples taken from Sacred Scripture. Again the Psalter is important: Why do you recite my justice (Ps 49/50:16-17); but it is also connected to Paul (1 Cor 9:27), and to the Sermon on the Mount (Matt 7:3).

Verses 11ff. provide inspiration for all those called to work as teachers, educators, and catechists, etc., and help them to put into practice the spiritual teachings and receive inspiration from these verses.

V. 11: Therefore, when one accepts the name of "abbot," he must guide his disciples with a twofold teaching. (*Ergo, cum aliquis suscipit nomen abbatis, duplici debet doctrina suis praeesse discipulis.*)

Starting with a strong *ergo*, this verse emphasizes the powerful teaching, the content of which was characterized by justice, fidelity, and salvation in the preceding verses. He is *Abbas*—teacher in a practical manner: he is to guide, preside, be in front (*praeesse*). He accepts the name of abbot (*suscipit*) and must not deny it, but with it he is to point to Christ, the father and teacher. The teaching is addressed to the disciples. Now we ask what the content of this twofold teaching is (*duplex doctrina*). It refers again to the title of abbot—teacher. The abbot becomes a father by his word. As we already saw, the meaning of the two titles flow into each other. With some changes, all these instructions apply also to all those who teach and educate in and also beyond the monastery.

V. 12a: That is, he should show all that is good and holy more by his actions than by words. (*id est omnia bona et sancta factis amplius quam verbis ostendat.*)

The *id est* is now made concrete: The content is the good and the holy! We are reminded of the words of Holy Scripture, which he is to show neither by words nor by actions only. The words are there, but the actions weigh even more. The method of teaching by actions (*facta*) is emphasized by the word *amplius*—more), which stands in the place of *magis* or *plus*. More by actions than by teaching! Both are directed to the conduct of the hearer. This also means that the teacher has interiorized the words of Holy Scripture and is expressing them in his way of life. We might say, he should become a living Bible, in which we can easily read what is to be done. Cassian has Abbot Chaemeron say, "How could I presume to teach what I myself do not do? Or should I instruct another person in what I know that I do less of or more lukewarmly? Hence I have allowed none of the younger men to live with me at this point in my life, lest someone else's strictness be slackened by my example. For the authority of the instructor will be valueless unless he has fastened it in his hearer's heart by what he has himself achieved."[46] In his comment on this verse, Smaragdus says: "A voice more readily penetrates the hearers' heart when the speaker's life commends it because his example helps the doing of what he commands by speaking" (130).

Now Benedict looks at the various kinds of listeners:

46. *Conf.* 11.4.3.

V. 12b: Therefore he is to present the commands of the Lord to receptive disciples in words, but to those who are hard of heart and the simpler ones he will show the divine commands by his actions. (*ut*[47] *capacibus discipulis mandata Domini verbis proponere, duris corde vero et simplicioribus factis suis divina praecepta monstrare.*)

The receptive disciples are distinguished from the hard hearted and the simpler persons. *Capacibus*—receptive—replaces the *intellegentibus* of RM. *Capax* denotes a person who is open and who can receive. This does not necessarily mean that one must be very intelligent (RM); and someone who is intelligent is not always receptive; he might even be haughty and think he does not need any teaching. Those who are receptive can even accept a teaching that is not fully exemplified in actions.

Those hard of heart (*duris corde*): the Word of God cannot enter such disciples because they have laid a thick cover around their hearts; they can be convinced only by actions. Both authors (of RM and RB) may have had Isaiah in mind: "Listen to me, you who are hard of heart and far from justice."[48] RB Prologue 10 (a text proper to Benedict) admonishes: "Today, when you hear his voice, harden not your hearts."

Simpliciores is used rather than *simplicibus* as in RM, meaning the *simpler* ones; they are somewhat limited, not so capable, do not understand quickly, perhaps they are rather slow and might also be simple minded, which is not necessarily of less value. Lentini sees in this word a "fatherly tenderness."[49] One must first demonstrate everything to them so that they will understand. Gregory mentions that in Benedict's community there was one "poor in spirit" (*pauper spiritu*).[50]

V. 13: Everything, however, which he teaches his disciples not to do, he is to show in his actions as not to be done so that he himself, after preaching to others, will not be rejected. (*omnia vero quae discipulis docuerit esse contraria in suis factis indicet non agenda, ne alliis praedicans ipse reprobus inveniatur* [1 Cor 9:27].)

Once again, the twofold teaching is restated, now in the negative sense. And this applies to *omnia*—everything that is *contrarium*, which means opposed, harmful, not necessarily forbidden. This is an admonition to the abbot. Yet

47. The *ut* in v. 12b is a consecutive "so that" (Lentini, 62); Smaragdus (130) says it simply means *et*. One may also consider it an *ut* indicating type or manner (Hanslik, 336).
48. Isa 46:12 as translated from the Vulgate and VL; in Latin: *Audite me, duro corde qui longe estis a iustitia.*
49. Lentini, 62: "paterna delicatezza."
50. *Dial* II.6.1-2.

after bitter experiences Benedict—in a text proper to him—addresses the monks in RB 4.61: "To obey the commands of the abbot in everything, even if he himself—far be it—should act otherwise, remembering the Lord's precept: 'Do what they say, not what they do.'" But only a monk with prudent understanding can do so, one who has learned to distinguish and has a strong faith.

The words of Paul here are interpreted as pertaining to the Last Judgment. "I drive my body and train it, for fear that, after having preached to others, I myself should be disqualified" (1 Cor 9:27).[51] *Reprobus* is the opposite of *probus*—what is honest and grows well, thus *reprobus* means that something is valued for nothing, declared guilty, condemned. Throughout the entire Rule, Benedict is well aware that the superior, too, may have faults (as well as the officials). While the Master states this clearly in this chapter, he treats this topic rather lightly in the second part of his Rule. We might wish to omit this sentence or at least soften it, yet RB here focuses on decisions that result in either salvation or condemnation.

V. 14: so that God not will say to the sinner later: "Why do you recite my just norms and talk of my covenant? You yourself have hated discipline and have thrown my words behind you." (*ne quando illi dicat Deus peccanti: Quare tu enarras iustitias meas et adsumis testamentum meum per os tuum? Tu vero odisti disciplinam et proiecisti sermones meos post te.*)

It is not sacrifices that God wants from the people but actions of justice and deeds of love. *Iustitias*—pertain to just commandments (or laws) and *testamentum* refers to the covenant, the promises.[52] It is certainly good that the abbot teaches the commandments and the covenant of God. It must, however, be a teaching which is confirmed by actions (as already emphasized in 2.12-13). "You yourself have hated discipline," here presumably means hating the commandments; it is a strong word. Benedict then adds to the Master's text the last part of Psalm 49/50:17, that the abbot threw God's words behind him. Its positive form would have meant that he always kept God's words before his eyes. Throwing them behind him is followed by not observing them. The abbot acts on his own, he does not use the divine word, Holy Scripture, as his guideline, he makes himself the norm for what he himself wants or what is agreeable to him. Stating the opposite shows us more clearly how a good

51. *Castigo corpus meum . . . ne forte cum aliis praedicaverim, ipse reprobus efficiar.*
52. RM has *sumpsisti*: you took on yourself. He looks at the past. Earlier he had *narrasti*: you told. This is logical, thinking of the Last Judgment; for the second part of this sentence also uses the perfect tense. In the first part, did Benedict think of a punishing word from God for the present time? Or did he more likely decide to use the text of Roman Psalter? One can notice repeatedly that he uses the original text of the Bible.

abbot would act. The Sarabaites in RB 1.6-9 are not tested by any (objective) Rule, their law is what they desire and like; what they think they call holy. When a superior is animated by such a bad spirit, the whole community suffers evil consequences. Arbitrary decisions predominate; all are subject to a superior's moods. What shall they use as a guide? We may again recall 4.61 (Benedict's proper addition): Do as they say, not do as they do.

V. 15: And "You saw the splinter in your brother's eye and did not see the log in your own." (*et qui in fratris tui oculo festucam videbas, in tuo trabem non vidisti.*)

Matthew 7:3 is quoted, following directly on the quotation from the psalm; everything is placed in the mouth of *Deus*. This clearly denotes Christ as *Deus*—God. The word of judgment is hard. It does not say the brother has no splinter in his eye, but it is here compared with a log in the abbot's eye.[53] It seems to me that RB 64.13 refers back to this verse when it states that the abbot should always be mindful of his own fragility. For the log in his own eye, his own brokenness, acts like a magnifying glass for the splinter in the brother's eye. And recognizing one's own fragility makes us more objective and merciful toward the failings of the other person.

This brings us to the nucleus of chapter 2.

VV. 16-22: EQUAL LOVE FOR ALL

The logical structure is:

a) exhortation to give equal love
b) biblical reason (*quia*)
c) conclusion (*ergo*).

Written in the form of a chiasm:

C 16 He is not to show favoritism in the monastery.
   D 17 One is not to be loved more than another,
   except if he find him better in good deeds and in obedience.
      E 18 One who enters the monastery as a slave
      is not to be outranked by one born free
      (unless there is another good reason.

---

53. Here the monk is indirectly (even though in a Scripture text) referred to as the brother of the abbot. One would like to expand this line (cf. however, there is also son: *filius* in 2.29).

19 If the abbot thinks it right, for reasons of justice,
To change anyone's rank, he may do so.
Otherwise each one is to keep his proper place.)
    F 20 For, whether slave or free,
    we all are one in Christ
    bearing the same burden of service under the one Lord
    for with God there is no favoritism.
  E' 21 Only in one way are we distinguished in his sight,
  When we surpass others in good deeds and being humble.
  D' 22 Therefore, the abbot is to show equal love to all,
C' and to apply the same discipline to all according to their merits.

In the central part of RB 2 the abbot does comparatively little (almost no direct action); the entire attention is focused on the members (not disciples). They become the subject (2.20-21). This is surprising, since the chapter is about the abbot. Even the style changes to "we" in the middle of the section (v. 20, cf. 21); the abbot is included among the brothers.

Compared with the text of RM, RB has two additional verses: verses 2.18-19 about the exception to rank, a concretization which reflects a later concern in the Rule. Benedict at the end also omitted one sentence of RM, which said: "Nevertheless to show his loving kindness to all alike, God commands the elements to serve sinners as much as the just" (RM 2.21, cf. Matt 5:45). Thus, the abbot should imitate God; perhaps Benedict thought this too lofty or too theological.

RB 2.16-22 is different from the other text of RB 2, but of course Benedict does want to place important content in the center of the chapter. Disagreements among former slaves and free persons may have been present from the very beginning. This can also be glimpsed in RM.

V. 16: He is not to show favoritism in the monastery. (*Non ab eo persona in monasterio discernatur.*)

Expressed in negative form this is, so to speak, the heading of the section, while verses 17 and 22 draw the conclusion. No favoritism, no distinction on the basis of background, family, or former wealth! Similarly, verse 21 says that God distinguishes persons by different criteria.[54] What is meant by *personam discernere* is expressed in the next verse.[55]

---

54. *Discernere* originally meant to sort out, separate, keep away; only by connotation does it mean to distinguish and later to select.

55. Here I do not agree with Guevin, "Beginning," 200–2.

V. 17: One is not to be loved more than the other, except he find him better in good deeds and in obedience. (*Non unus plus ametur quam alius, nisi quem in bonis actibus aut oboedientia invenerit meliorem.*)

The expression "or in obedience" was added by Benedict, similarly to "and humble" (et humiles) in verse 21. They are signs of how much importance Benedict attaches to these chief virtues and interior dispositions (obedience and humility here possibly used as synonyms?). It is always easy for antipathy or sympathy to creep in and be expressed in deliberate or unintended visible gestures. Benedict knows there are great differences among the monks. But one is to be loved as much as another and to know he is loved (cf. v. 22 "equal love," *aequalis caritas*). He means a love which is basically of equal strength but which can manifest itself in different treatment as individuals need it. The abbot must be considerate to each one, and this is precisely a sign of his basic love for all. We could say that this is a commonplace of nearly all cenobitic Rules.[56] Yet this also applies to every educator.

Vv. 18-19: One who enters the monastery from slave status is not to be outranked by one born free, unless there is a sound reason. If the abbot thinks it right, for reasons of justice, to change anyone's rank, he may do so. Otherwise each one is to keep his proper place. (*Non convertenti ex servitio praeponatur ingenuus, nisi alia rationalis causa existat. Quod si ita, iustitia dictante, abbati visum fuerit, et de cuiuslibet ordine id faciet. Sin alias, propria teneant loca.*)

We need to recall that RM provides the abbot with the right to determine the rank of the monks entirely at his own discretion, without regard to age or profession, and to change ranks quite often (RM 92.33-37), which instigates the monks to an unhealthy competition. Benedict sets clear rules for determining rank in the community to protect it against arbitrariness. In his time and environment, rank was important to him; he refers to it several times in the course of writing his Rule.

Entering from slave status . . . one born free (convertenti ex servitio . . . ingenuus). Among those entering, two great opposites are named here: those who came from slave status and those who were born free when they came.[57]

---

56. *Reg4Patr* 11-12 E: *Hoc ante omnia praecipimus vobis qui huic officio praesto estis ut personae a vobis non accipiantur, se aequali affectu omnes diligantur et correptione omnes sanentur.* LibHors 9: *Ideo, o homo . . . cavere quam maxime ne alterum ames et alterum oderis; sed et cunctis exhibeas aequalitatem, ne forte quem tu diligis Deus oderit, et quem tu odisti, Deus diligat* (cf. ibid., 16). Cf. also Caesarius, *Exhort Vg* 4.

57. *Ingenuus* means from this country, that is, not a foreigner, but one born free, born of a known father.

Social inequalities do not count for Benedict and the Master.[58] Today, it is other kinds of differences that cause difficulty. The verb *converti* means entrance into the monastery; it is also understood as a conversion (cf. 63.7, *ut convertuntur ita sunt*). The Master had stated: "One who enters as a slave shall not be outranked by a free man on the basis of his rank of birth" (2.18). He had directly designated the one entering as *servus*—slave. Benedict seems to be more specific. He says that the future brother comes from the condition of a slave (*ex servitio*). Old Rules state that slaves at times escaped from their masters and fled to a monastery. They and other former slaves had to be set free before their entrance. So they were, speaking precisely, no longer slaves when they entered.

Benedict adds some comments about rank. There may be reasonable grounds, *alia rationabilis causa*,[59] for changing the order of rank. What were these reasons? Perhaps good deeds or obedience, maybe also according to RB 62.6-7, based on an office or according to the wish of the community. Benedict himself cites "merit of life" in 63.1 (*vitae meritum*, cf. 2.22, *secundum merita*).

In verse 19 Benedict shows himself as a coolheaded Roman. For juridical thinking, a monk's excellence becomes concrete in a higher rank. But even this exception is safeguarded in several ways: "as justice dicates" (*iustitia dictante*), which is similar to Prologue 47: "for reasons of justice" (*aequitatis ratione*). But the reason is certainly not social difference, greater learning, greater esteem of family, or the personal wish of the abbot. Benedict arranges rank according to what he considers just and beneficial for the common welfare (cf. 63.2). In RB we get a glimpse of how difficult it must have been to maintain some measure of peace and good order among very different types of people. Benedict creates order partially by the order of rank (but also by other measures, as can be seen clearly in RB 34–35; 48; and 72, among others).

V. 20: For, whether slave or free, we are all one in Christ and bear the same burden of service under the one Lord since there is no favoritism with God. (*Quia sive servus, sive liber, omnes in Christo unum sumus et sub uno Domino aequalem servitutis militiam baiulamus, quia non est apud Deum personarum acceptio.*)

In this verse, Benedict returns almost literally to RM. The Codex of Justinian[60] had stated: "Being free or a slave does not matter: for all receive the same

---

58. At this point in RM the Master rouses our curiosity by inserting a "Why? Why?"

59. According to Lentini, 65, *rationabilis* is a "word of popular origin, frequently used in juridical language."

60. *Codex Iuris Civilis, Nov.* 5.2: *eo quod neque liber neque servus: omnes enim in Christo unam mercedem percipere.*

reward in Christ." There is surely a link between the two times Christ is mentioned, which Benedict has indeed taken over from RM, but to which he assigns a special location in RB 2, once at the beginning, like a title, then as a core and key sentence in 2.20: "whether slave or free, we are all one in Christ." This is a blending of Galatians 3:28[61] and Ephesians 6:8.[62] Like RM, Benedict omitted the name of "Jesus" from Galatians 3:28. The text is constructed in fine style. First, the two big opposites of slave and free are named, linked by *omnes* (all), then united into one with *unum sumus* (we are one); but unity is possible only "*in Christ*." Benedict added to the quote from RM an "in" which is characteristic of Paul;[63] besides, he intensifies it by repetition, *sive* servus, *sive* liber. Certainly we can also recall Acts 4:32, which Augustine quoted at the beginning of his Rule: they were "of one heart and one soul" to which Augustine added "in God" (*in Deum*, Praec 1.2).

In the next sentence, both authors refer to the one Lord under whom we do battle. That is, we all are servants, slaves of the one Lord, Christ. Experience seems to have proved that without Christ the unity of a monastic community in its diversity is not attainable. By striving for "equal love" (2.22), which the abbot is to bestow on each one in his uniqueness, he experiences that he has to hold on to Christ whose image he should be: Christ = father. In this core of 2.20, Benedict draws the practical conclusion from the theological basis of the abbot's office (2.2-3). In both of these important passages there is an indirect reference to the reality of baptism. Christ is the father of this monastic community in all its diversity, yet all are his sons. In baptism he has given all of them new life in fraternal relationship. This new life was deepened by profession, by which all became brothers at the altar. After the "petition" is placed on the altar and the *Suscipe* is sung and repeated by the community (58.23), the name of 'brother' is explicitly used for the first time; unfortunately, this word is not present in all translations.[64] "In Christ all are one" and are running on the way together, led by him (cf. also 34.5 and 72.12). In patristic literature, especially in Ambrose and Augustine, "one in Christ" occurs repeatedly.[65]

The reason given for the oneness in Christ is: We all bear the same load of military service under the one Lord (*servitutis militiam*, RM has *servitium*):

---

61. *non est servus, neque liber . . . omnes . . . vos unum estis in Christo Iesu* (Vulgate).

62. *Scientes quonium unusquisque quodcumque fecerit bonum hoc recipiet a Domino, sive servus sive liber* (Vulgate).

63. Only one manuscript (A) of RM says "*in* Christo." To be precise, according to Ms P, one would need to translate: "For Christ, we are all one."

64. E.g., in RB 80, which says "The novice prostrates" rather than "the new brother" (*frater novicius*).

65. Cf. Cetedoc; I, under *in Christo unum*. In similar context: Ambrose, *In Ps.* 123.12; *In Lc.* 5.85; *Exhort Vg*, 1.3; Augustine, *Contr Faust* 24.1.

We all are slaves, servants of Christ. Each one has the same Lord, we are his. The diverse origins and distinctions do not constitute a basic difference among persons because all are given for service. The Latin word *baiulare* for "to bear" reminds us of Luke 14:27: "Whoever does not carry his own cross" (*baiulat*). In Latin, this word is used for carrying a load, a burden. The monk's service also includes bearing the cross; for Benedict its essence is determined chiefly by obedience (cf. Prol 3, 40, 45). *Servitutis militiam* can be a genitive of identity; this means that being a soldier of Christ is to serve him. In Benedict's text (not in RM), two kinds of "service" are compared: the social (servant, slave)—which no longer applies—and the "service under the Lord," which applies to everyone and therefore unites the persons who were so different before.

The reason for "God has no favorites" probably is derived from Romans 2:11, which has, however, a broad biblical background.[66] A similar conduct was demanded of the abbot in verse 16; thus, he must imitate God. For everything in the monastery should be aligned with the law of God (cf. 2.4). Just as in verse 17b, Benedict added an exception, he does here in verse 21: "Only in one way are we distinguished before him, when . . ." RB 34.2 draws from this the very practical conclusion that all necessary items are to be distributed justly according to need, not according to respect for persons. This biblical truth of avoiding favoritism or human respect is often mentioned in patristic literature. Certainly because it was revolutionary and not easy to accomplish, yet became the basis for Christian fraternity. The thought is found most frequently in Augustine.[67] Not judging on the basis of a person's prestige is important for all those who are responsible for others. Humanly speaking, it is very easy to prefer someone who comes from a better family and is more intelligent and approachable.

V. 21: Only in one way are we distinguished in his eyes, when we surpass others in good works and being humble. (*Solummodo in hac parte apud ipsum discernimur, si meliores ab aliis in operibus bonis et humiles inveniamur.*)

Each person receives the same loving affection from God, but there is a difference in what each one does with it. "In good works and [being] humble" (*in operibus bonis et humiles*) reflects verse 17 which says: "in good works and obedience." In both cases the last words of the double expression are

---

66. Cf. the following versions as found in the Vulgate: Gal 2:6 *Deus personam hominis non accipit*; Acts 10:34: *Non est personarum acceptor Deus*; and in VL, Eph 6:9: *Non est personarum acceptio apud Deum*; Col 3:25: *Non est personarum acceptio apud Deum*; 1 Pet 1:17 (VL): *Patrem . . . qui sine acceptione personarum iudicat.*

67. Cf. Cetedoc I under "accept* persona*."

Benedict's addition: here "being humble," in verse 17 "and obedience." It seems important to him to emphasize that obedience and humility allow the gifts of God to grow. Besides, both times he points to the root of the good deeds. It seems to be a weakness of RM that too much attention was given to external observance.

V. 22: Therefore, he is to show equal love to all, and is to apply the same discipline to all according to their merits. (*Ergo aequalis sit ab eo omnibus caritas, una praebeatur in omnibus secundum merita disciplina.*)

Benedict omitted a sentence from RM 2.21: "to show his loving kindness to all alike, God commands the elements to serve sinners as much as the just." Verse 22 continues "Therefore (*ergo*) . . ." This is more logical. Benedict has to refer to verse 2.20 with his "ergo" and because of this, his verse 21 looks like an insertion or an exception.[68] We might like to equate the meaning of *caritas* with that of the Greek word *agape,* but in Benedict's time *amor* was already used in the same sense. Thus this short sentence is similar to verse 17a: "One is not to be loved more than another" (*ametur*). Here too we think of concrete situations where we are responsible for others. Benedict requires the same love that manifests itself in various ways to different individuals.

Subsequently Benedict again shortens the text of the Master, who had spoken of the same love for all and the same order (*disciplina*) for all. Benedict says "according to their merits," presumably of monastic life, embracing both good works as well as obedience and humility. Thus the *Regula Orientalis* also admonished the abbot: "He shall judge each one according to the merits of daily walking in truth."[69] The same love goes to the brothers not "according to their merit," but the same discipline does. In *caritas* we recognize the element of giving, in *disciplina* that of demanding or requiring; but *disciplina* also can be a form of love. From the abbot's point of view, it can mean good discipline and order in the monastery, correct conduct, or the dealing with individuals, and in this sense it may be a complement to *caritas.* We could even explain *disciplina* as a correction.

Caesarius had told the abbess: "Do not love one person more than another . . . Grant to everyone what they deserve, what is necessary."[70] In the writings of Pachomius we also find many admonitions of this type. It is a constant in the exhortation to superiors. On the other hand, we could write a long digression about how little this idea has been heeded in the course of history.

68. This is one of the texts that shows clearly that Benedict had the more logical text of the Master in front of him and made it less clear.
69. *RegOr* 1.7.
70. Caesarius, *ExhortVg* 4; cf. Orsiesius, *Lib* 16.

After this nucleus, the topic of teaching is resumed but is now applied even more concretely than in verse 12 to the different characters.

VV. 23-30: A DIFFERENT TEACHING FOR DIFFERENT CHARACTERS

This part of the text begins with the teaching (*doctrina*) and ends with a serious admonition to the abbot to take this really to heart, again in view of the Last Judgment.

The section can be subdivided as follows:

- 23-25 teaching according to the principles of the apostle
- 26-29 removing evil promptly (Benedict's addition)
- 30 final admonition to keep in mind who he is (or transition to the following)

The section's beginning and end contain the word "abbot." But he is also called "magister" (2.24). The verbs of teaching or educating predominate. "Correct, entreat, rebuke" *(argue, obsecra, increpa)* is the word of the apostle (2 Tim 4:2) that predominates in the first part, then also "reprove, punish" *(corripere, coercere)* in the application to the individual person. Toward the end, "remember" and "know" occur *(memor, meminere, scire)*. In the whole passage, the brothers are kept in view: they can be undisciplined and restless, or obedient, gentle, and patient but also negligent and scornful. In the part proper to Benedict, we see them as good and intelligent but also as bold, hard, arrogant and disobedient, and finally stupid—a whole range of behavior! The passage begins with the Scripture quotation from 2 Timothy 4:2; then Benedict mentions in his own addition the example of Eli and toward the end he quotes Proverbs 29:19 and 23:14 and in verse 30 refers to Luke 12:48.

Vv. 23-25: In his teaching the abbot must always follow the norm of the apostle who says: "Correct, entreat, rebuke;" that is, according to time and circumstances, combining strictness with mildness, the severe attitude of the teacher with the kindly one of the father. That is, he must reprove the undisciplined and restless strongly, but entreat the obedient and gentle and patient ones to progress to what is better, but we admonish him to reprove and punish the negligent and the scornful.

The whole person is to be educated: his will, his inclinations, and all his energies; thus argument, admonition, and correction are part of the teaching, here clearly meant to fit each individual. Theoretical learning fades into the background. Showing equal love to all is evident precisely in adapting the teaching to the individual. The passage is constructed logically. First in verse

23 the principle of the apostle; then a first, and still fairly general concrete application, with "that is" in verse 24; then the three ways of dealing with specific groups of monks, joined with another "that is." In the center we have the methods to be used with the obedient, gentle, and patient monks, "framed" by those for treating the undisciplined and negligent.

V. 23: In his teaching the abbot must always follow the norm of the apostle who says, "Correct, entreat, rebuke." (*In doctrina sua namque abbas apostolicam debet illam semper formam servire in qua dicit, Argue, obsecra, increpa* [2 Tim 4:2].)

This biblical text was also quoted in the Rule of the Four Fathers.[71] *Arguere* denotes to make clear, show, prove, make known, but in later Latin it denotes to accuse or denounce as wrong. *Obsecrare*, however, has more a sense of asking, even urgently, of imploring, possibly with religious motives. By its origin *increpare* is linked to sound and loud noise, arguing with someone loudly or reproving, scolding. It is regrettable that RM and RB did not include the words that follow in the Vulgate, "in all patience." The biblical quotation is usually called "the apostolic form" (*apostolica forma*); *forma* can mean form but also principle, norm, or Rule.

V. 24: That is, according to time and circumstances, combining strictness with mildness, the severe attitude of the teacher with the kindly one of the father. (*id est, miscens temporibus tempora, terroribus blandimenta, dirum magistri, pium patris ostendat affectum.*)

According to time and circumstances. The phrase "mixing the times with the times"—*miscens temporibus tempora*—probably was coined by RM and taken over by RB as a good formulation. The abbot must know not only what he says but also when and in what situation. Perhaps after overcoming his initial anger, he finds the other person more open to accept something. Only the right moment makes it possible for the abbot and the monks to find God's will together. Ecclesiastes says: "There is a time for everything" (3:1, *Omnia tempus habent*, Vulgate). Strictness (*terrores*) is a strong word in Latin, actually the plural of "terror, fright," but is joined

---

71. *Reg4Pat* 2:3-6 E: *Debet is qui praeest, talem se exhibere ut Apostolus ait: Estote forma credentibus, 4 hoc est pro qualitate . . . pietatis et veritatis fratrum animas ad caelestia de terrenis erigere, 5 dicente Apostolo: 'Argue, obsecra, increpa cum omni lenitate.'* The last two words of the imperative from 2 Tim 4:2 were already rearranged by Jerome in the Vulgate, and so this sequence is found in Ambrose, Augustine, and later several times in Cassiodorus.

here by "mildness" (*blandimenta*—mildness, what pleases the senses, and also careful, healing actions). This expresses a balance between two elements. It is a great pedagogical art to recognize the right moment for being either strict or gentle.

The terror or strictness of the teacher or master and the mildness and kindness of the father remind us of Prologue 1, where the instructions of the master and the kindly advice of a father are mentioned.[72] *Affectus* is a condition, a tendency, even an emotion, which is elicited from outside a person. The office of superior is to be fulfilled not only with regard to practical problems but also with concern for persons. It is of interest that Benedict assigns strictness to the master, although a master certainly is also kind, and assigns mildness to the father, although he must also be strict (2.29).

V. 25a: This means, he must reprove the undisciplined and restless strongly. (*id est indisciplinatos et inquietos debet durius arguere.*)

First there is *arguere*, to show something in a bright light, bring to light, to prove someone guilty. The abbot is to tear away the mask of the undisciplined and restless, a mask they hold in front of themselves. *Durius* is Benedict's addition; here it is not a comparative but rather an intensification, meaning energetically.[73] It is a drastic remedy. Basil in his Rule also speaks of a brother who is arrogant, restless, and undisciplined.[74] The undisciplined and restless are not likely to be open for arguments and gentle hints.

V. 25b: but entreat the obedient and gentle and patient ones to progress toward what is better. (*oboedientes autem et mites et patientes ut in melius proficiant obsecrare.*)

Here RM had "the very patient ones" (*patientissimos*); perhaps there are no such monks in Benedict's monastery? But he does mention obedient, gentle (*mites*; cf. Matt 11:29), and patient monks. They ought to be entreated, implored, and encouraged to make further progress (*ut in melius proficiant*). The word *proficere* occurs only one more time, in RB 62.4: The priest shall make more and more progress toward God (*magis ac magis in Deum proficiat*). So there is no end to making progress and going ahead.

72. See comments on Prol 1; cf. Jerome, *Ep* 82.1: *Blandiris ut pater, erudis ut magister.*
73. Cf. Lentini, 70.
74. *Reg* 98.2: *inquietus et indisciplinatus confundatur usquequeo discat loci sui ordinem custodire.*

V. 25c: but we admonish him to reprove and rebuke the negligent and scornful ones. (*neglegentes et contemnentes ut increpat et corripiat admonemus.*)

The "negligent" are the habitual neglecters of discipline. They go on their way without paying attention, literally, without reading (*neg [not]-legere*) what the community needs, what the superiors and the Rules say. They have blinded themselves to all but their own ego (today's gentle individualists might be a modern variant of these *neglegentes*). They can express their scorn for Rule and order in their hearts or even openly, thus justifying their own lifestyle. Here the abbot must be rigorous: *increpare* actually means getting loud, shouting, yelling harshly at someone.[75] Benedict adds *corripiat* to RM. Though it denotes to correct, reprimand, or grab hard, here the word even seems to have the meaning of punish. The word does not occur often in RM, but it does occur frequently in RB. Its components are *con-rapio*, to grab a person roughly, to take hold of him. One can almost feel Benedict's anger. Thus Benedict is not always more friendly and gentle than RM!

But we admonish (*admonemus*). This is the only time that the author of the Rule, as author, uses the plural in this chapter. It probably shows an important admonition and shows the involvement of the writer (the same applies to RM). One can get a glimpse of Benedict's bad experiences in the community. Yet in these sentences Benedict also describes how the abbot helps to foster unity in the community. Benedict omits a passage of RM, 2.26-31:

> He should in himself exemplify for them that norm of humility which the Lord presented to the apostles who were quarreling about the first place, 27 namely, when he took a child by the hand and brought him into their midst saying: 28 "If anyone wants to be great among you, let him be like this." 29 Therefore, whatever the abbot enjoins his disciples to do for God, he himself should first do, and then when he gives any orders the members will follow inline wherever he leads them. 30 He should have such love and kindness toward all the brethren that he will not prefer one to another, and will combine in himself the characteristics of both parents for all his disciples and sons 31 by offering them equal love as their mother and showing them uniform kindness as their father.

These are beautiful texts, but Benedict seems to be so concerned about his disobedient monks that he wants to stay with this topic while the Master takes off into the supernatural. The main idea is being childlike, humble, and that the members follow the head. This last image Benedict also avoids

---

75. It is strange that Benedict has changed the *increpet* of RM to *increpat*, which may have been the original way of reading it. Evidently he considered it a subjunctive of an infinitive *increpere*; cf. Linderbauer, 135.

in other places. The members are not the sons of the abbot and are not children. Therefore he also omits that the abbot should combine being father and mother in one person (RM 2.30-31).

In its place Benedict has a second major insertion in verses 26-29, which uses a harsher tone than RM.

Vv. 26-29: He must not overlook the sins of those who fail; but as soon as they appear, he is to cut them off at the root to the best of his ability, mindful of the death of Eli, the priest of Shiloh. But those of an upright and receptive disposition he is to admonish with words in a first and second warning; those who are evil, however, and the stubborn, arrogant and disobedient ones he is to correct with beatings and other physical punishments right at the beginning of a sin, knowing what is written: "The fool is not corrected by words" and again: "Strike your son with the rod, and you will rescue his soul from death."

V. 26: He must not overlook the sins of those who fail; but as soon as they appear, he is to cut them off at the root to the best of his ability, mindful of the death of Eli, the priest of Shiloh. (*Neque dissimulet peccata delinquentium; sed et mox ut coeperint oriri radicitus ea ut praevalet amputet, memor periculi Heli sacerdotis de Silo.*)

In the first sentence he alludes to 1 Kings 2:27-34, 3:11-14, and 4:12-18. Elsewhere Benedict shows his concern to cut off sins by their root *radicitus* (cf. 64.14; 33.1; 55.18); here he adds: "as soon as they appear." One might interpret this as emphasis or recall that it is really more merciful to eliminate evil right at the start, when it is still small, rather than to let it proliferate. The abbot might be in danger of overlooking faults, not to notice them (*dissimulare*), to delude himself; perhaps the abbot also does not want to create enemies for himself.[76] In 64.14, toward the end of the Rule, the manner of cutting off (*amputare*) is described by "prudent and loving." Here he adds "to the best of his ability" (*ut praevalet*).[77] The Corpus Iuris Civilis[78] said of the superior: "As soon as any small infraction of what

76. *Mox ut* here means "as soon as," that is, "quickly"; in this sense Benedict uses it in 66.3 (and similarly in 5.4).

77. *Praevalere* is used instead of *valere*, cf. Linderbauer, 177f. *Praevalere* actually means to be very capable, to have the power to do, be effective. Lentini, 71, translates thus: "with all the strength he has, with maximum energy." Others translate: "as far as lies in his power," or "for he has the power."

78. *Nov* 133.4, going back to Justinian: *Sicubi aliquid parvum fiat contra quam decet, hoc repente corrigere et non sinere maius fieri lapsum et perire animam.*

is proper occurs, he is to correct it immediately and not allow a greater failing and loss of the soul."

RB 28.4 mentions that sometimes all the abbot's zeal on behalf of a hardened brother has no effect. Perhaps our verses express some doubt born of long experience in the monastery? We might compare them with the more detailed treatment of the same topic in RB 64.11-14: "Let him hate evil but love the brothers. In correcting, he is to be prudent and not go too far, so that he does not break the vessel while trying to scrape off the rust too vigorously. Let him always consider his own frailty and remember that one must not break the bruised reed. By this we do not mean to say that he may let faults grow freely; on the contrary, he is to eliminate them, as we have said, prudently and lovingly, as seems best for each one." Benedict seems to proceed more gently, and we may assume this is due to insights into his own frailty.

Mindful of the death[79] *of Eli, the priest of Shiloh* (*memor periculi Heli sacerdotis de Silo*).[80] Caesarius describes this in more detail: "For I fear . . . the example of Eli the priest. Even though he heard that his sons were committing adultery, he failed to beat or excommunicate them but only admonished them gently."[81] In the same passage, Caesarius compares preachers and pastors with doctors. They must not neglect their duty, and often they must give a bitter medicine to drink. Early on, the monks saw Eli as model of the superior as physician of the monastic community. He becomes the example of a superior who is not conscious of his duty. One who, being in charge, ignores faults, and in the end also ignores the salvation of the others. Benedict has the courage to oppose the terror of unruly monks. The abbot's office requires something nearly impossible: uprooting the faults of the brothers at their very roots and, at the same time, being lovingly considerate. Today's danger might be excessive indulgence, whereas in earlier times superiors rather tried to uproot faults by close supervision. In both cases, there is a lack of energy, decisiveness, and trust.

In the next part we again have the image of diverse monks: first the open-minded, then the evil ones:

---

79. The word *periculum* actually means danger. Of course, Heli succumbed to the danger. But the word also can mean downfall, death, even accusation; cf. Linderbauer, 178.

80. Here I follow Steidle, "Memor."

81. s. 5.1: *Timeo enim et nimium expavecso Heli sacerdotis exemplum, qui pro eo quod audiens filios suos adulteria committere, dissimulavit eos aut caedere, aut de communione suspendere, sed tantummodo leniter ammonuit dicens: filii, non est bonum.*

V. 27: But those of an upright and receptive disposition he is to admonish with words in a first and second warning. (*Et honestiores quidem atque intellegibiles animos prima vel secunda admonitione verbis corripiat.*)

Honestiores can be translated as upright, refined, *intellegibiles* as understanding, receptive, open souls, similar to the *capaces* (in v. 12). Twice they are to be admonished verbally (cf. RB 23.2). The process of correction begins with words of admonition. In RB 23 it is the "seniors" who do so, while here it is the abbot (a contradiction that may indicate different times of editing). In the passages about correcting priests, deans, and the prior, verbal admonitions are mentioned. They seem to be the *honestiores*, who still might be in need of repeated admonitions.[82]

V. 28: Those who are evil, however, and the stubborn, arrogant, and disobedient ones he is to correct with beatings and physical punishment right at the beginning of a sin. (*Inprobos autem et duros ac superbos vel inoboedientes verberum vel corporis castigatio in ipso initio peccati coerceat.*)

Here we deal with corporal punishment. The monks are described as *improbi, duri, superbi, inoboedientes*, that is, wicked, hard, proud, and disobedient. This is similar to RB 23.1: correction by beatings (*verberum castigatio*) is contrasted with the "words" (*verba*) mentioned earlier. Corporal punishment, even right at the beginning of the sin, seems excessively harsh to us. It also contradicts RB 23.5, where corporal punishment is mentioned as the ultimate effort, when the monks cannot understand excommunication (*neque intellegit*; cf. RB 30.2). Not all understand the correction, be it by excommunication or by admonition; the abbot should adapt himself according to their insight. We also must consider that the present exhortation is in the spiritual part of the Rule, showing the basic direction, whereas RB 23 is part of the correctional code that pertains to the actual events. I am inclined to think that 2.28 was edited later than RB 23 and thus is an insertion here.

Presumably Benedict became stricter in the course of his life (and more often annoyed?). We might say this much: that Benedict is opposed to hesitant or long-suffering conduct on the abbot's part, which may cause him to miss the opportune moment. Thus he may here have said deliberately "right at the beginning of the sin." It is a restatement of verse 26, "as soon as they (faults, sins) arise." *Coerceat* means to put together but also to tame, rein in, call to order, or impose discipline. In the Last Judgment the abbot will only be declared not guilty if he fights faults energetically and thoroughly, and

---

82. "The need for multiple corrections suggests they might need more vigorous checking at times," Kardong, 59.

always begins again with the root. If the abbot is too gentle and lacks firmness, the whole monastic community suffers.

Vv. 28-29: knowing what is written: "The fool is not corrected by words" and again: Strike your son with the rod, and you will rescue his soul from death." (*sciens scriptum: Stultus verbis non corrigitur et iterum: Percute filium tuum virga et liberabis animam eius a morte.*)

The paragraph now culminates in two Scripture texts. The abbot knows (*sciens*), it is written. Earlier it was said that he remembers (*memor*) Eli the priest. According to the last Scripture texts, Benedict is concerned about "correcting" and "rescuing from death." For the fool does not understand a verbal correction, he belongs to the evil, wicked, hard, arrogant, and disobedient ones (2.28). Again we may be shocked by the words "rescuing his soul from death." The whole human person, in view of his eternal goal, is in danger of going astray. It is a very serious situation. Here Benedict refers to Wisdom literature.[83] We may note how freely he quotes though generally following the *Vetus Latina*. Only in a text from Scripture is the word "son" (*filius*) used to refer to the monk; it is the only time in RB. The abbot usually is dealing with the "disciples," the "brother/monk," or with "fellow servants" (*conservis*, 64.21).

According to many editions, verse 30 may also be considered as the introduction to the next paragraph. In my opinion, this verse is rather a summary of the middle section.

V. 30: The abbot must always remember what he is, remember what he is called, knowing that from the one to whom more is entrusted, more will be required. (*Meminere debet semper abbas quod est, meminere quod dicitur, et scire quia cui plus committitur, plus ab eo exigitur.*)

Now Benedict returns to the text of RM.[84] The meaning of *credere* in the sense of entrusting is familiar to both authors (cf. RB 2.39; 27.5).[85] The similarity to the beginning of the chapter on the abbot is striking (2.1, 6, 7); with its three verbs of "remembering" (*meminere, meminere, scire*), verse 30 is another call to accountability at the close of this earnest admonition. The "entrusting"

---

83. In VL Prov 29:19: *verbis non emendabitur servus durus.* Prov 23:14: *Tu quidem percuties eum (parvulum) virga; animam autem eius liberabis a morte.* Prov 18:2: *Non recipit stultus verba prudentiae.*

84. Only two words are rearranged and then *creditur* is replaced by *committitur*.

85. *Committere* in this context is more common for Benedict. The RM has no further use of *credere* in the sense of "entrusting."

(*committitur*) is matched by the demand (*exigitur*): a greater task means greater accountability. At any rate, it is clear that the community is not the abbot's property but is only entrusted to him. Ambrose said: "More is required of him to whom more is entrusted," and Jerome made a similar remark.[86] RM had quoted Jerome exactly. The sentence is derived from the Bible text in Luke 12:48, that much will be required of the one to whom much is given. In RM this text provides a good introduction to further admonitions in view of eschatological accountability (RM 2.33). Benedict, however, moves on to the service of many and diverse brothers, and this also puts verse 30 in a different light.

VV. 31-40: CONCLUSION

This conclusion, which emphasizes the abbot's chief task and his accountability in the Last Judgment, forms an inclusion to the beginning of the chapter (vv. 1-10). As can be seen, here is the third and longest addition of Benedict in verses 31-36. Equally long is the omission of the RM text between verses 38 and 39.

This final section consists of three paragraphs, two of which are added by Benedict:

- 31-32: directing souls—adaptation
- 33-36: a task in difficult times: seeking the reign of God; together with RM (though 2.35-38 are omitted) a third part
- 37-40: In the care of guiding souls and in view of the Last Judgment, the abbot himself is being purified

Vv. 31-32: Let him know what a difficult and wearisome task he assumes, guiding souls and serving the particularities of many, one with kindness, another with reproof, another with convincing arguments; and according to the character and capacity of each one, he is to adapt and adjust himself to all so that he not only will suffer no loss in the flock entrusted to him but also can rejoice in the growth of a good flock.

Regarding the activities of the abbot the "let him know" (*sciat*) stands for emphasis right at the beginning; it repeats the "knowing" of verse 30. Serving includes adapting (*conformare*) and adjusting oneself (*aptare*). The flock occurs not just once but twice in the final sentence (v. 32). The abbot's counterpart are the "many, the one, the other, the other, each one, all." Community and the diverse individuals—both poles are emphasized. In the center

---

86. Ambrose, *Apol Dav.* (10) 51: *Plus ab eo exigitur, cui plus commissum est.* Cf. Jerome, *Ep* 14.9: *Cui plus creditur, plus ab eo exigitur.*

Benedict placed the second part of verse 31 with the three different forms of service according to character (in Latin: *alium . . . alium . . . alium*).[87]

V. 31: Let him know what a difficult and wearisome task he assumes, guiding souls and serving the particularities of many. (*Sciatque quam difficilem et arduam rem suscipit regere animas et multorum servire moribus.*)

The term *guiding souls* (*regere animas*) seems difficult to us. It is used two more times in the last part of this chapter. "To guide, lead, souls, set them on a straight path" would be the precise translation. In English and in other languages we speak of "spiritual direction." Guiding (*regere*) in this sentence is a parallel to serving rather than a contrast. Perhaps we may think of leadership—leading, even guiding, on the straight way. English has a fitting term in "servant leadership." The word "souls" (*animae*) points to the eternal salvation involved in such guiding of persons. The abbot has to guide all persons in their wholeness, especially in regard to their ultimate destination. Guiding souls does not express any dualism (body against soul).[88]

"Serving" is a much-used word for the office of the abbot and of others. The ideal becomes painfully concrete in serving many unique persons. It does not mean becoming the servant of all decisions, wishes, or moods but understanding diverse attitudes, assessing them correctly, and influencing them in view of their continued formation. According to individual characters this guidance will vary, even go in various directions, but always toward the ultimate common goal.

The first part of this sentence is interesting: "Let him know what a difficult and wearisome task he assumes" (*rem difficilem et arduam suscipit*); the abbot has taken up this task; and he knows that it is a difficult and hard job, a steep path. Benedict shows understanding for the abbot's burden; presumably he himself has experienced it as hard—and I could imagine—as getting increasingly harder. This is different from the Master's concept, for whom the office of abbot seems quite desirable and honorable, even to the very end of his Rule.

V. 31: Serving . . . one with kindness, another with reproof, another with convincing arguments. (*et alium quidem blandimentis, alium vero increpationibus, alium suasionibus.*)

Serving shows itself concretely in adapting to various characters and capacities and in the choice of the appropriate means, such as kindness, mildness,

---

87. Cf. Puzicha, "Multorum."
88. Cf. Böckmann, "Der Mensch," 44; the translation "guiding persons" in SÄK seems too general.

then correction, then persuasive words, and encouragement (*blandimenta, increpationes,*[89] *suasiones*; cf. vv. 23-25). Yet in his own addition Benedict is more positive than before.[90] *Blandiri* means to caress, flatter, win over, invite, and *blandimentum* is a caress as a means (cf. v. 24) of winning someone over, usually used in the plural. The word only occurs in RB 2 and only two times. It describes the attractive and inviting manner of Christ as he stood before us in the Prologue. The word *suasiones* denotes the gentle behavior of someone who talks to us, advises, recommends;[91] in the same way, Benedict advises us in 49.2 to keep our life pure and in 61.9 advises a visiting monk who adjusts well to stay (Regarding *increpatio*, cf. v. 25).

V. 32a: and according to the character and capacity of each one, he is to adapt and adjust himself to all. (*et secundum uniuscuiusque qualitatem vel intellegentiam, ita se omnibus conformet et aptet.*)

According to the *qualitas*—that is, the nature, type of person, and the *intelligentia*—that is their judgment and insight! It is typical for Benedict to show consideration for such particular traits (cf. RB 30.2; 23.4). He addresses himself first to each individual person and then gathers all of them together again (*omnibus*, cf. the double use of flock [*grex*] in v. 32b). Holzherr writes: "Such 'discreet' pastoral care is characterized by mutual personal attentiveness; it requires a 'knowledge of hearts,' also to avoid demanding too much and to prevent the abbot from using an impersonal egalitarian treatment toward everyone."[92] Of Honoratus it is said that he saw through the uniqueness of each person. "If one improved, he adapted his correction to him. He met one sternly, another one kindly. . . . He carried, as it were, the souls of all in his own soul." He is said to have had a "God-given insight," so that he knew "the strengths, the emotional condition, even the stomach and the sleep of each one, [was] able to rein in the enthusiasts and to spur on the sluggish. He knew how to mingle friendliness with sternness."[93] The Rules for monks do not contain many parallel passages about such adapting pastoral care. And

---

89. The repetitions, among other things, prove that vv. 31-32 were added. Presumably Benedict is aware that these are repetitions and inserts them because he has experienced more and more just how important it is to guide souls by adapting to characters.

90. There are two positive concepts; only in the middle are the loud correcting words while in v. 23 the positive term was framed by two negative behaviors (cf. also *increpat* in v. 25).

91. It is also used a few times with regard to the soft way by which the devil sneaks in (Prol 28; 58.28).

92. Holzherr 2007, 87.

93. Hilary of Arles, *VitHon* 3.17-4.18; 6.26.

it is clear that all this can be easily used by all who are involved in pastoral care, spiritual direction, and education of youth and adults.

V. 32b: So that he not only will suffer no loss in the flock entrusted to him but also can rejoice in the growth of a good flock. (*Ut non solum detrimenta gregis sibi commissi non patiatur, verum in augmentatione boni gregis gaudeat.*)

It is typical of Benedict that he again leads the persons to the community with a final "so that" (*ut*). The individual monks belong to the whole, to the flock (used twice). The goal is expressed first negatively, then positively: suffering no loss or harm but rather seeing a good flock increasing.[94]

The negative image is also evoked in John 17:12 in the concern that none of the sheep be lost, as it is also used in RB 27.5. The entire flock shall grow and increase, not just individuals. When the abbot devotes himself to individuals, he must simultaneously take care that the unity of the whole grows and that the brothers treasure and love one another. *Detrimentum* (from *detero*) is actually a rubbing away, then a decrease, a lessening, a damage, loss. *Augmentatio*, however, occurs only once, and is derived from *augere*, which Benedict uses twice, and which means not only to increase but also to grow, to let flourish, to strengthen. In our situation this not only means a numerical increase of the community but also a strengthening and enlivening of the community. There might even be a danger if one were to use a growing number of candidates for assessing the more or less excellent quality of the abbot. Growth (*augmentatio*) is also applied to the individual who may possibly surpass the abbot. And this is to be a joy to the superior. He is here portrayed as truly selfless, solely concerned with the benefit of the others, following the example of Christ and his successors. One could round it off with the key sentence of 72.7: "to do what is more useful to the other."

Vv. 33-36: Above all, he must neither overlook nor underestimate the salvation of the souls entrusted to him and be more concerned about transitory, earthly, and perishable things; but he must always bear in mind that he has assumed the task of guiding souls of whom he will have to give an account. And he must not give a possible lack of resources as an excuse, but remember what is written: "Seek first the reign of God and

---

94. CanAp 40. PL146B: *ne ecclesia detrimentum patiatur.* The *Sacramentarium Gelasianum* states in 38.358: *ne grex tuus detrimentum sustineat.* Orsiesius, *Lib* 17 speaks of *commissum sibi gregem.* Perhaps still more clearly, the *Sacramentarium Leonianum* 957: *incrementum gregis atque salubritas gaudium est . . . corona pastorum.*

his justice, and all this will be added besides." And again: "Those who fear him will lack nothing."

In this paragraph the language becomes urgent. It begins with "above all" (*ante omnia*),[95] which is Benedict's way of introducing sentences that are very important to him. This corresponds to the fact that the abbot must always bear in mind (*sed semper cogitet*). Benedict begins with the caring about material things to which he returns in verse 35, contrasting it each time with a spiritual principle such as guiding souls or seeking first the reign of God. Verbs of awareness predominate in this part of the text: "overlook, underestimate, think, be mindful" (*dissimulans, parvipendens, cogitet, meminerit*). "That not" (*ne*) occurs three times; that the following must not happen: neglecting the salvation of the souls, being more concerned about material things, or being too concerned about lack of resources. These demands are hardly found in directories for abbots of the old Rules.

V. 33a: Above all, he must neither overlook nor underestimate the salvation of the souls entrusted to him. (*Ante omnia, ne dissimulans aut parvipendens salutem animarum sibi commissarum.*)

Absolute priority is the salvation of the souls (*salus animarum*), not good organization, not even discipline or any other monastic value. The precious nature of each individual person in view of his salvation is pointed out. The souls are entrusted to the abbot (*commissae*: cf. in v. 32 *gregis sibi commissi*). It may happen that the abbot shuts his eyes (*dissimulare*—to hide, to conceal), he might also underestimate, undervalue (*parvipendere*, that is, to consider less important or to disregard). With material things he can point to success, but this is not possible when serving persons, and not at all when one is concerned about their salvation, not simply that they are well cared for. These demands have few parallels in the directories for abbots in older Rules.

V. 33b: and be more concerned about passing, earthly, and perishable things. (*ne plus gerat sollicitudinem de rebus transitoriis et terrenis atque caducis.*)

The abbot's task is to be concerned (*sollicitudinem gerere*), to have a wholistic, eager concern, to be totally (*sollus*) present to this task. *Sollicitudo* is an important word in RB, which is used several times concerning the abbot but also for the cellarer and for the community in general in regard to the poor and strangers (e.g., 31.9; 53.15). It is characteristic of Benedict that these

---

95. Cf. Puzicha, "Ante omnia."

intensive efforts are to be directed chiefly to persons, specifically the weaker ones (this is one of the differences in word usage between him and RM). Souls are contrasted with business, material things, that is, with the management of the monastery's property. Of course the abbot must deal with those concerns as well, but they are secondary to his primary concern. It is worth noting that the word *sollicitudo* is given an explicitly negative sense here (and only here in RB), when it is directed to material things rather than to persons. Similar terms are used by Augustine, Cyprian, and Cassian,[96] when they compare heavenly things with earthly values. In RB 2 this does not signal a negative assessment of material things in themselves, as if they had no value. What is passing (*transitoria, caduca*) is contrasted with what is eternal, as the earthly is contrasted with heaven. Earthly things are transitory, ephemeral; this does not mean, however, that they are bad or evil.

This passage touches on a very important problem of our times: the value of each individual human being versus the value of money! Benedict's Rule can give us direction and encourage us to take—perhaps only—small steps in the right direction. This admonition applies to areas that go beyond the monastery.

V. 34: But he must always bear in mind that he has assumed the task of guiding souls of whom he will have to give an account. (*Sed semper cogitet quia animas suscepit regendas, de quibus et rationem redditurus est.*)

Insistently the abbot is admonished always to bear in mind his main task and with it his accountability for each one of the monks (cf. vv. 31, 37). This part of the sentence is almost identical with RB 64.7: "He must always remember what a burden he has assumed and to whom he must give an account of his stewardship."[97] The abbot is only the representative, the administrator; the flock belongs to Christ, the *paterfamilias,* who will require an account. This is also a consolation, for in some situations the abbot can tell the Lord: This or that person (who is giving me such a hard time) is your property. Please, take him into your special care.

Vv. 35-36: And he must not give a possible lack of resources as an excuse, but remember what is written: "Seek first the reign of God and his justice, and all this will be added besides." And again: "Those who fear him will lack nothing." (*Et ne causetur de minori forte substantia, meminerit scriptum: Primum quaerite regnum Dei et iustitiam eius, et hae omnia*

---

96. Augustine, *s.* 113.6; Cassian, *Conf.* 10.24; 16.9.1. Cf. also Fulgentius, *De remiss pecc* 1.21.5; Cyprian, *De mortal* 2.

97. Cf. Augustine, *Praec* 7.3.

adicientur vobis" [Matt 6:33], *et iterum: nihil deest timentibus eum,* [*Ps 33/34:10*].)

Lack of resources (*de minori forte substantia*)! This may not always be the case, but this remark presumably points to the material situation of the monastery at the time this addition was inserted after chapter 2 as a whole had been written. One can assume that during the Gothic Wars the goods of the monastery were in fact insufficient. Why else would such an addition have been necessary? We may recall the Dialogs of Gregory who writes of shortages in Monte Cassino.[98] The lack of material resources could serve as an excuse for caring primarily about the daily bread and thus forgetting the care of souls. The abbot might cause the brothers to feel insecure, overly worried, or to become stingy and greedy. If the complaint "we have no money" keeps getting repeated, the priorities for all may be shifted as a result.

Give as an excuse (*causetur*) is used in the sense of being anxious, worried, or of using excuses, even a pretense.[99] We can think of 55.7, where the monks are not supposed to worry (*causentur*) about the color or rough texture of the material for their habits. One uses what can be obtained more economically in the locality.[100] While the reason given may be a fact, repeating it all too frequently may harm the spirituality of the community.

An actual lack of resources is certainly difficult, and the attitude desired in such a situation is even more demanding. Therefore the term "he must bear in mind" (*meminerit*) refers here to two Scripture texts, one from the psalm which was discussed in the Prologue (Ps 33/34:10) and one from the Sermon on the Mount in Matthew 6:33.[101] The entire text of Matthew 6:24-34 pertains to this topic and supplies the foundational context of this passage in the Rule: to decide whether to serve God or mammon, not to worry and be anxious about physical needs, food, or clothing, but to be concerned about one thing only: the reign of God. What does "seeking the reign of God and his justice" mean in concrete terms? In verses 33-36 the emphasis is on the priority of the spiritual over the earthly, on salvation of souls over material gain. The psalm verse also mentions those "who fear him." Fearing God here seems to mean looking to him, living in his presence, and letting him set the priorities. Then the conclusion applies as well: Everything else will be given them besides;

---

98. *Dial* II.21.1; cf. also 27.1; 28-29.

99. Linderbauer, 183 considers the last most likely.

100. Concerning the poverty of the monastery, see Böckmann, *Around*, 93–101; also "Arme," 191f.

101. RM has this text in a different form in other places, e.g., RM 16.14 in the chapter about the cellarer: "Seek the kingdom and the justice of God, and all will be given to you," whereas Benedict follows the Vulgate more closely.

they will lack nothing. This is the radical stance of the Gospel that Benedict requires of the abbot and certainly also of the community: profound trust in God. This is equally true for all those who are responsible for others.

Vv. 37-40: And he must know that one who takes on the task of guiding souls must be ready to give an account; and whatever the number of the brothers in his care, he must realize with certainty that on the day of judgment he must give an account for all these souls, and no doubt also for his own soul. And thus, always fearing the future examination of the shepherd about the sheep entrusted to him and caring for the condition of others, he will also care for his own. And as he helps others to make progress by his exhortations, he himself will be purified of his own vices.

The final passage once again begins with an emphatic "and he must know" (*Sciatque*, cf. v. 31, and similarly v. 35). It is used one more time in the next verse with "he must realize with certainty" (*scierit, agnoscat*). This is a crescendo, an intensification. Benedict again follows the text of RM.

Vv. 37-38: And he must know that one who takes on the task of guiding souls must be ready to give an account; and whatever the number of the brothers in his care, he must realize with certainty that on the day of judgment he must give an account for all these souls, and no doubt also for his own soul. (*Sciatque quia qui suscipit animas regendas paret se ad rationem reddendam, et quantum sub cura sua fratrum se habere scierit numerum, agnoscat pro certo quia in die iudicii ipsarum omnium animarum est redditurus domino rationem, sine dubio addita et suae animae.*)

Verse 31 is practically repeated, reinforced, and emphasizes that the abbot must give an account for all souls, now explicitly before the Lord. The text states again that the sheep are entrusted to the shepherd (*creditis*). Among the souls he has accepted into his care there is finally also his own. The ending of the section also turns attention to his own soul and his own spiritual development. It certainly would not be in Benedict's intention if the abbot were to neglect himself.

Since the ideas and expressions of the chapter are being repeated, a summary exegesis of this passage is sufficient. The thought of the Final Judgment becomes stronger. This may be due to the situation of Benedict's historical era with its sense of an "end of the world" in connection with the political and social events and upheavals. Recurring ideas of judgment in the Rule give us a real feeling for the atmosphere of the period (cf. also Gregory the Great).

Between 2.38 and 2.39 Benedict omitted the following verses (2.35-38 of RM):

for, so as not to do their own will in the monastery, the brothers always served
in all obedience to his [the abbot's] commands. When they are called to account for all they have done they will say to the Lord at the judgment that they
did everything in obedience by command of the master. Therefore the master
must always see to it 38 that everything he commands, everything he teaches,
every correction he gives, is manifestly in accord with the precepts of God, as
justice demands, so that he will not be condemned in the judgment to come.

The Master thinks that the monk must only obey and is not accountable
for the content of his obedience. In RM 7.53-56, the same idea is expressed
even more bluntly:

Furthermore, under the care of the abbot, not only are they not forced to
worry about temporal necessities, that is, food, clothing, and footwear but also
solely by rendering obedience in all things to the master, they are made secure
about the account they will have to give of their soul and about whatever else
is profitable for both body and soul. This is so because, whether for good or
ill, what happens among the sheep is the responsibility of the shepherd, 56
and he who gave orders is the one who will have to render an account when
inquiry is made at the judgment, not he who carried out the orders, whether
good or bad.

With a sure instinct Benedict omits this text, but he too maintains that the
abbot is responsible for the souls of the others.

**Vv. 39-40: And thus, always fearing the future examination of the shepherd
about the sheep entrusted to him and caring for the condition of others,
he will also care for his own. And as he helps others to make progress by
his exhortations, he himself will be cleansed of his own faults. (*Et ita,
timens semper futuram discussionem pastoris de creditis ovibus, cum de
alienis ratiociniis cavet, redditur de suis sollicitus, et cum de monitionibus
suis emendationem aliis subministrat ipse efficiatur a vitiis emendatus.*)**

An account will have to be given for each individual soul. This seems to be
asking almost too much. In his time, Benedict probably was faced with a
"lazy" abbot who did not care about his individual monks. The abbot is a
model for a new kind of society; he is accorded a large sphere of action and
freedom. Therefore he must grow in being accountable to a higher authority,
that is, to the Lord. Every official is accountable to one above himself. We find
a similar text in Orsiesius: "From all this we learn that we must stand before
the tribunal of Christ and will be judged not only for our individual actions
but also for our thoughts; and after having given an account of our own life
we also must give an account of the others who are entrusted to us . . . we

were entrusted by God with a good, namely, the conduct of our brothers. When we labor for them, we can expect an eternal reward."[102]

The abbot saves himself precisely by helping others—and this holds true for every office of service. While he is correcting and accompanying others, they hold up a mirror to him and, as it were, correct him. His admonitions to others to improve and be cleansed of faults, are also an admonition to himself.[103] By his serving as Christ served, he is saved.

He himself is cleansed of faults (*ipse efficitur a vitiis emendatus*). It is interesting how frankly Benedict (together with RM) talks of the faults (*vitia*) of the abbot, of which he must be cleansed. For our two authors it seems quite normal that the abbot has not yet progressed so far that he would no longer be on the way of purification. This verse is parallel to the last verse of RB 7: "All this the Lord will graciously manifest by the Holy Spirit in his laborer now cleansed of faults and sins" (7.70). Here we see the abbot as one among brothers who is on the way and as such is also the shepherd of his flock, who on the one hand represents Christ but is not yet identical with him and must still grow into Christ. On the other hand, his own fragility is both cause and reason for dealing mercifully with the weaknesses of the brothers.

At this point RM adds the verses about the counsel of the brothers (2.41-50) as an appendix and a transition to the chapter about the holy art in 2.51-52: "The abbot, therefore, must be a master of this holy art, not attributing the performance of it to himself but to the Lord, whose grace achieves in us whatever we do that is holy. 52 This art must be taught and learned in the workshop of the monastery, and it can be practiced with the use of spiritual instruments."

Benedict, however, has written a separate chapter (RB 3) about the counsel of the brothers. He lacks the transitions from one chapter to the other (cf. introduction to RB 1-3). And chapter 4 in Benedict's Rule is not a book from which the master teacher gathers his wisdom. It belongs to all the monks.

Now one ought to compare RB 2 as a whole with RB 64. Certainly RB 2 was edited earlier than RB 64, which was written under the influence of Augustine. But it is interesting that Benedict's insertions in RB 2 show a closer link with 64. Moreover, it seems important to compare RB 2, especially its insertions, with RB 27-28 in order to sketch a portrait of the abbot according to RB. The insertions in particular shed light on Benedict's own later experience with difficulties in the community, as well as on his view that being an abbot is a heavy burden.

102. *Lib* 11.
103. It is worth noting that Benedict (similar to RM) uses the same word in the final verse: *emendationem aliis subministrat . . . ipse efficitur a vitiis emendatus.*

One might say that this portrait of the abbot also seems to be a model, an orientation for all, since the abbot normally is chosen from the community. Besides, similar qualities are desired for the cellarer and also, to a lesser degree, for the deans. All these officials don't fall from heaven; they were formed within the community. Today the following qualities might especially apply:

- Each one is, as it were, in the role of father/mother in respect to certain persons,
- most of them are in a certain sense teachers—instructing and educating,
- each one is in some sense a shepherd—responsible for certain groups and individuals,
- each one is accountable before the judgment of God,
- each one needs to preserve the priority of the spiritual over the material,
- each one needs to respect the basic equality of the others and simultaneously their uniqueness, to which one must adapt.

RB 72 is the hermeneutical key with which ultimately everything needs to be read. Reverence, patience, selfless mutual love to each other, so that Christ can lead us all together.

Another important line: The abbot has done a thorough *Lectio Divina*. We can practically recount the entire chapter using Scripture quotations and allusions; they are like the scaffolding. The word of the Bible is pondered, repeated, called to mind; it is present in the heart. This also guarantees that the superior teaches nothing but the Word of God (cf. RB 7.10-13). The chapter is permeated by the divine command.[104]

With regard to style we notice that Benedict often uses "not, but," "not, if not," and similar words; this means that he wants to consider both, or even several, sides (while the Master more often uses "therefore," and "that is"). We could say that the Master's teaching style is generally more rational, while Benedict in his teaching intuitively perceives existing differences.

Looking back on the entire chapter with regard to the description of the community, we may be shaken by the fact that Benedict assumes so many faults and vices; but there are also very good monks, and in all of them Benedict emphasizes the differences not only in their social origin but also in their moral qualities. Humanly speaking, we would have to say that it is

---

104. Cf. Giurisato, "Regola," 98–100. He lists: (4) the commandments of the Lord, (5) divine justice, (9) your justice, your truth, your salvation, (12) the Lord's commands; the divine precepts, (14) my just norms, my covenant, my words, (23) the apostolic form, (28) as is written, (35) as is written.

impossible to be entrusted with a community—as described in this chapter—and to accept the position as its pastoral leader. Yet Benedict has great trust in the divine grace: "they praise the Lord who works in them" (Prol 30). Or we recall the hopeless case mentioned in RB 28 in which the Lord, who can do all things, is called on (28.5).

The unity of the community will be a principal concern of the abbot, as verse 2.20 states: "we are all one in Christ and bear the same burden of service under the one Lord." With this Benedict already distances himself from the half-eremitical ideal represented by the Master. Benedict is a truly a cenobitical abbot whose concern for the community never lets him forget the individual members with all their needs and particularities. Still today the chapter will assist superiors in finding ways to deal with their own faults, as well as those of others, thus seeing situations not only realistically but also in the light of God and thereby growing in mercy and compassion. These thoughts are more clearly formulated in the second directory for the abbot (RB 64.7-22). The first chapters of the Rule must especially not be interpreted without looking at the later ones, and certainly not without RB 72.

Calling the Brothers for Counsel

CONTEMPORARY CONTEXT

Consultation, counsel, joint decision making—all these terms and concepts are timely in church and society today. Authoritarian modes of acting are generally unacceptable. Therefore, a chapter in the Rule on taking counsel together is timely and welcome.

The word "dialogue," especially since the Second Vatican Council, has become very attractive to religious. Yet most of us still can remember instances when its opposite was, or still is, practiced. Our ecclesiastical context enables us to approach chapter 3 with positive expectations.

It might be both amusing and enriching to imagine role playing a council meeting in its extreme forms: first in a monastery governed in an authoritarian style and then in a monastery characterized by a laissez-faire style. After such an activity, we might do a first reading of the chapter and be surprised by many of its statements. The players of the authoritarian monastery might marvel at the great confidence Benedict has in the brothers. The players of the more liberal monastery might possibly be disappointed that Benedict gives so much weight to his abbot.

We also could read the chapter from the perspective of an authoritarian abbot and note what he might like or dislike, and then from the perspective of a modern brother, noting what might suit him and what he would not like at all. Another possibility would be to rewrite this chapter in the spirit of a supermodern brother or in the sense of an authoritarian abbot.

A preconciliar abbot might make the following statements: (1)[1] Fairly often when I want to show my power to all my sons, I call them all together (or: all those who agree with me) to state what I think and what I want, how well I have planned things, and what good ideas I have; (2) From my sons I expect attention and approval; (3) No need to call the younger members; they

---

1. The numbers of these imaginary statements refer to the verses in RB 3, thus are not always consecutive.

are still immature. The Lord usually reveals to me what is better; (4) When
the sons express their agreement, they must do so reverently and with proper
bows. On no account should they dare to express their own views; (6) It is
clear that they all obey me as their master; (7) And all of them are to follow
me and not to deviate even an inch from my instructions to follow the desires
of their own hearts; (9) There are never to be any arguments with me, their
abbot, since I do everything according to my mind, and this is best.

From the perspective of the antiauthoritarian brother, the chapter might
be rewritten thus: (1) Whenever there is any decision to be made in the monastery, we are entitled to be called and to decide for ourselves; (2) The abbot
does not really need to state the subject matter, for we know better anyway.
But in any case, he should listen well, while we all weigh the matter, think,
and discuss it fully; (3) The Lord always reveals to the brothers (never to the
abbot) what is better; (4) The brothers are to express their opinions fearlessly
and forcefully, so that the abbot will obey them in everything; (8) Every
brother should follow the will of his own heart for only good things flow
from his heart; (9) Arguing with the abbot is part of honesty; he needs to
be corrected. The Rule is just a limitation and hinders creativity; (12) Above
all, the abbot must consult the brothers in all affairs and must obey them.

CONTEXT IN BENEDICT'S TIME[2]

In this chapter Benedict deals with two types of council meetings: one with all
the brothers and one with the seniors. The latter form is already found in the monastic tradition of the desert.[3] In the Coptic *Vita* of Pachomius we learn[4] that the
superior general called together the seniors of the community in order to select
his successor, to have appointments confirmed, and finally also for the sad case
of a brother who had to be excommunicated. Cassian reports that the hermits
were meeting from time to time to take counsel about questions of discipline.[5]

In the Rules of Basil, though only in their later versions, we read of a
council of brothers to assist the superior. They take counsel with him and
check into matters of common concern. Basil cites Sirach 32:24.[6] Also the
Shorter Rule 104 states that the superior must keep in mind to do everything
with counsel. Newcomers must be accepted with the knowledge of all the
brothers.[7] In the official version, known to us in Latin, there is only the state-

---

2. Cf. Steidle, (Abt); Luislampe, "Geistliche Entscheidungsfindung." This chapter was
first published in *EA* 69 (1993): 95–113, 200–22; for this book it was revised.

3. Cf. e.g., *Alph*, Moses 2, 5.

4. Cf. Lefort, *VitPach*, 424; cf. Pachomius, *Praef* 8.

5. *Conf.* 18.5; cf. also *VitPat* 5.9.5; 5.16.2 etc.

6. *Regfus* 48.

7. *Regbrev* 112.

ment that the community needs to contribute its counsel in difficult matters so that a solution can be found more easily.[8]

Outside the monastic tradition, there is a letter of Cyprian in which he writes that he wished to do nothing without the counsel of the priests and their consent but rather to treat things together as mutual respect requires.[9] Finally, we need to consider Roman law. Justinian's Code[10] requires the cooperation of all the monks, for example, in the sale of goods of the community. The superior is not the sole owner; the goods belong to everyone, so all must be consulted.[11]

This also seems to be the Master's view (RM 2.41-50). His Rule mentions counsel with all since the goods of the monastery belong to all and to none. Therefore, they are all to be consulted and then the abbot decides. He also has the list of all the goods. Practically, however, the abbot acts as the owner.

Later monastic Rules also mention a council of the brothers, for example the *Regula Ferrioli* refers to a council when a slave is to be set free (36). The goods belong to all the monks in common (35). The *Regula Aureliani* 43 even authorizes the monks to protest in case the abbot wishes to donate or sell something of the monastery's property. Isidore of Seville[12] writes of a council in connection with the excommunication and the reconciliation of a brother. The later Rules clearly show that in the course of time, such a council of brothers constituted a protection against an abbot who acted too arbitrarily.

In looking at the tradition, two forms can be noted: the council of the seniors from the desert and Basil; then the council of all from Roman law, the church, and RM. Benedict combines the two traditions.[13] We realize how independent he is, even while depending on others; why he insists so strongly on adhering to the Rule and also why he forbids the brothers to be presumptuous.

IMMEDIATE CONTEXT

The reality of Benedict's community can be gleaned to some extent from intensive or negative terms: Apparently the abbot did not always want to summon *all* (vv. 1, 3), nor for *every important matter*! Verse 3: Like today, there was a danger at that time of not consulting the youngest members. Verse 4 mentions that some presumed to defend their opinion stubbornly so that, as shown in verses 9f., they actually argued boldly with their abbot (and outside the monastery at that). Therefore the strong emphasis on humility! The threefold warning against "presuming" (*praesumere*) points to an evil

8. *Reg* Prol 12-13.
9. *Ep.* 14.4.
10. *Nov.* 123.6; cf. also *Nov.* 120.6-7.
11. Concerning the idea of common ownership, cf. Vogüé, "Blecker."
12. *Reg* 18.4.
13. Cf. Hilpisch, "Rat"; Puzicha, 95f.

in Benedict's monastery, which in Miquel's view is probably a danger for strong characters (cf. below).[14] Likewise, it seems to have been necessary to appeal to the abbot's conscience and to remind him that he had to arrange *everything* with foresight and fairness (without exceptions! v. 5) and that he was accountable to the "most just" judge (v. 11) for *all* his decisions. *All* are to obey him, even those who are displeased with a decision (v. 5). Verses 12-13 show that the community had probably already increased in size or that the author anticipated this development, so that calling the entire community for every problem would have been too unwieldy. Verses 7-9 are particularly intense and negative. It seems necessary for Benedict to emphasize that all, the brothers *and* the abbot, are to obey the Rule and by no means ought to deviate from it by yielding to the desires of their own hearts. In council meetings this may be a particularly sore point with each monk running the risk of defending his own ideas and not observing the rules of dialogue, which also means no longer being open to other views, and lastly to the will of God.

We might reflect what we would emphasize today, or whether we still have the same weaknesses.

OVERVIEW OF THE CHAPTER

First let us try to see the structure of the chapter and to identify its core. Borias discussed this,[15] locating five parallel parts and considering verse 7 as the center. In my opinion the individual and corresponding verses are less important here than the paragraphs containing similar sequences of thoughts and words.

RB 3: CALLING THE BROTHERS FOR COUNSEL

A 1 As often as anything important is to be done in the monastery, the abbot is to call together the whole community and to explain himself what the business is;

2 and listening to the advice of the brothers, let him ponder it and then do what he judges the more useful course.

3 The reason why we have said all are to be called for counsel is that the Lord often reveals to the young what is better (cf. Matt 11:25).

B   4 The brothers, for their part, are to express their counsel thus:

14. Cf. Miquel, *"Praesumere"*; Zorzi, *"Vivere."*
15. Borias, *"Chiasme."*

with all humility and submission,
not presuming to defend their own
views obstinately.

5 The decision is rather for the
   abbot to make,
so that when he has determined
   what is more salutary,
all will obey him.

6 Yet, just as it is proper for the
disciples to obey their master,

so it is fitting for the master
to arrange everything with
   foresight and fairness.

C 7 Therefore, in everything
all are to follow the Rule as their mistress,
and no one is to deviate rashly from it.
8 In the monastery no one is to follow his own
   heart's desire,

B'

9 and no one is to presume to
   argue
impudently with his abbot,
or outside the monastery.
10 Should anyone presume to do
   so,
let him be subjected to the
   discipline
of the Rule (*disciplina regularis*).

11 The abbot, however, must fear
   God and keep
the Rule in everything he does,
knowing that without doubt he
   will have to
give an account of all his
   judgments
(*iudicia*) to God, the most just of
   judges.

A' 12 If less important affairs of the monastery are to be treated, he is to
   take counsel with the seniors only,

13 as it is written: Do everything with counsel, and you will not be sorry
   afterwards (Prov 31:3 VL; Sir 32:24).

It is evident that the beginning and end of the chapter, A – A', are parallel. Verses 1-3 are matched by verses 12-13 at the end. Both passages contain the same train of thoughts: As often as anything is to be done in the monastery (*agenda sunt in monassterio*), counsel is needed (*consilium*). Then a biblical reason follows (v. 3 alluding to Matt 11:25; v. 13 from Wisdom literature). Some contrasts are inserted into these parallels: At first important matters (*praecipua*) are treated, later less important things (*minora*); at first the entire community is to be summoned to meet (*congregatio, fratres*), later only the seniors (*seniores*). In the first part, the reference to Sacred Scripture is only indirect with "for/because" (*quia* is often used for introducing a scriptural foundation) while the second part states explicitly "as it is written."

At the beginning and at the end we find not only the indispensible facts that concern the foundation and their basis in Sacred Scripture but also the manner of proceeding in the council, especially on the part of the abbot. Basically, these two sections would almost be enough. According to Borias, a chapter consisting of just verses 1-3 might have been sufficient. Only later might the council of seniors (vv. 12-13) have been added, harking back to an older tradition.[16] We could, however, also imagine a chapter having consisted of A and A'. In a second or third step, Benedict may have realized that he ought to add something about the manner of the brothers in giving counsel, as well as more about the pondering and acting on the abbot's part. The vocabulary used in B and B' indicates that these verses correspond mainly to the RB chapters that were written later (see below).

In B and B' Benedict addresses the brothers and the abbot in turn, verse 4 beginning with the brothers, verse 5 being addressed to the abbot, verse 6 beginning with the brothers and closing with an admonition to the abbot. These admonitions to both parties are characteristic of RB, as Vogüé points out in various parts of the Rule. Part B is matched by B' (vv. 9-11). Benedict first addresses the brothers, then the abbot. In both B and B' the brothers' part mentions the danger of "presuming" (*praesumere*) and of speaking boldly or impudently (*procaciter, proterve*), while in the abbot's part his judgment (*iudicare, iudicia*) is mentioned and how he is to arrange "everything" (*cuncta; omnia; de omnibus iudiciis suis*). Benedict seems to stand in the center between the abbot and the brothers, mediating and giving admonitions to the right and the left. Each part has its climax, the first in verse 6 and the second in verse 11. The beginnings of B and B' also match, speaking of presuming impudently or obstinately in verse 4 and verse 9.

In the center is a small part (C), verses 7-8, which concerns both the abbot and the brothers. In this core the beginning and the end again correspond to

16. Cf. Borias, "Comment."

each other: verse 7: "All are to follow the Rule as their mistress" has its counter-point in verse 8: "No one in the monastery is to follow his own heart's desire" (twice the word "follow," *sequi*). This central part (vv. 7-8) is especially radical: "in *every* instance . . . *all* are to follow . . . *no one* is to deviate . . . *no one* is to follow . . ." Abbot *and* brothers are in danger, both are admonished to obey, both are subject to the Rule. If at first glance the chapter seemed charming, we might by now feel disappointed with this nucleus. Why is it so negative and seemingly restrictive? Perhaps we would have preferred to see verse 3 as the high point, which emphasizes the democratic element. But our present concern is to let the statements of RB stand as they are raising questions in us.

This center part is connected to the entire chapter. It emphasizes, as does the entire chapter, the "all; no one; in every instance." It marks the danger expressed in the adverb *temere*—doing something rashly (which relates to "impudently" in v. 9 or "obstinately" in v. 4). Rashness is contrary to the fear of God (v. 11). The Rule appears again in verses 10 and 11. The word "follow" (*sequi*) or its opposite "deviate" (*declinare*) mark all three verses. The concern here is the guideline, the straight way, for coming as close as possible to the will of God.

These verses describe the basic attitude of the chapter, without which there is no common seeking of the will of God and no discernment. In Ignatian terms it might be called holy indifference. Benedict expresses this attitude as obedience which is based on open-minded listening. Self-will, selfishness, is the greatest enemy of the objective search for God's will. The danger of self-will exists not only in the brothers but also in the abbot. The guarantee for this objective listening and obeying lies for Benedict in the following of the Rule as master guide; the Rule is the fruit of *discretio* in the sense of making distinctions and observing moderation and trains in this essential attitude.[17]

The beginning of the sentences throughout the chapter reveal an author who is both resolute and reflecting, giving reasons (see for example the use of "therefore," "however," "but," "rather").

Taking a look at the semantic fields, we can see that the abbot is specifically named four times. Once he is given the title "master" (*magister*). Three times the term "he himself" (*ipse*) is used for him. This may already indicate how much weight is given to his person. Many actions of the abbot are stated: He includes the brothers, calls them together, explains, listens, ponders, acts, judges, arranges, does, knows, gives an account, uses, etc. This may be another correction in our dream for RB 3 as modeling a democratic assembly. All the verbs with the exception of "listen" (v. 2) are more or less active. Three times the word "do" occurs (vv. 1, 11, 13), three times the word "judge" (*iudicare* or *iudicia*, vv. 2, 5, 11). All this gives the chapter a rather energetic tone. But

17. See Böckmann, "Discretio."

it also stresses *how* the abbot ought to act: "providently and justly" (*provide et iuste*, v. 6), "in the fear of God and observing the Rule" (v. 11) and "with counsel" (v. 13). We might say: this is resolute acting, but with care and wisdom, with human deliberation as well as supernatural motivation!

What topics are to be treated in council? First the important affairs of the monastery are mentioned (v. 1), later the less important ones (v. 12). Benedict clearly distinguishes between the two types of councils. More striking, however, is the fact that the abbot is admonished to do *everything* justly, *all* in the fear of God, and *everything* with counsel, that is, not only the important matters (all three verses also state *how* the abbot should deal with everything: vv. 6, 11, 13). These three sentences have a significance that goes beyond the present context.

On the other side are the brothers: three times they are designated as "brothers" (*fratres*, in the title and in vv. 2, 4), three times as "all" (*omnes, cuncti*, vv. 1, 3, 4). They are also called "the entire community" (v. 1) or referred to in the singular as "no one" (v. 9). Among these brothers there are the younger and the older ones (vv. 3, 12). All are "disciples" (*discipuli*) in relation to the abbot-teacher (v. 6). We could say: Each brother is important, yet there is a certain ranking or order (which God can turn upside down).

Since on the abbot's part the action receives emphasis, it follows logically that on the side of the brothers receptivity is stressed. They are called (v. 3), they are to obey (vv. 5, 6). The only real active word for them is that they offer counsel (v. 4). The term "presume" (*praesumere*) is used three times about the brothers (vv. 4, 9, 10) but along with the comment that this is not to happen. Yet three times the statement is also made that all are taking part in the consultation (title, vv. 1, 4). On the one hand we sense a great respect for each brother, on the other the effort to keep the brothers within bounds, clearly warning them, after they have had their say, of the danger of insisting obstinately on their opinion. How are the brothers to act? "With all humility and obedience" (v. 4); twice they are told how not to talk: "stubbornly" (*procaciter*, v. 4) and "impudently" (*proterve*, v. 9). Again the emphasis is on safeguarding authority.

There is, however, one more agent. At first he is identified as the revealing Lord (v. 3), later as God, the most just judge (v. 11). This provides the perspective for the whole chapter. The council takes place in the presence of God the Lord who can take part by his revelations, but who, as the final judge, also sees and knows everything and to whom all of us are accountable. Concretely we can think of the great "council" of a papal election in the Sistine Chapel. On the wall in front of the cardinals is the very impressive painting of the Last Judgment. Yet the least person can be the gateway for God's revelation. Both statements are deliberately viewed together in this chapter.

Finally, in the core of the chapter (vv. 7-8), which deviates from the pattern, *all* are joined as one, both the abbot and the brothers, in their obedience to the Rule as their mistress teacher and with the warning that no one is to deviate from it carelessly so as to follow the will of his own heart. It seems that neither side is immune to such dangers.

The Rule is a help for finding the will of God more readily. How is this direction described? It is not always "what they think" (v. 4), what seems conspicuous and evident from one perspective. The abbot is to decide what is more "useful" (*utilius*, v. 2), or a little later, what he "considers more salutary" (*salubrius*, v. 5). The abbot is bound to seek the common good and needs to keep the entire community in view. But he also cannot solve all problems. The Lord reveals "what is better" (v. 3, *melius*). In my opinion this is an intensification. Human beings, including the abbot, can judge by human standards, aided by the fear of God, the Rule, and Sacred Scripture (*scriptum est*). But only the Lord knows what is truly "better." And here we again meet the paradox that a lowlier member may open the door to an inspiration for what is better, probably because he is open and less rigid and fixed in his thinking.

Chapter 3 is marked by opposites and contrasts:

The brothers should give their views

"with all humility and submission"— and not "defend them obstinately" (v. 4).

It is fitting for the disciple to obey— it is fitting for the Master to arrange everything justly and carefully (v. 6).

All are to observe the Rule,— they are not to deviate from it rashly (v. 7) or follow the desire of their own hearts (v. 8).

There is an awareness that finding the right way (the will of God) is no simple matter and that we can easily deviate from it to the right or the left. It is characteristic for Benedict the realist that his style is often marked by the expressions "not so," "but so," or "on one hand," and "on the other."

If we list all the elements mentioned at least three times in this chapter, we can find the essential components of community life:

God

Monastery

Brothers
Abbot (older/younger) Rule
all

council and giving counsel

Three types of acting are named three times: judging, doing, and as a negative not presuming. Also three times the manner of acting is described (vv. 4, 11, 13). As Vogüé has often pointed out, Benedict favors sets of three, indicating both dynamism and balance.

Since this chapter talks about many actions, a narrative sequence can be set up:

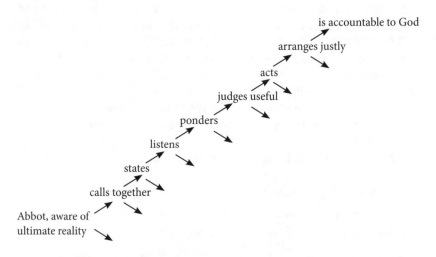

For the abbot RB 3 has only a positive sequence of actions. A new line begins wherever an (implied) decision has been made and where the next step could be different. We can add the potential negative at each point: knowing but not acknowledging; he does not call the brothers together; gives no information; does not listen; does not judge what is useful; does not ponder/consider but acts immediately; or does not act after considering. From verses 7-8 we can add: he easily departs from the Rule and follows the will of his own heart. These last remarks could be added to the narrative sequence.

What does such a narrative sequence look like from the brothers' side?

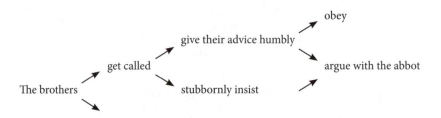

For the brothers, too, there are some possibilities for a decision. For example, they might not gather when called. In this short narrative sequence, the negative response of the brothers is mentioned twice. They could stubbornly insist on their own views and argue with the abbot. They, too, are to follow the Rule and not their own hearts, which again applies to the entire sequence (vv. 7-8).

In this chapter it is also instructive to examine the modality of the verbs. Most of them are admonitions in the subjunctive form, as is customary for Rules. But we also find some indicatives: When something important is to be done (*agenda sunt*, v. 1), when less important matters are concerned (*agenda sunt*, v. 12). The abbot explains the business at hand (*unde agitur*, v. 2). In this way the concrete reality with its problems and questions is placed before us.[18] Two more indicatives concern God's action or Sacred Scripture. The Lord often reveals (statement) to the younger one what is better (v. 3); this is a fact of faith. In verse 13: "It is written . . . you will not regret." This is a message of hope for the future which is proven and firm. We often find these two types of indicatives in the Rule concerning the strong reality of experience on the one hand and the truth of faith on the other.

The two Scripture references seem to be important hinges for the reality of the council. A wise word that stems from human experience and is passed on from generation to generation as a proverb concludes the chapter and serves as a firm foundation for RB 3. But human wisdom can also be turned upside down by an "inversion of values," especially by a principle from the New Testament (v. 3). As is often emphasized in the gospels, God can invert hierarchies and prefer the younger, the poor, and the powerless while placing the elders, the rich, and the powerful last.

CHAPTER 3 WITHIN THE RULE

RB 1.2 describes the cenobites as monks living in a monastery and serving under a Rule and an abbot. The second chapter deals with the abbot. Chapter 3 belongs to the basic structure of the monastic community. Both abbot and community are subject to the Rule. After chapter 3 follow the spiritual foundations: tools for good works, obedience, silence, and humility (RB 4–7). These virtues are already referred to in chapter 3 (cf. below). The structural elements connect our chapter with the preceding ones while the principal virtues link it with the chapters that follow.

When comparing chapter 3 with the Rule as a whole, we immediately are faced with the question of how the Rule was written. Is it possible that chapter 3 as a whole or in some parts was written as a later addition? Some notable

---

18. We also find indicative forms in the manner of wisdom literature in v. 6: "It is fitting for one—the other has the right/duty to." Yet these indicative forms are intended not only to state facts but also to inspire an appropriate conduct.

words in this chapter are quite interesting, occurring only here (*hapax*). On the one hand, one should decide what is more useful (*utilius*) or salutary (*salubrious*). On the other hand, the reality of arguing (*contendere*) or the manner of talking and acting is explicitly named only here and very negatively: stubbornly (*procaciter*), impudently (*proterve*), rashly or lightly (*temere*). We can well imagine that such experiences colored later revisions of the Rule. The remaining vocabulary resembles the last chapters of the Rule rather than the first ones. We recognize right away that many expressions are typical, especially for chapters 63–68.[19] Vogüé and Borias agree that this chapter shows traces of having been revised later on, probably when Benedict wrote chapter 65. Chapter 3 acquires a new significance when we realize that it probably was revised by Benedict after long experience.

The greatest similarity exists with chapter 65. There Benedict first emphasizes the abbot's authority concerning affairs of the monastery (following the long introduction in vv. 1-13). But then we note how the community "reasonably and humbly" (*rationabiliter cum humilitate*, v. 14b) requests a prior (presumably during an assembly). The abbot considers it good. Then with a smaller council, presumably with the seniors (in 65.15 referred to as "God-fearing brothers"), he selects a prior. Thus there were two consultations: by the entire "congregation," then by the seniors concerning the person. The admonitions to the prior and to the abbot mirror the alternating admonitions in RB 3. Just as in RB 3 all are bound to observe the Rule, so in RB 65 the prior is exhorted to "keep what the Rule commands" (65.17). Then in both chapters penalties are mentioned, and in the end the abbot is reminded that he is accountable to God for all of his judgments.

RB 3	RB 65:14-22
3.1-2 procedure	65.14-15 community and special council
3.4-6 alternative admonitions	65.15f. admonitions to brothers and prior
3.7-8 adhering to the Rule	65.17 adhering to the Rule
3.9 rebellious brothers	65.18 rebellious prior
3.10 process of penance	65.19-22 process of penance
3.11 abbot gives an account	65.22 abbot gives an account

Seeking the will of God also connects RB 3 with RB 68 which deals with difficult or even impossible commands. It shows that the superior has authority and that finally obedience in love must be the basic attitude. But there also are many indicators of how to speak and how to dialogue in order to

19. See Borias, "Comment," 34–37.

recognize God's will more readily: without resistance, without contradicting, without pride, but in humility and patience. This is very similar to RB 3.

RB 3 is also related to RB 2. The chapter on the abbot emphasizes his accountability at the Last Judgment (e.g., vv. 2, 6, 9f., 14f., 38ff.) speaking of the master and of the harmony between his knowing and his acting (e.g., vv. 2.1, 11-15). RB 3 completes this by stressing shared accountability and keeping the Rule. Yet RB 3 also reflects RB 1. It is interesting to consider the statements about the Sarabaites (1.6-9) and imagine how they would behave during a council meeting. Presumably they would not even attend since they are "without a shepherd, not enclosed in the Lord's sheepfold, but in their own" (1.8). They deceive themselves and others and lie to God (1.7). With respect to RB 3.4-6, we can imagine that their law is what they like to do, whatever strikes their fancy. Anything they believe in and choose, they call holy; anything they dislike, they consider forbidden (1.8-9). The nucleus in RB 3.7-8 has a parallel in RB 1.6: The Sarabaites have been tried neither by a Rule nor by the school of experience (*experientia magistra*) as gold is tried in a furnace (1.6). Cenobites are the opposite: with them one can take counsel.

Since in RB 3 people are speaking and listening, there is also an affinity to RB 6. "Speaking and teaching are the master's task; the disciple is to be silent and to listen"; this admonition is also basic to RB 3. Yet our chapter goes further and allows the disciple, even the younger person, to speak (cf. 3.6 below). When a matter is discussed with the superior, RB 6.7 states it should be done "in all humility and respectful submission," which is also expressed also in RB 3.4.

In all the initial chapters, from the Prologue to and including RB 7, self-will is seen as the great enemy of obedience and humility, even of monastic life as a whole and of cenobitic life in particular. Thus the core of RB 3 is very closely linked with the preceding and successive chapters. If Benedict inserted this chapter after RB 2 at a later time, he fitted it very skillfully into the whole.

COMPARISON OF THE ENTIRE CHAPTER WITH RM 2.41-50

The Master does not have a special chapter about the counsel of the brothers; he integrates it into the chapter on the abbot. It is clear that Benedict knew this passage. The abbot proceeds in an authoritarian manner; the brothers only may state their opinion when the abbot orders them to do so. If the advice of the brothers does not seem good to the abbot, he himself decides how he wishes after having justified his view. Matters for counsel seem to be chiefly material concerns, for "the affairs of the monastery are the concern of all and not of any one person" (2.48). This is a pragmatic reason, just as the first one given: "So many people—so many views" (2.47). A further reason is that each brother expects that eventually he may become a successor of the abbot (2.49). Thus, each one must, of course, feel responsible!

Benedict took the institution of the council of the brothers and some expressions from RM, but in spirit he moves far away from it. Benedict's abbot is a listener. His pondering and weighing are more strongly stressed. The abbot is bound by the fear of God and by the Rule. Benedict seems to have far more experiences of council meetings; he also points out *how* one is and is not to speak. He holds both abbot and brothers to observing the Rule and forbids both sides to be guided by their own will. Finally Benedict does not justify the counsel with human principles but refers to the Bible. Thereby he shows more clearly that humans can decide what is useful and salutary, but that the Lord reveals what is better. Although Benedict may seem too authoritarian for us today, he is far more "democratic" than RM.

Recalling the monastic tradition in which Benedict stood, he proves to be one who listened to the various movements of his time, one who critically selects and uses discretion. Simplifying, we could describe his evolution thus: he turns away from his direct source (RM) and turns to the spirit of Holy Scripture. The Bible gives him two principles, one expressing human wisdom, the other relating to the paradox of God as agent who can overturn our human arrangements and can choose the least person as his mouthpiece.

Title: That the brothers are to be called for counsel (*De adhibendis ad consilium fratribus*).

The chapter title is written from the abbot's perspective, for it follows the chapter on the abbot and completes it. He does not govern alone but shall consult the brothers. The word *ad-hibere* literally means "to have them with him" (*ad-habere*).[20] It indicates that for recognizing what is best for the community, the abbot needs help; he needs each of the brothers, both for the group that gives counsel and for the function of giving counsel.[21]

Verses 1-3 are carefully crafted and directed at the climax of this part in verse 3. First the external circumstances are described, then the abbot's activities follow in their logical sequence—together with the aim of "what seems most useful to him"—and in verse 3 the reason follows. These initial verses already contain the important elements of the chapter *in nuce*.

V. 1: As often as anything important is to be done in the monastery, the abbot is to call the whole community together and to explain himself what

---

20. This word is also used in connection with the remedies for healing a sick brother (28.4) and for bringing in the bishop as a witness (62.9).

21. The Latin word *consilium* can designate both the group that is meeting (council) and the counsel that is given. In the chapter title it could have both meanings.

the business is. (*Quotiens aliqua praecipua agenda sunt in monasterio, convocet abbas omnem congregationem et dicat ipse unde agitur.*)

What might Benedict have considered as important (*praecipua*) matters that concern the whole community and for which each time (*quotiens*) the entire community is summoned for counsel? The Rule gives us some information. In chapter 65 it is the question of needing or desiring a prior; in 62.6 of assigning a higher rank to a priest; it may also be for faults that are confessed before the abbot and the community (46.3). Probably we may also include acceptance for profession, new foundations, sale of a house, excommunication, etc. Thus these matters are not only material affairs (note the difference to RM).[22] The community, which is to be called together in its entirety, is named *con-gregatio*. It is the actual assembly, the flock with its shepherd. Right at the beginning the importance of each one is already emphasized. No one is to be missing. After this initial preparatory act of the abbot, we can visualize the monastic community as present before us.

We recognize five steps (cf. narrative sequence, p. 174). Verses 1-2 describe various actions that are psychologically well graded.

1. *The abbot himself explains what the business is;* he himself begins and gives information. Generally one can assume that he is well informed about current problems. Information means power which is now being shared. Nowadays the superior might delegate someone who is better informed or who is a specialist in an area. The abbot does not say what he wants or hopes for, but he explains the situation and what is at stake (*unde agitur*). Stating a problem or important matter as objectively as possible is an art. The superior thereby also shows that he sincerely wants the brothers to share his responsibility.

V. 2: And listening to the brothers' counsel, let him consider it and then do what he judges the most useful course. (*Et audiens consilium fratrum tracted apud se et quod utilius iudicaverit faciat.*)

2. *Listening to the brothers' counsel;* the word *audire* is often (explicitly) used in connection with Holy Scripture and with obedience as well as with regard to the signal for the Divine Office. Here in RB 3 the abbot is shown as a listener, a trait lacking in RM. It is a listening for the will of God that may be revealed even to the least of the bothers (cf. 3.3). In RB we often see the abbot (implicitly) as a listener: In RB 68 he listens to the brother and his difficulties; in RB 61.4 he listens to a guest monk who voices a criticism and asks himself "whether the Lord has sent him for this very purpose"; in RB 65

22. See Hilpisch, "Rat," 225–30.

he listens to the community's request for a prior, even though he himself is convinced that the appointment of a prior is not good (65.14-15). Benedict himself is such a listening abbot. He listens to the difficulties of the monks who cannot be convinced that wine is not suitable for monks (40.6), or to the difficulties of the brothers in praying so many psalms in a day (18.22-25). He listens, so to speak, in every direction—to the brothers, the local situation, the climate; ultimately, he is listening to Holy Scripture, by which God's will is made known. Listening then becomes obeying; indeed, hearing and listening in its full sense already includes obeying (cf. Prol 1-3).

3. *Let him ponder/consider it.* Whereas RM 2:42 states that "there is a general discussion," here the concern is with an interior action in the abbot. Pondering it within himself (*apud se*)—this expression reminds us of monk's "due reflection" before making profession (58.14). The abbot listens to his own heart, in the center, where he stands before God. Later Gregory used a similar term to describe Benedict, *habitare secum*: he lived alone with himself (Dial. III.5).

The Latin verb *tractare* means weighing, considering all angles, being busy with something, discussing, but also meditating. It occurs only one more time in RB: When a visiting monk has with reason and humility expressed some criticism, the abbot should consider prudently (*tractet prudenter*), whether the Lord has not sent him for this very purpose (61.4). In the heart one can perceive whether the Lord speaks in such words. *Tractare* occurs in the Vulgate in connection with the heart (Sir 9:1, cf. 1 Kgs 9:18). In other chapters of the Rule Benedict used the word *considerare*—to take into account, to weigh—being chiefly concerned about listening to the weaker persons.[23]

4. *After this interior process follows the judging (iudicare).* The word occurs once more in verse 5 for the abbot, "when he has determined (judged) what is more salutary." And he must, according to verse 11, give an account to God for all his judgments and decisions. Benedict seems to be very fond of the word *utilius*[24] whenever he wants to have a situation evaluated in the light of God, following certain criteria. He is concerned to find what is better (18.22), what is salutary and liberating (65.14), and what is useful (32.2). According to the abbot's task, it is assumed that he will judge problems in view of the common good. Although the word is normally used for an activity of the abbot, we also find it used in RB 72, the climax of the Rule, as an activity for the monk: "No one is to pursue what he judges useful for himself, but instead, what he judges useful better for someone else" (RB 72.7, the core of the chapter). Apparently the brothers also are capable of judging (which

---

23. Cf. RB 37; 34; 48.25; 55.21.
24. With one exception, it occurs only in the texts ascribed to Benedict.

seems not to be true for the brothers in RM). This development in RB is extended today as we expect more than in earlier times that each member have a good measure of judgment, also in regard to community consultations.

To judge more useful—The Master, speaking of *utilitas monasterii* in the parallel section (2.41, 42, 45), seems to limit himself to material usefulness. In RB as a whole (cf. also the chapters on receiving members), usefulness pertains not only to the community's material matters but also to its supernatural goal.[25] In the chapter on the abbot, 2.33-36, Benedict inserted that the abbot, in the very instance when the monastery lacks resources, must not neglect the salvation of souls, for this ought to be his chief concern.

5. *And follow what he judges the wiser course (faciat).* In the Latin version the verb is deliberately placed at the end of the sentence and shows Benedict's energetic character. We already noted how this chapter emphasizes doing (cf. vv. 11, 13). One can conduct lengthy meetings and keep debating back and forth, but in the end, someone (the abbot) must have the courage to risk doing something, even though not everything is fully clarified and not yet all are sharing the same view. On the other hand, if the will to take action is lacking, we may use all the techniques of discernment and yet block the way for finding God's will that can be found only by those who are ready to fulfill it and to accept and bear the consequences. This approach to action is missing in RM. The Master only says that the abbot, when no clear advice is given, is free to decide as he wishes (2.47).

Thus there are five stages: stating, listening, considering, judging, and acting. Stating and listening can be seen as part of the basic search for information. Considering and judging are related. The last step is giving orders and acting. These three basic steps are contained in all the modern forms of communal discernment, though developed in different ways. This may be a good place for reflecting on modern discernment and comparing it with RB 3.[26] We may get the impression that this method could easily be applied, yet we may not immediately realize how challenging RB 3 is and how many basic conditions are presupposed (cf. vv. 4-6).

V. 3: The reason why we have said all are to be called for counsel is that the Lord often reveals what is better to the younger. (*Ideo autem omnes ad consilium vocari diximus quia saepe iuniori dominus revelat quod melius est.*)

After having used pedagogical wisdom, Benedict now gives reign to the spirit of faith. The ultimate reason for calling everyone for counsel is the

25. Cf. Borias, "Utilité."
26. See Böckmann, "Discretio," 366–73.

Lord's action. "Therefore" (*ideo*)—this introduction was repeated four times in the short text of RM (2.41-52), but with human, practical reasoning, for example: "Therefore, however . . . so many people so many opinions" (2.44); "therefore all shall be called . . . because the affairs of the monastery are the concern of all and not of any one person" (2.48). All the more we note Benedict's different motivation. In 63.6 he says that Samuel and Daniel in their youth had judged their elders. In 64.2 we read that even the youngest might be chosen as abbot of the monastic community. Benedict knows very well that God can overturn our normal ranking of values, as is shown repeatedly in the course of salvation history: the younger are preferred to the elder, the poor are chosen rather than the rich, and the children are placed ahead of the adults.

The small and insignificant person can be more easily the gateway for God's inspiration. In a similar manner, a Desert Father might have gone to a child in order to be told God's will. If God could open the mouth of Balaam's donkey to convey his message to the prophet, how much more can he manifest his will to us through any human person, even the least. It is reported that once a community of baptists held a council meeting. Among the members there was a child of ten years. When all were ready to depart after the decision had been made, the leader recalled all the members and made them aware that they had not listened to the child. When we listen even to the youngest in our consultations, it will make us respectful and open to everyone.[27] The younger one need not be the youngest. Unlike RM, Benedict often mentions the younger in relation to the senior, the younger members whom one shall love (4.71; 63.10), the younger monk whom one respects as well and whom one calls "brother" (63.12).

Here Benedict also clearly speaks of the Lord's "revealing." The Latin word literally means taking away the veil, the cover (*velum*). It does not occur anywhere in RB in this sense (nor in RM, but in Matt 11:25, 27, Vulgate). God has revealed it to the little ones and has concealed it from the clever; no one knows the Father, except the ones to whom the Son wishes to reveal it. The Gospel paradox, however, is also not unknown in human experience. Older persons love to argue from tradition. "That's how it was always done." Theirs is wisdom and life experience. The younger members tend to be more flexible, open to new ideas, not bound by historical prejudice. Thus it is good

---

27. Cassian, *Conf.* 16.12: "it often happens that a person who has a sharper wit and a broader knowledge conceives something false in his mind, while a person who has a slower wit (*tardioris ingenii*) and less prestige perceives something more correctly and truly. Therefore no one, however well endowed with knowledge should persuade himself with empty pride that he does not need anyone else's advice."

to hear both the counsel of the elders, human wisdom (vv. 12-13), and also the younger ones (v. 3), possibly a shocking novelty. Benedict points the way to "both and."

"What is better" is set as an intensification against what is more useful (v. 2) and what is more salutary (v. 5). Only the Lord knows what is truly better for the community. We can only hope to approach what is more useful, not what is better. Therefore in such meetings, prayer and openness to God's ideas and surprises are absolutely necessary.[28]

V. 4: The brothers, on their part, are to express their counsel with all humility and submission, not presuming to defend their own views obstinately. (*Sic autem dent fratres consilium cum omni humilitatis subiectione, et non praesumant procaciter defendere quod eis visum fuerit.*)

After the supernatural principle of verse 3, which highlights the younger one, some sobering admonitions follow. Some later copyists of the Rule, however, seemed to have found it shocking that the brothers were really allowed to speak; thus one version reads: In this manner the brothers should "listen" to counsel.[29]

The word "submission"—*subiectio*—only occurs one more time in 6.7. Requesting something of the superior, one "ought to do so in all humility and respectful submission" (a sentence added by Benedict in RB 6, which was taken from RM 8). A basic prerequisite for finding the will of God is the readiness to submit not only to what the abbot may command but also to what is decided by the community. The latter might be more difficult. In RB 3 submitting is seen together with humility (genetive of identity or *genetivus epexegeticus*). Moreover there is added emphasis: "with all (submission of) humility," which is similar to the attitude toward God in 20.1-2, "with humility and reverence, with all humility and purity of surrender." The artisans are to practice their craft "with all humility" (57.1). The guests are to be met "with all humility" (53.6). It would be worthwhile to examine how necessary humility seems to Benedict, not only in prayer and relating to God but also in mutual relationships, how it makes them fruitful and how it helps the community to grow and progress.[30]

The second part of the verse states the negative. The brothers are not to presume to defend their own views obstinately. There is an ongoing

---

28. According to Ignatius of Loyola, one might consider the view of a younger person based on revelation, a grace, not due to a previous cause. Cf. *Spiritual Exercises*, no. 175.

29. For differing versions, cf. Hanslik, 29–31.

30. All the preceding citations are Benedict's own texts.

discussion about the word *praesumere*.[31] From its root the word means to take something ahead of time, to take something for oneself before the time. It can also mean to set one's foot on another person's land, to confront another with an accomplished fact, to force one's will on another, to be arrogant, or to claim something without legal basis. In RM the word is used in a concrete sense of not taking food ahead of time (e.g., 21.8; 83.6). The use of *praesumere* seems to express the characteristics of a monastic epoch or possibly the psychology of the legislators. Benedict uses the term thirty-three times independently from RM. Miquel holds that this fact shows some strong personalities in Benedict's communities. Since he granted greater freedom (than, for example, RM), the danger of presumption on the brothers' part might have been greater.

What did the brothers presume or insist on? There were, first of all, things which one would claim for oneself without permission of the lawful authority (54; 33); one might act without proper authority, e.g., to punish or beat others (69; 70), or someone might proudly lead the singing (47). How such presumption affected a council meeting in practice can be easily imagined; also how such behavior might affect shy and sensitive brothers or the abbot.

Something can also be obstinately defended (*procaciter defendere*). The word *defendere* occurs once more in the same sense in RB 28.2, where the guilty one wants to defend his bad deeds. There may also be the case of defending another.[32] Romans 12:19 admonishes Christians not to defend themselves. The word *procax* means brash, insolent, shameless, obstinate. In RB 3 it is not a case of a good defense of rights or facts. A person whose arguments are not convincing needs to defend something obstinately and brashly. There are indications that such a person is not sincere, not trying to seek God's will together with others. Such a person is working against others and against authority, trying to impress or make others afraid, seemingly he is unwilling to submit. Benedict implies that such a person lacks humility.

This sentence of RB 3 is very pertinent for our communal deliberations today. As soon as someone starts insisting obstinately and impudently, the

---

31. Steidle in "Parrhesia" (44–61) thinks that *praesumptio* is a translation of the Greek term for parrhesia—frank speech or freedom of speech. A monk lacking this freedom would mean he is not a free human being but a slave without rights, not even the right to speak freely. Miquel, *"praesumere"* (424–36) first discusses the view of Christine Mohrmann (425) that the word comes rather from the Christian late Latin (cf. *Sacramentarium Leonianum*, Cassian and Caesarius), and has a generally negative meaning. Miquel concludes that the word seems to come neither from the liturgy, nor from law or the Bible, but from monastic experience and seems to be characteristic of the lawmakers of this epoch (436). Cf. also Zorzi, "Vivere."

32. RB 69, T,1; cf. Basil, *Reg* 26.

common seeking for God's will can easily become a struggle for the victory of certain persons rather than a concern for the will of God. To avoid the danger of defending something stubbornly, polemically, and obstinately, we do well to ask ourselves whether we would be ready to do the opposite of what we passionately desire, if that were God's will. If we are not ready, we can pray for this grace.

Defending something obstinately refers to that which "seems" good to the brothers (*quod eis visum fuerit*). It is only a part of the truth, and it is probably for this reason that there is the danger of defending it. Certainly we can only judge by appearances most of the time. The term "seems" occurs a number of times in RB in this sense.[33] To complement what seems right to us, we need the opinions of others. We must ask how they see the matter in order to come nearer to the truth. This requires accepting our human limits, or in older monastic terms, being humble.

V. 5: The decision is rather the abbot's to make, so that when he has determined what is more salutary, all will obey. (*Et magis in abbatis pendat arbitrio, ut quo salubrius esse iudicaverit ei cuncti oboediant.*)

When Benedict says that the decision is rather (*magis*) for the abbot to make, he is here more cautious than in the other situations in which he simply states that the abbot decides, for example, to judge the gravity of an offense (24.2) or to assign posts (65.11). For Benedict this seems to be a kind of juridical formula, used also in Cassian but not in RM.[34] *Arbitrium* denotes basically a subjective judgment.[35] Thus the abbot judges when the heat is great or when the situation requires giving the brothers more food or drink (*in arbitrio*, 39.6; 40.5). Such texts do not show tyrannical decisions on the part of the abbot but his weighing and judging of what is best for the common good so that the weak are not discouraged and the strong find what they need (cf. 64.19). Benedict is quite realistic: Someone must have the last word.

The word *salubrius*—more salutary—occurs only here; it is related to health, well-being, and salvation (*salus*). In other chapters this idea is

---

33. As it seems to the abbot: 2.19; if the candidate seems to bear the difficulties patiently: 58.3; if the brother who received a difficult command sees that it exceeds his measure: 68.2; or when it seems to the artisan that he is conferring a benefit on the monastery: 57.2.

34. Cassian, *Conf.* 24.16.14: "They remain in monasteries and are governed by the commands of elders; they act not according to their own judgment, but depend on the will of the abbot." Similarly, Sulpicius Severus had emphasized that the monks depend on the authority of the abbot (*Dial* 1.10).

35. Herwegen, 113.

described as follows: The abbot "is to regulate and arrange all matters . . . so that souls may be saved and the brothers may go about their activities without justifiable grumbling" (41.5). The abbot should prune faults "as he sees best for each one" (64.14); the Latin word *ex-pedit* could also be translated: how it helps him to pull his foot out of the snare, that is, how it frees him.[36]

All are to obey the abbot (*ei cuncti oboediant*). The readiness to obey is a condition for discernment. Even those who do not agree or who previously held a different view must be ready to submit at last to the result of the community consultation, to accept it in obedience. Chapter 68, which deals with impossible or difficult commands, closes in a similar manner with the word *oboediat*: he is to obey. What is said in 68.5 also applies to RB 3: "Trusting in God's help, he must obey in love." The individual brother has contributed all he could, stating his view, listening, perhaps modifying his view, supporting what seemed right to him, keeping himself open to the will of God; now he needs to obey, even if the outcome does not suit him or seems inappropriate to him.

We can find so many reasons for excusing ourselves from obedience. RB 4.61 says, "Obey the [abbot's] orders unreservedly, even if his own conduct—which heaven forbid—be at odds with what he says." Regarding a chapter meeting one might translate it thus: I can subject myself even when I think these or those brothers pushed through their own views from bad motives or insisted on certain ideals which they themselves are unwilling to live. To obey means living with the decision for the time being, trying it out with good will. If great difficulties appear, we can suggest reconsideration of the issue. Obedience, as RB 3 clearly shows, creates community. It is rendered in love, for love of Christ, but also for love of the community and for its oneness. Obedience, as in RB 68, is not blind but seeing, and for this reason may be all the more difficult.

Benedict emphasizes that *all* are to obey. No one is to exempt or excuse himself. In our time we experience on an international level that armistices and agreements are made but that the appropriate actions do not follow. Everything continues as if no negotiation or summit had taken place at all. Such an attitude could also be found in a monastery: "Let them decide as they please; I won't abide by it but will do what I think is good." If one or two monastics exempt themselves from obedience in this way, the whole community and future chapter meetings will suffer very negative consequences.

Benedict, living in the sixth century, placed strong emphasis on the abbot's authority. Today, according to constitutions and declarations, much of this authority is vested in corporate bodies. We distinguish between consulta-

---

36. RM twice mentions counsel that is healing and for the soul's benefit (87.12 and 91.48, *salubre consilium*).

tive chapters, which do not juridically bind the superior to the opinion of the community, and deliberative chapters. In this latter case, according to modern law, the chapter stands above the superior. But this does not make obedience easier for the individual.

While Benedict entrusts the final decision to the superior, he also requires much from the superior, especially that he be concerned about the common good and give real consideration to the weaker members. In this context, some admonitions of RB 64 can be added as an explanation. For example, the abbot must be well versed in Sacred Scripture, selfless, sober and merciful, prudent and loving, and seeking to be loved rather than feared. "He must not be excitable, anxious, extreme, obstinate, jealous, or overly suspicious. He must show forethought and consideration in his orders. In his orders he is to be farsighted and level headed. In spiritual as well as secular matters he is to be discerning and moderate . . . heeding the examples of discretion, the mother of virtues. He must arrange everything so that the strong have something to yearn for and the weak nothing to run away from" (64.16-19; 64:9-14).

V. 6: Yet just as it is proper for disciples to obey their master, so it is also fitting for the master to arrange everything with foresight and fairness. (*Sed sicut discipulos convenit oboedire magistro, ita et ipsum provide et iuste condecet cunca disponere.*)

This sentence is a masterpiece of Benedict's rhetoric.[37] The verse is a pleasing contrast to the parallel text in RM 2.47: "But if none of the brothers can give apt counsel, then let the abbot, after explaining his reasons, decide as he wills, and it is right that the members follow the head." In RB the two sides are named "disciples" and "master." With one exception, Benedict uses the word "disciple" only when following RM; we can safely say that it isn't his favorite word.[38] Its use here is probably a reminder of 6.6. It is the closest parallel to 3.6:

3.6	6.6
Just as it is for the disciples to obey	b. the disciple is to be silent and listen
so it is proper for the master	a. it is proper for the master to speak and to teach
to arrange everything with	
foresight and fairness.	

37. Caesarius in his *RegMon* 16 uses a sentence worded similarly: "Just as it is holy that they possess no property, so it is just that they receive from the holy abbot whatever they need."

38. After chapter 6, he uses it only one more time; in chapter 7 he always uses another term for the word "disciple." Benedict likewise avoids words that smack of school.

In 3.6 Benedict starts with the disciple, in 6.6 with the master. For the master he uses the term "it is proper" (*condecet*, which seems the stronger term to me). He speaks and decides, but he is also admonished to practice foresight and fairness. The disciple's part "is" (*convenit*)[39] silence, listening, and obeying. One builds on the other. Chapter 3 goes beyond RB 6, however, for the younger has spoken, not only kept silent; because he listened, he was able to give counsel, and this in humility and obedience. He has done what in chapter 6 is not yet permitted to him. The master,[40] here the abbot, has spoken and taught but also kept silence and listened. RB 3 indicates a later stage of RB revision than does RB 6, and we may assume that 3.6 was meant to correct the earlier verse 6.6.

The abbot is to organize, regulate, command, and arrange. Thus Benedict himself arranged the psalmody for the various hours of the Office (18.20: *disponere*). The abbot is to arrange (*disponere*) everything so that souls will be saved (41.5) and he is to arrange nothing unfairly (63.3: *disponere*). In RM this is not stated so emphatically about the abbot. The word occurs in the Latin Bible primarily in the Wisdom literature. Wisdom orders everything strongly and lovingly (*disponens omnia fortiter, suaviter* [Wis 8:1]). Summarizing, we can say that these and other texts about the abbot show that according to Benedict, the abbot should be a wise person.

"With foresight" (*provide*) is always used for the abbot in RB. It should be in the abbot's foresight to order everything in such a way that it serves for the well-being of the brothers (41.4-5). He must show foresight and consideration in all his orders (64.17). This word also occurs primarily in the Latin Wisdom literature of the Bible. Foresight is especially required for a leader. The superior must think of the direction and the future of the whole community. A decision might seem hard at the moment but more merciful in view of the future.

"Just" (*iuste*)! The same warning, though expressed in negative terms, occurs in 63.2: "The abbot is not to disturb the flock entrusted to him nor make any unjust arrangements (*iniuste disponat*), as though he had the power to do whatever he wished." A similar expression is inserted in 2.19 from Benedict's own pen: "for reasons of justice" (when he considers it just), the abbot may change a monk's rank. Justice is a typically Roman virtue and means that one gives to everyone what he needs.

RB 3.6 makes great demands on the abbot: to arrange everything with foresight, with the long view toward the human and divine future, with justice, without human favoritism, without fearing the elders, but in a manner

---

39. Both terms, *condecet* and *convenit*, only occur in RB in 3.6 and 6.6.
40. *Magister* only recurs until RB 6, then Benedict no longer uses it.

that promotes the common good and the welfare of the individual. Today, when every member is responsible to help with planning, these demands also apply to everyone.

Verses 7-8 are the nucleus of the whole chapter and are very carefully constructed:

7 A In every instance all	B are to follow	C the Rule as their mistress
A' and no one	B' is to deviate from it	C' rashly
8 A" No one in the monastery	B" is to follow	C" his own heart's desire

Some manuscripts have introduced changes into the text. One says to follow the Rule as master (instead of the Rule as mistress).[41] The following verse 8 reads logically that no one is to deviate from him, that is, the master (instead of: her, the mistress = Rule). In verse 7 one manuscript says: No one may deviate "from this way" (instead of rashly; *itinere* instead of *temere*). Perhaps the word rashly sounded too daring in referring to all, monks and also abbot. Most of these changes show how difficult people found it in later times to sustain this coresponsibility, how easily the abbot could take more power and authority to himself. How can anyone write in the text of the Rule that even the abbot should follow it as his mistress! But all the more the original text highlights the spirit of Benedict.

V. 7: Therefore, in everything, all are to follow the Rule as their mistress, and no one is to deviate rashly from it. (*In omnibus igitur omnes magistram sequantur regulam, neque ab ea temere declinetur a quoquam.*)

The word used here for "therefore" (*igitur*) occurs only one more time in RB 63.10, as the summary of the first part: "The younger monks therefore (*igitur*) must respect their seniors, and the seniors must love their juniors." It is one small indication that these are Benedict's own words. (The word does not occur in RM.)

The Rule as mistress (magistram . . . regulam). The feminine counterpart to the master (RB 6.3) here is the Rule. In RB 1.6 experience is called the teacher, the mistress. "The sarabaites are not tested by any Rule as mistress of experience, like gold is tested in a furnace." It is interesting that RM 1 does not know this word and in the very same place speaks of experience as the master (*experientia magistro*). This, like the alternate versions of RB 3.7, gives

---

41. In Latin this reads *omnes magistri sequantur regulam* (instead of *magistram sequantur regulam*). One small change of just two letters has changed much of the meaning! Cf. also n32 in the chapter on RB 1.

the abbot more power. The intention of 3.7 is certainly to limit the abbot's power; he, too, is under the authority of the Rule. The master mentioned in the preceding verse has a mistress. She is born from experience with people, with tradition, from contact with Sacred Scripture, and above all with God.

RB 1 states the negative side of 3.7: The sarabaites pen themselves up in their own sheepfolds and do whatever strikes their fancy; they follow neither the master nor the mistress as their norm (see RB 1.6-9). But if we truly seek God's will, we need a norm and a mistress. Otherwise we would be disregarding the tradition and God's salvific plan, who has given us Sacred Scripture and rules of conduct to help.

Regula denotes a ruler or tool for drawing straight lines or erecting walls vertically. So the Rule helps us live straight lives. In the manuscripts of the Rule we read after the list of titles and before chapter 1: *Regula appellatur ab hoc quod oboedientium dirigat mores.* "It is called a Rule because it directs, makes straight the conduct and way of life of those who obey." It seems then that in 3.7 the Rule specifically means the Rule of Benedict. In comparison with RB 7.55 (referring to the common Rule of monasteries) this expression implies at least the approximate end stage of Benedict's revisions of the Rule. As shown above, RB 3 as a whole is more directly related to the last chapters of the Rule and in its present form might have been written at about the same time as RB 65.

The word "follow" (*sequi*) in its concrete sense is used a few more times in RB. One follows Christ: Prologue 7; 4.10. This is done practically by following in obedience the voice of the person giving the command (5.8), by seeking peace and pursuing it (Prol 17), and finally, by following what will truly benefit another (72.7). When we act in this manner, the Rule is really our mistress and will lead us to none other than Christ himself.

"*In everything . . . all (in omnibus . . . omnes)*" is a very radical expression and with its intensity is also the climax of the chapter. Benedict here touches on something that is truly essential and therefore quite radical. Everyone, the abbot as well as the brothers, are to follow the Rule in everything and must make no exceptions. In RB 3 this means, for example: The abbot must each time call everyone when weighty affairs are to be decided; he must listen, must arrange things fairly and with foresight; the brothers shall humbly state their views and obey. One must pay attention whether the Lord might not manifest his will to a younger member.

"*And no one is to deviate from it rashly.*" This is the same radicality expressed in the negative. "No one," that is, neither the abbot nor an older nor a younger member.[42] "Rashly" (*temere*) means at random, blindly, without

---

42. In this verse the singular form begins, also concerning the brothers.

considering, without reason. Might one interpret this to mean that at times one might deviate for an important reason? In the entire Rule we see that the abbot adapts the regulations according to circumstances. Benedict has great regard for *epikeia*, i.e., the reasonable treatment of specific situations not specifically foreseen in the Rule or any law. To me this interpretation seems justified. One deviates from a written document to meet the current situation by following the criteria of the Rule as a guide but applying it differently to the present. This then is no "rash" deviating, no disobedience.[43] Other interpreters feel that here any deviating from the Rule is called "rash action"; this is, however, a bold assertion. Basil[44] calls the words spoken by Peter when he did not want Jesus to wash his feet "rash" and "presumptuous." It was self-will and presumption. Such reactions are forbidden in RB 3. Rashness is related to presumption and the desire to follow one's own ways and wishes. Cassian[45] speaks of a young person who started monastic life "rashly and carelessly" (*temere incauteque*); he lacked discretion. *Temere* is the opposite of counsel, prudence, following the Rule, foresight, and fairness. One should carefully consider: Must one really deviate from the Rule in this case? "Deviate" (*declinare*) is used one more time in the Rule in the sense of turning toward what is evil (7.29 and in this sense, oftener in the RM). When we do not strive for what is good, we decline (decadence; cf. also RB 73).[46]

V. 8: In the monastery no one is to follow his own heart's desire. (*Nullus in monasterio proprii sequator cordis voluntatem.*)

This "no one" (*nullus*) again pertains to the abbot as well as the brothers. "In the monastery" concretely implies all of the monks, for even when a monk is outside the enclosure (v. 9) or on a journey, he should not follow his own will.

"*His own heart's desire*": from the context of the chapter it means self-will, stubbornness, egotism, wanting to dominate (vv. 4, 9). Someone only thinks of his own benefit, not the well-being of the community.[47] The word "own"

---

43. Already Smaragdus interpreted this in a broad sense: One may deviate with reason and discretion, "and with great care and out of necessity" (*rationabiliter et cum discretione, cum magna cautela et pro necessitate*). (157)

44. *Reg* 184.

45. *Conf.* 2.6.3.

46. Cf. Böckmann, *Perspektives*, 90–91.

47. In the first part of the Rule, until chapter 7, self-will is always used in the negative sense. One must renounce self-will (Prol 3), even hate it, i.e., not love it (7.31, 4.60), and relinquish it (5.6; 7.12, 19). In nearly all of these texts Benedict follows RM. In the second part, however (RB 8–73), self-will is positive in one instance. The monk voluntarily offers God something from his own initiative, his own will (RB 49.6). As the negative counterpart, one might recall RM that is branding self-will as a bad enemy in the

in the first part of RB is nearly always negative in meaning and is usually used with self-will; in the second part we find it also in the sense of individual property that one exempts from what belongs to all. But it can also be positive, for example, when one's "own gift" is used for others (40.1), or when something is joyfully offered to God "of one's own free will" (49.6).

In verse 8 it is the heart that has its own will and is not concerned with the well-being of the whole community and the will of God. Benedict does not think of the human person as having good and evil parts. The heart can be capable of the noblest sentiments, such as love of God, of truth, of purity, and intense devotion (4.1; 52; 20), but from it also come evil thoughts (4.24), murmuring (5.17f.), arrogance, and here self-will. Self-will is only linked to the heart in RB 3 in a text proper to Benedict. The author seems intent to emphasize that a person's interior is the center of all these negative and positive drives and dynamisms. The egotistical heart is contrasted with the obedient heart that is open to God and is here marked by the will to serve the common good. The common good is concretely served through the will to follow the common Rule.[48]

Basically, verses 7-8 challenge our will's readiness to seek God with the community under the Rule and the abbot. In the context of seeking the will of God, Benedict could simply have said: No one shall follow only his own thoughts and opinions. But he addresses the fundamental problem by asking from where such behavior comes; he is concerned about the human heart. The root of the barriers that prevent the common seeking is here: in the heart that is not obedient to God. "Thy will be done"—this must be the basic attitude of heart in all participants, both in prayer and in all of life and therefore now in the communal decision-making.

Verses 7-8 point out two ways: one can follow the way of community, that is, the Rule (cf. 1.2), or the will of one's own heart, one's own desires (cf. 1.6, 11).

VV. 9-11

In this fourth section of the chapter, there are more admonitions to both sides, yet only once to a brother and once to the abbot, but they are all the more emphatic. The brother's conduct is set against the conduct desired of the abbot. The obstreperous brother is described as confronting the abbot. The abbot, for his part, is placed beyond the human level, standing before God.

---

chapters on receiving members. Self-will is always negative in RM. Benedict does not seem to hold the same opinion, but he requires that even the positive self-will be subject to the abbot's approval (RB 49).

48. Regarding "heart" (*cor*), cf. Böckmann, "Mensch," 44f.

V. 9: and no one is to presume to contend with his abbot defiantly, or outside the monastery. (*neque praesumat quisquam cum abate suo proterve out foris monasterium contendere.*)

At first Benedict seems still to be thinking of the council meeting but then extends the situation to include a case outside the monastery. Perhaps this verse is still inspired by verse 8: Where can self-will lead? Someone contends obstinately with his own abbot, not only with the brothers but also with his abbot and this even in the presence of everyone. The abbot is "his" abbot, destined for him, but the brother arrogantly claims a right he does not have.

The word "contend" (*contendere*) is used only here in RB, but the noun is found also in RB 4.68: "Do not love quarreling" (thus also in RM). A brother may also be quarrelsome (71.5); he is to be admonished. The Latin word *contendere* is used for a string instrument when its strings are tightened. All one's energy is exerted for something that is passionately desired. Of course, we may do this for the will of God; yet no one owns God's will, all are seeking it, and each one sees only a portion. Whoever quarrels fanatically wants to push through the part he sees (cf. defend in v. 4). In the Bible, the word *contendere* often occurs in a negative sense. Second Timothy 2:14 admonishes: "Do not engage in controversy with words; it is useless and causes harm to the listeners." RB 3 talks not about good arguments but about verbal battles.[49]

Proterve means arguing vehemently, shamelessly, impetuously, defiantly, and impudently.[50] In the Vulgate it is used together with *contumax*—defiant, disobedient. Cassian speaks with embarrassment about a defiant monk. His defiance (*protervia*) consisted in answering arrogantly after having been corrected a second time by his abbot: "But I did not humble myself for remaining always a subordinate." This unbridled and proud response left the elder speechless.[51] When an argument becomes polemical and vehement, any communal seeking of the will of God is finished. God can be sought only in open dialogue, in humility and obedience. Benedict admonishes us to shun arrogance, resistance, and contradiction (68.3)—which would signal the end of discernment.

Interestingly enough, we see here both abbot and brothers outside of the monastery. Some of the manuscripts read: "in or outside the monastery" (*intus aut foris*). But Benedict probably wants to forbid defiant arguments in general. He deliberately mentions the place as being outside; perhaps he thinks that other people also will learn about the disagreement and that

---

49. Basil mentions the word in the context of competing for the top places, which is opposed to humility (*Reg* 10).

50. The word occurs only here and is not used in RM.

51. *Inst.* 12.28.

scandal may easily result. It is also possible that the phrase "outside the monastery" was added later, for it goes beyond the setting of communal counsel.

V. 10: Should anyone presume to do so, let him be subjected to the discipline of the Rule. (*Quod si praesumpserit, regulari disciplinae subiecerat.*)

Much as Benedict would want to avoid this, he still assumes that it can happen and adds a disciplinary measure. This is typical for him as he distributed his threats of punishment throughout the entire Rule. The term *regularis disciplina* is used frequently in the texts proper to Benedict. Should it be translated as "punishment"? The Latin word *disciplina* can also mean learning. Discipline is a process for the brother to improve after faults such as murmuring, talkativeness, claiming private property, pride, and refusal to be reconciled. Just how the regular discipline proceeded in concrete cases cannot be deduced from the entire Rule. The brother should be "subject" to this process; he is subjected. Presumably the brother would not be asking for it on his own initiative. Someone must step in and subject him to the process. One might also say that he automatically is subject to the "discipline." Its goal is the healing of his tendency to quarrel.

V. 11: The abbot, however, must fear God and keep the Rule in everything he does, knowing that without doubt he will have to give an account of all his judgments to God, the most just of judges. (*Ipse tamen abba cum timorem Dei et observatione regulae omne faciat, sciens se procul dubio de omnibus iudiciis suis aequissimo iudici Deo rationem redditurum.*)

This verse is very compact and once more summarizes the essential admonitions for the abbot in a brief and memorable manner. The abbot is now described in contrast to the quarrelsome brother: not bent on anything, he is acting in the fear of God, is fully integrated into the monastery with its Rule and is standing before the most just judge. In this way verse 11 emphasizes the vertical dimension, whereas in verses 4-6 the horizontal dimension was central.

The fear of God (timor Dei) recalls the first degree of humility, as well as obedience (RB 5.9). It is characteristic of Benedict to require persons with the fear of God for all important offices, for example the cellarer (31.2), the infirmarian (36.7), the brother in charge of guests (53.21), the brothers in the council (65.15), the porter (66.4) and, of course, the abbot. All are to live in God's presence and from this vantage point assess people and the monastery's practical affairs. All these officials have to deal with weak brothers, with the poor and the insignificant. Thus the fear of God helps to pay attention to these very people and guarantees that the least are respected in a special way. The fear of God also can preclude that in the council meeting someone feels inhibited by the fear of others, of reality, or of the consequences of a decision. Such fears can dominate persons and thus prevent a free discernment.

"*Keep the Rule in everything he does.*" This and similar expressions occur particularly in the last chapters of RB.[52] Benedict did not take the emphasis of observing the Rule from RM; the words "keep/observe the Rule" (*observare regulam*) do not occur there. In RB the abbot is admonished to observe the Rule in everything he does and to exempt nothing from this observance. In the course of his life in community, Benedict probably realized more and more how important it is to have a sound and wise rule of conduct. Though he doesn't call his Rule "holy" (as often is the case in RM), it is for him also the fruit of experience of a life with Sacred Scripture. In a community, not everyone can craft his own Rule. There must be norms that apply to everyone. As RB 73 shows, Benedict also knew that his Rule was only a beginning. Observance of the Rule is not a static attitude; rather, the Rule keeps leading us beyond itself and beyond ourselves.

In insisting on observance of the Rule in RB 3, Benedict means that in a council meeting there are some principles that are not subject to discussion; for example, that we walk under the guidance of the Gospel (Prol 21), that our communal liturgy is a priority (43.3), and that we are cenobites (1.2). Observing the Rule also means to practice the "discretion" of the Rule, to call and to really hear everyone, to arrange everything justly, not to slide into defending and obstinate quarreling, and to respect everyone, especially the little ones.

"*Knowing . . . without doubt.*" Here the constant awareness of being accountable to God is stressed. "Knowing"—*scire*—is often demanded of the abbot, as in RB 2 and 64. It means knowing the ultimate realities (e.g., 2.30; 2.37f.) and the deeper reality (e.g., 2.7; 2.31; 64.9). It is not an intellectual kind of knowing but an existential one, a knowing with the heart.

"*The abbot must give an account of all his judgments.*" Just as he is to do "everything" with the attitude required earlier, so now none of his decisions are exempt from judgment. The Rule allows the abbot much latitude in deciding; but the closer Benedict comes to his final chapters, the more he emphasizes that the abbot is accountable to God for all his decisions (55.20; 63.3; 65.22).

God is "the most just judge"—*aequissimo iudici Deo.* With this expression we stand before the final reality. How will the decision hold up before it? This question likewise fosters objectivity in discernment. Just as the liturgy takes place under the Lord's eyes according to RB 19, so the community discernment is before the most just of judges. Both chapters speak of the fear of the Lord and paint a picture of the whole community as it should be. Today verse

---

52. For example, in 58.10; 60.9; 65.17; 73.

11 certainly applies not only to the abbot but also to every brother in the council: the greater his authority, the more he is accountable to God. God's justice is strongly emphasized here.

Aequitas denotes the fittingness and the justice that gives everyone his due according to his need; the law is not rigorously applied to persons but takes personal situations into account. Benedict is characterized by this attitude throughout his entire Rule.[53] In RB 3 this quality of justice is attributed to God, who examines the heart. The abbot should take this attribute of God as his guideline. God not only is just but also knows all the circumstances that need to be considered. Therefore the abbot should strive to know and consider them.

Vv. 12-13 (A') to some degree reflect the beginning (vv. 1-3) and have a parallel structure.

12-13	T, 1-3
12 When	Whenever
less important business	anything important
is to be transacted	is to be done
for the benefit	
of the monastery	in the monastery
he is to take counsel	the abbot is to call
with the seniors only	the whole community together all,
as it is written	because . . .
do everything	he is to do

As stated earlier, this may be an addition: it certainly broadens the concept of RM. The council of senior brothers is mentioned also in RB 65.15. On the other hand, the council of seniors was a tradition (cf. introduction to RB 1–3). Benedict is practical enough to think that the entire community cannot be convoked for each and every matter. Two kinds of council meetings are mentioned already in the Bible in Exodus 18:13-26f.: Jethro, Moses' father-in-law, did not see why Moses should labor from morning to night to solve the peoples' problems. "You are wearing yourself out, and the people as well" (18:18). An arrangement was made to have the easier problems decided by judges. Only the weightier ones were brought before Moses.

53. It is found especially after RB 31 as far as content is concerned; the word occurs in Prol 48: Sometimes a little more strictness is required "when reason and fairness demand it."

V. 12: If less important business for the benefit of the monastery is to be transacted, he is to take counsel with the seniors only. (*Si qua vero minora agenda sunt in monasterii utilitatibus, seniorum tantum utatur consilio.*)

In practice, what might the less important business for the benefit of the monastery be? Excluding weighty matters (v. 1), the less important ones might be issues the abbot cannot decide by himself or ones he is unsure about. There might be questions of discipline or problems regarding material goods. In RB 65 the council of seniors acts in the nomination of a prior after the entire community has desired to have one. Today such cases are determined by the constitutions or the norms.

"*He is to take counsel with the seniors only.*" Actually, the text says he should use the council. The elders (*seniores*) in the language of the Rule are spiritual persons; sometimes the adjective *spiritalis* modifies it, as in RB 4.50. They generally share in the responsibility of the abbot, in contrast to RM, which provides for deans who are chiefly supervisors. In RB the seniors help provide a good spiritual atmosphere (48.17f.). A senior is master of novices (58.6), and there are the seniors who are honored and who in their turn love the younger members (4.70f.; 71.4). There are also the wise elders on whom the abbot may call in the healing process of the community (27.2f.), but they also supervise, as in 22.3, 7; 56.3 and 48.17. A senior is someone with life experience, but he need not necessarily be older in years; one must possess maturity and wisdom (human and spiritual), and a younger person may also have these. In Daniel 13:50 it is said of Daniel that God gave him the "honor of being old" (*honorem senectutis*). And St. Gregory also says of St. Benedict that from his childhood he had the heart of an elder (*cor gerens senile*).[54]

V. 13: As it is written: "Do everything with counsel and you will not be sorry afterwards." (*sicut scriptum est: Omnia fac cum consilio et post factum non paeniteberis* [Prov 31:3 VL; Sir 32:24].)

"*As it is written.*" Benedict favors this expression when he departs from RM. The following texts are typical: In RB 2.33-36 the abbot is admonished not to neglect the spiritual welfare of those entrusted to him; "he is to remember what is written: Seek first the reign of God." In 31.14 the cellarer is advised to give a kind word (*ut scriptum est*). Each one should receive what he needs (34.1: *sicut scriptum est*). The brothers should try to be the first to show respect to each other (63.17; *quod scriptum est*). Here in RB 3 it is one solid sentence from the Wisdom literature. The second half is found in the Latin Bible in Sirach 32:19. The first part comes from the Old Latin translation of

54. Cf. the first antiphon for Vespers or Lauds for the feast of March 21.

Proverbs 31:3, "*cum consilio omnia fac*."[55] This proverb provides homely wisdom from experience. Benedict does not immediately require supernatural motivation when not necessary.

"*Do everything with counsel.*" This is addressed to the abbot but could just as well be said to each one. Take counsel with the right kind of persons when you need to make an important decision! Do nothing on your own, only according to your own instinct, feeling, or opinion! Be open to good advice. This is very human and good wisdom! From the beginning of monasticism, we encounter this principle: one should not begin living the Gospel on one's own, without a guide or counselor, nor continue alone.

The promise says: "And you will not be sorry afterwards." How often we regret having acted too quickly or according to a biased opinion! On the other hand, if we have done what in our view seemed possible, we can more calmly accept the consequences, even though they are not always positive. We need not regret. As a negative example, one might think of Rehoboam, who first took counsel with the seniors. But he dismissed the good advice of the elders, took counsel with others, and followed them. This led to the division of the kingdom (1 Kgs 12:6-15).

This chapter grew out of the Rule as a whole. Its present form was not part of the first version of the Rule but rather seems to have been developed slowly with experience. It reflects both the spiritual foundation and the spirit of the last chapters.

Taking one more look at the chapter, we can see that it is linked with RB 4–7 chiefly by its spiritual teachings: the danger of self-will and emphasis on obedience and humility. The more practical regulations and admonitions (council, community, Rule, and abbot) of RB 3 also point to the later chapters of RB, as well as to RB 1–2.

This chapter also needs to be interpreted with RB 72 as the key. According to RB 3, the evil zeal of bitterness (72.1) would be quarreling, boldness, stubbornness, defending, and presuming. The most fervent good zeal (72.2f.) would be: listening to one another, mutual respect, giving advice with humility, being concerned with justice and the common good, obeying, and doing everything in the fear of God and with counsel. Anticipating one another in showing respect (72.4) finds a wide field of implementation during a council meeting. Besides, patience with the physical and character weaknesses is needed (72.5). We can practice mutual obedience and love one another selflessly (72.6, 8).

Above all, we ought to follow that which is useful (nucleus of RB 72 in 72.7), not for the individual neighbor, but for what is helpful to the whole

55. Cf. Ambrose, *In Ps.* 36.66.1: *cum consilio omnia fac!*; cf. Augustine, *Spec* 23: *Sine consilio nihil facias, et post factum non paeniteberis* [speaking about Sir 32:24].

monastery in view of its goal. The brothers who conduct themselves during a council meeting according to the Rule are abiding in the fear of God and joined by love of God (72.9). They can also practice love for the abbot, just as Benedict says, "sincerely and humbly" (72.10); that is, with courage voicing their own opinion, being conscious of their own limitations, and in the proper manner. All together, who thus seek the will of God, want to prefer nothing whatsoever to Christ (72.11), not even their own advantage, their own opinion, their own honor . . . They are totally directed toward Christ and the will of God and eager to be guided by him together, and to attain eternal life as a community (72.12).

The important persons of monastic life need to do their part here. There is God, the most just of judges, the Lord who reveals, presumably Christ. We see the abbot and the brothers engaged in communal discernment. They are true cenobites with a Rule and an abbot. Among the brothers some are older and some younger. All of them together are on the way to their final goal: God. They need to decide what is more wholesome, better. Another person, as it were, is the mistress, the Rule that is personified here. It educates the monks in the basic virtues. The following are named in this chapter: listening, obeying, humility, fear of God, awareness of the ultimate realities. Faith in the priority of grace is expressed indirectly in RB 3.3. The entire chapter is governed not only by fairness and foresight but also, above all, by *discretio* in the sense of discerning and deciding according to the will of God and avoiding extremes to the right and to the left. The older and younger members are asked for their view, the seniors having more experience, the juniors being perhaps more open for the surprising revelations of God. Benedict shows his sense for the uniqueness of each person.

He is radical in regard to essential matters, even harsh in forbidding presumption, bold quarreling, and defending, also in the battle against the "will of one's own heart" and "rash deviating," yet at the same time also shows balance. He appeals to the abbot's conscience to be just and concerned about the welfare of the whole, arranging everything with foresight and observing the Rule. Throughout RB and in this chapter in particular, the abbot bears a very great responsibility. Yet Benedict also charges him squarely to be accountable to God. As more coresponsibility is given to individual monastics today, they must help share the burden and responsibility of the abbot. The chapter shows Benedict as a realist with a good knowledge of his community but also as one who with firmness keeps setting the ideal before the members.

The spirit of this chapter also applies today when we have discernment at various levels: discernment undertaken by the entire community with deliberative or consultative voice, or of a council, again with either deliberative or consultative voice. Not everything applies literally to us—for example, the abbot does not always make the final decision. The chapter as a whole can show us how Benedict and we must and can strive to seek the will of God together with all our strength in complex situations.

Conclusion

Looking back on the entire volume, the importance of reading slowly becomes clear: each line has to be read in the context of the chapter, the Rule, and its possible sources. It is indispensable to do both the synchronic reading of the text itself and the diachronic reading of the text with its sources. And for the first three chapters of the Rule of Benedict, it is particularly important to compare each one with its immediate source, the Rule of the Master. By doing this we better recognize the person of Benedict. It seems that, at first, he was quite impressed with RM and thus copied much of it, especially in the Prologue, but also in the first part of RB 1 and RB 3 and the main section of RB 2. But he also deviated from it and put forth his own ideas. He omits the satire of the gyrovagues with its exaggerations as well as the questionable theology of monastic life. And it is Benedict who, in the very center of RB 2, clearly states that the abbot has to be guided by care and concern for the community and then also omits the Master's statement that the disciples have no responsibility at all. RB 3 is developed by Benedict, giving more weight to the community as a whole and even to the younger members. The abbot tries hard to discern the will of God and does so together with his community. Benedict has the courage to bind not only the brothers but also the abbot to the Rule in the same way and reminds all of them to forego following the will of their own hearts. And in all the texts discussed here, additions and insertions shed much light on the person of their author, Benedict.

At the end of the Prologue the important insertion of verses 46-49 is very characteristic for Benedict. He is convinced that monastic life expands the heart, and it seems that he has experienced himself that, in spite of the strictness of the beginning, one is able to run the way with the unspeakable sweetness of love.

Rule, abbot, and community are the three pillars of this listening community. The abbot is chosen from among the community, and the Prologue especially shows what listening entails so that—as the nucleus of the Prologue states in verse 21—all can go forward on this way under the guidance of the Gospel toward their final goal.

Abbreviations

A. PERIODICALS, ENCYCLOPEDIAS, SERIES, EDITIONS

(Series of English translations are added. English translations are given in parentheses.)

ABR	*The American Benedictine Review.*
ACW	Ancient Christian Writers.
ANF	Anti-Nicene Fathers; ANF 10 [1994] contains useful indeces to ANF and NPNF. (NPNF both first and second series, given as NPNF[1] and NPNF[2].)
Ben	*Benedictines.* Atchison, Kansas, USA.
Boon	A. Boon, *Pachominiana latina.* Louvain, 1932.
CC	Corpus Christianorum, Series Latina.
Cetedoc	Cetedoc I. Library of Christian Latin Texts (CD). Louvain, 1996.
CollCist	*Collectanea Cisterciensia.* Forges.
CS	*Cistercian Studies.*
CSCO	Corpus Scriptorum Christianorum Orientalium. Paris, Louvain, 1903ff.
CSEL	Corpus Scriptorum Ecclesiasticorum Latinorum. Vienna, 1866ff.
DIP	Dizionario degli Instituti di Perfezione. Rome, 1973ff.
DS	Dictionnaire de Spiritualité. Paris 1937ff.
EA	*Erbe und Auftrag* (previously *Benediktinische Monatsschrift*). Beuron.
FC	Fathers of the Church.
GuL	*Geist und Leben.* Würzburg.
LL	*Lettre de Ligugé.* Ligugé
MonInf	*Monastische Informationen.* Eibingen.
Mst	*Monastic Studies.* Mount Saviour.
NPNF[1, 2]	Nicene and Post-Nicene Fathers, series 1 and 2.
PG	Patrologia Graeca. Ed. J. P. Migne. Paris, 1878ff.
PL	Patrologia Latina. Ed. J. P. Migne. Paris, 1878ff.
PsRom	Psalterium Romanun. Ed. Robert Weber. *Le psaultier romain et les autres psautiers latins.* Rome, 1953.
RBén	*Revue bénédictine.* Maredsous.
RBS	*Regula Benedicti Studia.* Hildesheim.
SC	Sources chrétiennes. Paris 1941ff.

SMGBO	*Studien und Mitteilungen zur Geschichte des Benediktinerordens und seiner Zweige*. Ottobeuren–Augsburg.
StA	*Studia Anselmiana*. Rome.
StMon	*Studia Monastica*. Barcelona.
StSil	*Studia Silensia*. Silos.
SupplRBS	Supplementa, Regulae Benedicti Studia. Hildesheim 1974ff.
Tj	*Tjurunga*. Tarrawarra, Australia.
VL	Vetus Latina: Die Reste der altlateinischen Bibel. Beuron, 1949ff.
VS	*La Vie spirituelle*. Paris.
Vulg	Vulgata; quoted according Biblia sacra iuxta Vulgatam versionem. Ed. Robert Weber, I–II. Stuttgart, 1969.
WSp	*Word and Spirit*. Still River.

B. OTHER ABBREVIATIONS

Art.	Article (in encyclopedias)
Ed.	Edited by
Ep.	Epistle
n	Footnote
ibid.	*ibidem* (in the same place)
Lib.	*Liber* (book)
Praec.	*Praeceptum, Praecepta* (Precept[s])
Praef.	*Praefatio* (Preface)
Prol	Prologue
Ps	before a name: Pseudo.
s.	*sermo* (sermon)
Th	*thema* (RM: theme in the sense of a brief explanation)
Thp	theme/explanation on the *Pater Noster* (Our Father) in RM
Ths	theme/explanation on the psalm in RM
T	title (of a chapter e.g., in RB)
V(v.)	Verse (s)
Vit.	*Vita* (life of a saint)

Bibliographies

BIBLIOGRAPHY I: EDITIONS OF THE RULE OF BENEDICT AND THE RULE OF THE MASTER

Rule of Benedict

RB (Hanslik) *Benedicti Regula,* Edited by Rudolf Hanslik. Wien,[2] 1977. CSEL 75.

RB 80 *The Rule of St. Benedict in Latin and English with Notes.* Edited by T. Fry, et al. Collegeville, MN: Liturgical Press, 1981.

Vogüé, Adalbert de. *La Règle de S. Benoît.* Edited by A. de Vogüé and J. Neufville, 2 vols. SC 181–82. Paris, 1972. Quoted as Vogüé I, II. (Engl. trans. *A Critical Study of the Rule of Benedict.* Translated by Colleen Maura McGrane. Vol. 1: Overview, Theology and Faith. Hyde Park, NY: New City Press, 2013. Vol. 2: Prologue, Chapters 4, 6, 7, and 73. Hyde Park, NY: New City Press, 2015.)

SÄK (Salzburger Äbtekonferenz) *Die Benediktusregel lateinisch/deutsch.* Beuron, 1992.

The Rule of the Master / Regula Magistri

Bozzi, Marcellina and Alberto Grilli, Eds. *La Regola del Maestro.* 2 Vols. Brescia, 1995. Vol. 1 quoted as Bozzi 1 with page reference. Edition with commentary.

Eberle, Luke. *The Rule of the Master.* Translated from the Latin in the critical edition by A. de Vogüé. Kalamazoo, MI: Cistercian Publications, 1977. Quotations from RM are from this translation.

Frank, Karl Suso. *Die Magisterregel.* St. Ottilien, 1989.

Vogüé, Adalbert de. *La Règle du Maître.* Edited by A. de Vogüé. 2 Vols. SC 105–6.

BIBLIOGRAPHY II: PATRISTIC AND MONASTIC TEXTS

As we are dealing with texts that were available to Benedict, we are citing primarily editions that contain the Latin text, or a Latin translation, even if they are not the original source. English translations are given in parentheses.

Alph *Alphabetikon: Apophthegmata Patrum. Collectio alphabetica:* PG 65.

Ambrose of Milan

ApolDav	*De Apologia Prophetae David I*: PL 14.851; CSEL 32.2.
ExhortVg	Exhortatio Virginitatis. In F. Gori, ed. *Opera omnia. S. Ambrogio.* Biblioteca Ambrosiana, 14.2.
In Lc.	*Expositio Evangelii secundum Lucam*: CC 14.
In Ps.	*Explanatio Psalmorum* 12: CSEL 64.
De Paenit.	*De Paenitentia*: SC 179.

Augustine

A new English translation of Augustine's works is being published: *The Works of Saint Augustine: A Translation for the 21st Century*, 1990ff. Though this translation was not used, its volumes (*AW*) are cited for the Letters and the *Expositions on the Psalms*.

Contr Ep Parm	*Contra Epistulam Parmeniani*. CSEL 51; PL 43.33.
Contr Faust	*Contra Faustum Manichaeum*: PL 42–207; CSEL 25.1; NPNF[1] 1.4.
Ep	*Epistulae*. PL 38–39; PLS 2.742 (selected letters and sermons in NPNF[1] 1.219; 5.260, 281, 437–40; FC 11.38; ACW 5.15; *AW: Letters*. Translated by R. Teske. Part II, Vols. 1–4 (2001–2005).
In Joh.	*In Joannis Evangelium tractatus*: PL 35.1379; CC 36 (NPNF[1] 7.7).
In Ps.	*Enarrationes in psalmos*: PL 36.67; CC 38–40 (NPNF[1] 8.1); ACW 29–30; *AW: Expositions on the Psalms*. Translated by M. Boulding. Part III, Vols. 15–20 (2000–2004).
MorEccl	*De Moribus Ecclesiae catholicae et de moribus Manichaeorum*: PL 32.1309 (FC 56; NPNF[1] 4.41).
OpMon	*De Opere Monachorum*: CSEL 41; PL 40.547 (FC 16; NPNF[1] 3.503).
Praec	*Praeceptum*; Verheijen, *Règle. The Monastic Rules*. Translated by G. Bonner. Hyde Park, NY: New City Press, 2004.
Spec	*Speculum*: CSEL 12.

Aurelianus

Reg.	*Regula Aureliani ad monachos*: PL 68.385.

Basil the Great of Caesarea

Reg	*Regula (Asceticum parvum)*: PG 31. Translated into Latin by Rufinus: PL 103.483; Clarke (below) describes Rufinus's translation as a "conflation of the 55 Longer and 313 Shorter Rules to make one book of 203 Rules." (*The Ascetical Works of St. Basil*. Translated by W. K. L. Clarke. London: SPCK, 1925); also FC 9.33 *Discourse on Ascetical Discipline*.
Reg fus.	*Regulae fusius tractatae*: PG 31 (cf. Clarke "The Longer Rules," 145–228; also FC 9.223).
Regbrev.	*Regulae brevius tractatae*: PG 31 (cf. Clarke, "The Shorter Rules," 229–351).

Caesarius of Arles

ExhortVg	*Exhortatio ad Virginem Deo dicatam*: SC 345.

RegVg   *Regula ad Virgines*: SC 345; this volume *Oeuvres monastiques de Césaire d'Arles* (Paris, 1988) also contains Vogüé's "Introduction à la Règle des Vierges" (35–168). (*The Rule for Nuns of St. Caesarius of Arles*. Translated by M. C. McCarthy. Studies in Medieval History, new series, vol. 16. Washington, DC: The Catholic University of America, 1960.)

RegMon   *Regula ad monachos* or *Regula monachorum*: PL 67.1099, Ed. G. Morin. *S. Caesarii opera omnia*, vol. 2. Maredsous, 1942.

s.   *Sermo(nes)*: CC 103f. Ed. G. Morin (FC 31, 47, 66).

Ep ad Caes   *Epistula ad Caesariam*: SC 345.

Canons of the Apostles

CanAp   *Codex Canonum Apostolorum, Canones . . . Apostolorum*: PL 67. Edited by F. Funk. *Opera Patrum Apostolicorum*, Vol. 1. Tübingen, 1887.

Cassian, John

Conf.   *Conlationes*: PL 49.477; CSEL 13, SC 42, 54.64 (NPNF[2] 11.293 [omits Conf. 12, 22]; and ACW 57; *The Conferences*. Translated by B. Ramsey. New York: Paulist, 1997.

Inst.   *De institutis coenobiorum et de octo principalium vitiorum remediis libri xii*: PL 49.53; CSEL 17; SC 109 (NPNF[2] 11.199 [omits Inst. 6]; ACW 58; *The Institutes*. Trans. B. Ramsey. New York: Newman, 2000.

Cassiodor

In Ps.   *Expositio Psalmorum*: CC 97–98, PL 70 (ACW 51-53).

Peter Chrysologus

s.   *Sermo(nes)*: CC 24, 24A.

Clement of Rome

Ad Cor I   Ed. G. Morin. *Anecdota Maredsolana*. Maredsous 1894 (Old Latin translation).

Ad Cor II   Ed. F. Funk. *Opera Patrum Apostolicorum*, vol. 1. Tübingen, 1887.

Cyprian of Carthage

De dom. or.   *De dominica oratione*. PL 4.520; 47.1113; CSEL 3/1 (ACW 20; ANF 5.447).

De mortal   *De mortalitate*: CSEL 3.1.

Ep.   *Epistulae*: PL 4.224; CSEL 3/2 (ANF 5.275; with different numbering: FC 51).

Diadochus of Photice

Cent   *Cent chapitres gnostiques. Oeuvres spirituelles*: SC 5b.

Dorotheus of Gaza

Instr   *Instructions*: SC 92.

Evagrius

Sent.   *Sententiae ad monachos*: PG 40 (*The Mind's Long Journey to the Holy Trinity: The Ad monachos of Evagrius Ponticus*. Translated by Jeremy Driscoll. Collegeville, MN: Liturgical Press, 1993; also Evagrius Ponticus. *Ad monachos*: Translation and Commentary. New York: Newman, 2003. ACW 59).

Fulgentius of Ruspe

De remiss pecc   *De remissione peccatorum ad Euthymium*: CC 91A.

Gregory the Great

Dial   *Dialogorum libri IV*: SC 251, 260, 265. (Engl. trans. T. Kardong. *The Life of St. Benedict by Gregory the Great*. Collegeville, MN: Liturgical Press, 2009).

Hilary of Arles

VitHon   *Vita Honorati*: SC 235; PL 50.1249 (*The Western Fathers*. Translated by F. R. Hoare, 247–82. New York, 1954; FC 15).

Hilary of Poitiers

In Ps.   *Tractatus super psalmos*: PL 9.231; CSEL 22, Bk 1 NPNF^2 9.236; includes only Pss 1, 53, 130.

Hildemar

                Expositio Regulae ab Hildemaro tradita: R. Mittermüller. In *Vita et regula SS. P. Benedicti una cum expositione regulae a Hildemaro tradita*, vol. 3. Ratisbon: Pustet, 1880. Numbers in parentheses indicate the page in this edition.

Isidore of Seville

De eccl offic   *De ecclesiasticis officiis*. CC 113. (Translated by Thomas L. Knoebel. ACW 61, 2008).
Reg.   *Regula monachorum*: PL 83; 103.

Jerome

Ep   *Epistula(e)*: CSEL 54–56 (ACW 33, letters 1–22; NPNF^2 6.1).

PsJerome

In Ps.   *Breviarum in Psalmos*: PL 26.

Justinian

Nov.   *Corpus Juris Civilis III, Novellae*. Ed. R. Schoell, W. Kroll, Berlin ^{6}1954; new edition, Hildesheim, 2005.

Martène

Martène, Edmond: *Regula S .Benedicti commentata*: PL 66.

Origen

Job Fragm.	*Fragmenta in Job*: PG 12, PG 17.
In Num.	*Homeliae in Numeros*: SC 415, 442, 461.
In Ps.	*Homeliae in Psalmos 36–38*: SC 411. Translated by Rufinus.

Orsiesius

Lib	*Orsiesii liber, versio latina—Pachomiana latina.* Ed. Armand Boon. Louvain, 1932. Cf. Pachomian Koinonia, III. Ed. and trans. A Veilleux. Kalamazoo, MI: Cistercian, 1982.

Pachomius

VitPach	Lefort, L. Th. *Les Vies Coptes de S. Pachôme et de ses premiers successeurs.* Louvain, 1943.
Praec	*Praecepta.* Ed. A. Boon (cf. Orsiesius).
PraecInst	*Praecepta et Instituta.* Ed. Boon.
PraecIud	*Praecepta atque Iudicia.* Ed. Boon.
Praec Leg	*Praecepta ac Leges.* Ed. Boon.
Praef	*Praefatio Hieronymi.* Ed. A. Boon.

Paulinus of Nola

Carm.	*Carmina*: CSEL 30 (ACW 40).

Philo of Alexandria

De migr Abr *De migratione Abrahami*: SC 47.

Rules

RegEug	*Regula Eugippii*: CSEL 88.
Reg4Patr	*Regula quattuor Patrum*: SC 297; PL 103; cf. *Early Monastic Rules.* Translated by C. Franklin, Collegeville, MN: Liturgical Press, 1982; also *ABR* 54, no. 2 (2003): 142–80, trans. T. Kardong.
RegulaFerrioli	*Regula ad monachos*: PL 66
RegOr	*Regula Orientalis*: PL 103; SC 298. Ed. A. de Vogüé. *Benedictina* 23 (1976) 241–71; cf. also *Early Monastic Rules.*

Sacramentuam Gelasianum

Sacr Gelas *Liber Sacramentorum Romanae Aecclesiae ordinis anni circuli*; Ed. L. C. Mohlberg. (Series maior, Fontes IV). Rome,[3] 1981.

Sacramentum Veronese (Leonianum)

Sacr Veron *Sacramentarium Veronese.* Edited by L. C. Mohlberg. Series Rerum Ecclesiasticarum Documenta, Series maior, Fontes I. Rome,[3] 1994; Edited by Ch. Feltoe: *Sacramentarium Leonianum.* Cambridge, 1896.

Smaragdus

Expositio in Regulam S. Benedicti: CCM 8. Siegburg: Schmitt, 1974. (Smaragdus of
     Saint-Mihiel. *Commentary on the Rule of Saint Benedict.* Translated
     by David Barry. Kalamazoo, MI: Cistercian Publications, 2007. Page
     numbers refer to this translation.)

Sulpicius Severus

Dial.   *Dialogorum libri II*: PL 20.175; (FC 7; NPNF² 11.24).

Visio Pauli

"The Revelation of Paul." In *Apocryphical Gospels, Acts and Revelation.* Edited by
     A. Walker. Anti-Nicene Library, Vol. 16. Edinburgh, 1870.

Vitae (Lives of the Saints)

Vit Ant.   *Vita Antonii*: PG 26.835; PL 73.127 (ACW 10; NPNF² 4.195).
VitCol   Jonas v. Bobbio: *Vita Columbani.* Ed. G.M.S. Walker. *Sancti Columbani
               opera.* Dublin, 1970.
VitPat   *Vitae Patrum III-IV-V*: PL 73.

BIBLIOGRAPHY III: SECONDARY SOURCES AND STUDIES

For authors with several entries books are mentioned first. Articles are arranged
alphabetically according to the first important word.

Art. "Abbas." *DIP* 1 (1973): 23–26.
"Abbot" in RB 80. Collegeville, MN: Liturgical Press, 1980, appendix 2, 322–89.
Art. "Endurcissement." *DS* 4 (1960): 642–52.
Art. "Girovaghi." *DIP* 4 (1977): 1302–1304.
Art. "Logismos." *DS* 9 (1970): 955–58; *DIP* 5 (1978): 715–19.
Blaise, Albert. *Dictionnaire latin-français des auteurs chrétiens.* Turnhout, 1954.
Böckmann, Aquinata. *Perspectives on the Rule of Saint Benedict.* Collegeville, MN:
     Liturgical Press, 2005.
———. *Around the Monastic Table: Growing in Mutual Service and Love.* Collegeville,
     MN: Liturgical Press, 2009.
———. "Arme und Armut in der Benediktsregel." *EA* 67 (1991): 187–94.
———. "Benedictine Mysticism: Dynamic Spirituality in RB." *TJ* 57 (1999) 85–101.
———. "Benediktinische Mystik: Dynamische Spiritualität in der *Regula Benedicti*."
     EA 72 (1996): 367–84; also as *Zu den Quellen: die Spiritualität der Wüstenväter
     und des hl. Benedikt.* Edited by J. Kaffanke. Freiburg, Switzerland, 1997. 42–59.
———. "The Experience of God in the Rule of St. Benedict." *Ben* 51, no. 2 (1998):
     6–19; "Gotteserfahrung nach der *Regula Benedicti*." *EA* 75 (1999): 282–96;
     also *MonInf* 100 (1999): 20–28.
———. "*Discretio* im Sinn der Regel Bendikts und ihrer Tradition." *EA* 52 (1976):
     362–73.

————. "Der Mensch nach der Regel Benedikts (RB) auf dem Hintergrund ihrer Tradition, besonders der *Regula Magistri* (RM)." *RBS* 20 (2001): 35–58.

————. "Zum Prolog der Regel Benedikts. I: Prolog 5-7." *EA* 79 (2003): 5–16; II: "Prolog 8-13." *EA* 79 (2003): 124–37; III: "Prolog 14-20." *EA* 79 (2003): 224–35; IV: "Prolog 21-22." *EA* 79 (2003): 308-13; V: "Prolog 23-25." *EA* 79 (2003): 389–407; VI-VII: "Prolog 36-39; 40-44 (45-50)." *EA* 79 (2003): 487–96; VIII: "Abschluss." *EA* 80 (2004): 28–33.

————. "Die *Regula Benedicti* und die Psalmen." In *Il monachesimo tra eredità e aperture*. Edited by M. Bielawski and D. Hombergen. Studia Anselmiana 140. Rome, 2004. 607–40.

Borias, André. "Le Chiasme dans la Règle." *RBén* 95 (1985): 25–38.

————. "Comment Benoît a élaboré le ch. 3 de sa Règle." *RBS* 12 (1985): 29–37.

————. "La foi dans la Règle de Saint Benoît." *Revue d'ascétique et de mystique* 44 (1968): 249–55.

————. "L'utilité d'autrui." *LL* 236 (1986): 17–26.

Casey, Michael. *Strangers to the City: Reflections on the Beliefs and Values of the Rule of Saint Benedict*. Brewster, MA: Paraclete, 2005.

Choi, Bonitas. "Listening: The Fundamental Symbolism in Benedictine Life." *Ben* 49 (1996): 28–46.

Colombás, García. *La Regla de San Benito*. Madrid, 1979.

————. "El *Abad*, Vicario de Cristo: Commentario critico de RB 2.2-3. Hacia una relectura de la Regla de S. Benito." *StSil* 8 (1980): 89–116.

Egli, Beat. *Der 14. Psalm im Prolog der Regel des hl. Benedikt*. Sarnen, 1962.

Farmer, David Hugh. *Early English Manuscripts in Facsimile*. Vol. XV: *The Rule of Benedict* (Oxford, Bodleian Library, Ms Hatton 48). London, 1968.

Fischer, Balthasar. *Die Psalmen als Stimme der Kirche*. Trier, 1982.

————. "Zu Benedikts Interpretation von Röm 8:15." In *Colligere Fragmenta*. Festschrift. Edited by A. Dodd., B. Fischer, and V. Fiala. Beuron, 1952. 124–26.

————. "Die Psalmenfrömmigkeit der *Regula S. Benedicti*." *Liturgie und Mönchtum* 4 (1949): 22–35; 5 (1950): 64–79.

Gertler, Thomas."Herausgefordert vom Bösen." *GuL* 70 (1997): 83–98.

Giurisato, Giorgio. "La Regola riflette la *lectio divina* di San Benedetto." *Ora et labora* 59 (2005): 97–109.

Gordan, Paulus. "Gnadenfrist." *EA* 56 (1980): 425–26.

Guevin, Benedict. "*Dominici scola servitii*: A School of the Lord's service or A School of the Lord's way of Service?" *Downside Review* 114 (1996): 294–312.

————. "The Beginning and End of Purity of Heart: From Cassian to the Master and Benedict." In *Purity of Heart in Early Ascetical Literature*. Edited by H. A. Luckman and L. Kulzer. Collegeville, MN: Liturgical Press, 1999. 197–215.

Herwegen, Ildefons. *Sinn und Geist der Benediktsregel*. Einsiedeln, 1944.

Hilpisch, Stephan. "Der Rat der Brüder in den Benediktinischen Klöstern des Mittelalters." *SMGBO* 67 (1956): 221–36.

Holzherr, Georg. *Die Benediktsregel*. Freiburg, Switzerland, 2007. Cited as Holzherr 2007.

Huerre, Denis. *Von Tag zu Tag*. Kellenried, 1983.

Kardong, Terrence G. *Benedict's Rule. A Translation and Commentary.* Collegeville, MN: Liturgical Press, 1996. Cited as Kardong.

———. "The Abbot as Leader." *ABR* 42 (1991): 53–72.

———. "The Demonic in Benedict's Rule." *TJ* 37 (1989): 3–11.

———. "The Devil in the Rule of the Master." *StMon* 30 (1988): 41–62.

———. "*Iustitia* in the Rule of Benedict." *StMon* 73 (1982): 43–72; also under the same title in *Commentaries on Benedict's Rule.* Richardton, ND: Assumption Abbey Press, 1987. 124–54.

Kasch, Elisabeth. "Das liturgische Vokabular der frühen lateinischen Mönchsregeln." *RBS* Suppl. 1 (1974).

Kasper, Clemens M. "Faustus von Riez. Predigten an die Mönche (III)." *EA* 67 (1991): 461–63; (IV) *EA* 68 (1992): 117–20.

Kurichianil, John. "As We Progress in Monastic Life and Faith (Prol 49)." *A.I.M. Bulletin* 84 (2005): 70–86; 85 (2005): 8–15.

Lauer, Christina. "Der Gnadenbegriff Benedikts und sein theologischer Hintergrund." *RBS* 13 (1986): 17–34.

Leloir, Louis. "Il Diavolo nei padri del deserto e negli scritti del Medioevo." *Ora et labora* 39 (1984): 176–91.

Lentini, Anselmo. *S. Benedetto. La Regola.* Monte Cassino, ²1980. Cited as Lentini.

Linderbauer, Benno. *S. Benedicti Regula Monachorum.* Metten, 1922.

Luislampe, Pia. "Geistliche Entscheidungsfindung in der Regula Benedicti: Textanalyse zu Kapitel 3 und Folgerungen für die Praxis." *MonInf* 47 (1986): 7–14.

Malone, Janet. "Listening with the Heart." *Human Development* 21, no. 3 (2000): 13–17.

Marrion, Malachy. "Perichoresis in the Prolog of the RB" *StMon* 25 (1983): 11–29.

Michels, Thomas. "Attonitis auribus audiamus." *SMGBO* 50 (1932): 336–42.

Miquel, Pierre. "La lumière dans la Règle de S.Benoît." *Irénikon* 53 (1980): 331–40.

———. "L'oeil et l'oreille." *Lettre the Ligugé* 228 (1984): 3–19.

———. "*Praesumere - praesumptio* dans l'ancienne littérature monastique." *RBén* 79 (1969): 424–36.

Nowack, Petrus. "*Quid dulcis nobis ab hac voca Domini invitantis nos.*" In *Ecclesia Lacensis* (Münster, 1993): 462–88.

Peifer, Claude J. "The Use of Romans 8:15 in the *Regula Magistri* and the *Regula Benedicti.*" In *Benedictus: Studies in Honor of St. Benedict of Nursia.* Edited by R. Elder. Kalamazoo, MI: Cistercian Publications, 1981. 15–22.

Posset, Franz. "The Sweetness of God." ABR 44 (1993): 143–78.

Puzicha, Michaela. *Kommentar zur Benediktusregel.* St. Ottilien, 2002. Cited as Puzicha.

———. "*Ante omnia.*" *MonInf* 57 (1988): 16–19.

———. "Leitworte altkirchlicher Taufpraxis im Prolog der Benediktusregel." *MonInf* 98 (1998): 19–24.

———. "*Multorum servire moribus—der Eigenart vieler dienen.*" *MonInf* 142 (2010): 11–17.

Quartiroli, Anna Maria, ed. *La Regola di San Benedetto.* Introduzione, traduzione e commento. Scritti Monastici. Praglia, 2002. Cited as Quartiroli.

Roth, Anselm. "Ursprung der Regula Magistri: die Kontroverse zwischen M. Masai und A. de Vogüé." *EA* 60 (1984): 119–27.

Ruppert, Fidelis. "Nur Stellvertreter." *EA* 76 (2000): 107–18.

Schmidt, Albert. "Jetzt." *EA* 77 (2001): 193–94.

Schuth, Gabriele. "Die Süsse Gottes: Zur Sprache der religiösen Erfahrung." *Geist und Leben* 57 (1984): 420–24.

Schwager, Raymund. "Hörer des Wortes. Eine empirische Anthropologie für die Theologie?" *Zeitschrift für Theologie und Kirche* 114 (1992): 1–23.

Stasiak, Kurt. "Four Kinds of Monks: Four Obstacles to Seeking God." ABR 45 (1994): 303–20.

Steidle, Basilius. *Die Benediktusregel lateinisch-deutsch*. Beuron, ² 1975.

———. "Der Abt und der Rat der Brüder. Zu Kapitel 3 der Regel S. Bendikt's." *EA* 52 (1976): 339–53.

———. "Memor periculi Heli sacerdotis de Silo: Zum Abtsbild der Regel St. Benedikts (Kap. 2.26)." *EA* 52 (1976): 5–18.

———. "Parrhesia - praesumptio in der Klosterregel St. Benedikts." In *Zeugnis des Geistes. Benediktinische Monatsschrift*. Beiheft, 1947. 44–61.

Studer, Basil. "Die *schola Christi* in der Regel des heiligen Benedikt." In *Lebendiges Kloster*, Festschrift für Georg Holzherr. Edited by M. Löhrer and M. Steiner. Freiburg, Switzerland, 1997. 59–75.

Thevenet, Jean-Marie. "Essai d'analyse sémiotique du Prologue de la Règle de S. Benoît." Mansucript. Institut Catholique de Paris, 1976.

Vagaggini, Cipriano. "La posizione di S. Benedetto nella questione semipelagiana." *Studia Benedictina in memoriam gloriosi ante saecula XIV transitus S. P. Benedicti*. StA 18–19 (1947): 17–83.

De Vogüé, Adalbert. *La règle de S.Benoît*. SC 184–86. Paris, 1971. Quoted as Vogüé *IV, V, VI*.

———. *La règle de S.Benoît: Commentaire doctrinal et spiritual*. Paris, 1977. (Engl. trans. *The Rule of St. Benedict: A Doctrinal and Spiritual Commentary*. Translated by J. B. Hasbrouck. Cistercian Studies 54. Kalamazoo, MI: Cistercian, 1983. Cited as *RB-DSC*).

———. *La communauté et l'abbé dans la Règle de S. Benoît et du Maître*. Paris, 1961. (Engl. trans. *Community and Abbot in the Rule of Saint Benedict*. Cistercian Studies 5/1, 5/2. Kalamzoo, MI: Cistercian 1978, 1985).

———. "The Abbot, Vicar of Christ in the Rule of S. Benedict and in the Rule of the Master." *WSp* 6 (1984): 41–57; also "Der Abt alsStellvertreter Christi bei S. Benedikt und beim Magister." *EA* 59 (1983): 276–78; also "L'Abbé, vicaire du Christ chez S. Benoît et chez le Maître." *CollCist* 44 (1982): 89–100; also "El Papel del Abad según la Regla de San Benito en una cultura che cambia." StSil 25 (2003): 29–41.

———. "The Fatherhood of Christ in the Rules of St. Benedict and the Master." *Mst* 5 (1968): 45–57; in French: "La Paternité du Christ dans les Règles de S. Benoît et du Maître." *VS* 110 (1964): 55–67.

———. "Le *De generibus monachorum* du Maître et de Benoît: Le Maître, S. Eugippe et S. Benoît." *RBS* Suppl. 17 (1984): 163–87.

————. "Les recherches de François Masai sur le Maître et S. Benoît." *StMon* 24 (1982): 7–42, 271–309.

————. "*Sub regula vel abbate.*" *CollCist* 33 (1971): 209–41 ("*Sub regula vel abbate:* The Theological significance of the Ancient Monastic Rules." In *Rule and Life*, 21–63).

————. Blecker, M. P. "Roman Law and '*Consilium*' in the *Regula Magistri* and the Rule of S. Benedict." In French: "Le Maître, Eugippe et S. Benoît." *RBS* Suppl. 17 (1984): 187–92.

————. "The School of Christ." *CS* 24 (1989): 16–24; "L'Ecole du Christ." *CollCist* 46 (1984): 1–12; also in "Etudes sur la Règle de S. Benoît: Nouveau Recueil." *Spiritualité monastique* 34 (1996): 221–23.

————. "Trois expressions du Maître et de Benoît, éclairées par Augustin, *La Vita Antonii* et d'autres texts." *StMon* 26 (1984): 205–14.

Zelser, Klaus. "Zu Geschichte und Überlieferung des Textes der *Regula Benedicti.*" In *Il monachesimo tra eredità e aperture*. Edited by M. Bielawski and D. Hombergen. Studia Anselmiana 140, Rome, 2004. 739–51.

Zorzi, M. Benedetta. "Vivere i limiti e talenti in relazione: Glosse sull'uso del verbo *praesumere* nella Regola di S. Benedetto." *Inter Fratres* 57 (2000): 165–87.

Index of Subjects, Authors, and Works

The words *abbot* and *brothers* are only referenced outside of RB1, 2, and 3. *Cenobites/cenobitic/al*, *gyrovagues*, and *sarabaites* are referenced throughout the text.

Index of RB References

Note: RB references treated in a chapter of their own are referenced only in places outside that chapter.

Index of Hebrew Scriptures: Old Testament

Index of Christian Scriptures:
New Testament